MORAG SMYTH

A Walk in Deep Time

First published by © Morag Smyth 2022

Copyright © 2022 by Morag Smyth

All rights reserved. No part of this publication may be reproduced, stored or transmitted in any form or by any means, electronic, mechanical, photocopying, recording, scanning, or otherwise without written permission from the publisher. It is illegal to copy this book, post it to a website, or distribute it by any other means without permission.

Morag Smyth asserts the moral right to be identified as the author of this work.

First edition

ISBN: 978-1-914398-14-8

This book was professionally typeset on Reedsy. Find out more at reedsy.com

For my family, with love.

Contents

Acknowledgement	iv
Part One Belonging and Dislocation 1951 - 1967	1
Fault Line	2
Muckhart Mill	6
Tigh na Feile	10
Dollar Academy	18
Road to the Isles 1	22
Hillfoots Way	28
Scarsdale	34
Knowle and Dorridge	41
Netherlee	45
Howard's Way	49
Ladygrove	56
Bakewell	69
Part Two Design and Romanticism 1967 – 1983	76
Hasland	77
Newbold Road	86
Snake Pass	97
Road to the Isles 2	107
Cakor Pass and Cheshire	112
Somerset	118
The Folly	126
Bath	133
Bristol	141

Road to the Isles 3	147
Part Three Deconstruction and Transformation 1984 – 1997	151
St Michael's Hill	152
Chewton Mendip	159
Greenfields	166
Litton	170
Szczecin	176
The Road to the Isles 4	185
Wallisdown	191
Bournemouth	197
Cardiff	203
West Moors	212
Glasgow School	222
Tarrant Launceston	230
Bonnington Square	238
Dartington	245
Part Four Change, Backlash, Continuum 1997 – 2018	254
Woodbury Close	255
Claverton Down	264
St Andrews Stream	272
Don Valley	278
Blue Mountains	284
Poacher's Pocket	292
Eastwood Lodge	302
Scots Pine	311
The Parade	320
Road to the Isles 5	329
Bibliography	337
Images	339

About the Author	342
Testimonials	343

Acknowledgement

I am deeply grateful to Rosie Jackson for facilitating this autobiography and memoir in her memoir workshops and to my sister memoirists and writers, Caroline Mair, Sue Orgill, and Gaie Vickers for their support and many memorable and moving shared times.

As a poet I have a tendency to edit out the story. I thank my fellow poets in Wells Fountain Pens, Ama Bolton, Sara Butler, Rachael Clyne, Michelle Diaz, Jinny Fisher, Jo Waterworth; in the *Tears in the Fence* writing and festival groups, Val Bridges, Lesley Burt, John Freeman, Richard Foreman, Jeremy Hilton, Gerald Killingworth, Joanna Nissel, Mandy Pannett, Maria Stadnicka; and from Bath Writers and Artists Verona Bass, Ama Bolton, Sue Boyle, Eileen Cameron, Claire Coleman, Marilyn French, Peter Reader, Graeme Ryan, Linda Saunders, Sue Sims; and Wells Writers Mark Mapstone, Pamela Morley and Christine Head; and Sheila Page, Susan Milland, Averil Pike; Stephen Boyce, Chaucer Cameron, Dawn Gorman, Ruth Sharman for patiently encouraging me to "write it all down".

Extracts from the chapters Dollar Academy and the Parade, have appeared in my column *Electric Blue in Tears in the Fence* and I am indebted to David Caddy for his support and encouragement. And thanks to Westrow Cooper for his help with the cover and support for this book during the pandemic.

My dear friends Sharon Edwards and Karen have been unwavering in their support for me, their belief in my writing my story, and were generous and willing readers of the first drafts. I am also grateful to many dear friends and colleagues, you know who you are, who appear at various points in my story. Thank you all.

None of this would have been possible, and much of the story would not have existed, without the steadfast support of my partner Andrew Henon, and of all my family: Tom Kiziewicz, Marie Claire, Peter and Lily, David, my dear sister Sheila, Alan and Simona, Sofia and Monica, Anne Marie and Tasmin, Tom B, my dear brother Alan and Donna, and Karen Browning, Karen and Kiera who have all walked with and beside me with love on the journey.

Part One Belonging and Dislocation
1951 - 1967

Path End, painting by Helen Lees

Fault Line

Path End, woodcut by Helen Lees

I was born on a fault line on a brilliant summer's day in the bedroom of our cottage named Path End. I was a small baby and my mother was in constant fear for my survival. She worried that I was not getting enough nourishment, that she was breastfeeding me for too long, that I may have contracted tuberculosis from the unpasteurised cow's milk we collected from the neighbouring farm. My three-year old sister was dark haired, rosy cheeked and bonny. I was a thin, pale, blonde and scrawny baby who could not be consoled. Nanny sent a telegram on the day of my birth, "welcome home, long life, happiness, love".

Outside my mother's womb the first sound I was aware of was the river. The river's roar and rumble was to be a constant source that held me to this place, this time, this moment. The ground shook and rumbled, a deep resonance. Repeated minor swarm activities of seismic events occur in this area. A restlessness in the earth meant I grew used to listening to the ground, to crawling in the mud and hearing this strange deep language, a guttural downwards movement, a creaking and shifting of things.

In the Ochils the hills rise dramatically forming a southern facing ridge that goes down as far as it goes up. The valley has filled with rich accruements over the millennia and our cottage rested on this halfway point beside the river that carries the mountain to the sea. Path End's deep stone walls, central front door, small windows and sloping roof with two chimneys promised warm comfort for harsh winters. We produced electricity from our own generator that my father had placed in the river and we had a solid fuel stove, paraffin stoves and open fires.

The light we are born into, the height of the sun, magnetic forces, the air that we breathe and the water we drink, seem to me to be intimately linked to our cellular structure, to who and what we are. And we are transient, mere flickers or impressions on the land on which we stand. The earth moves and breathes and sometimes remembers.

In Scotland the geology of the planet is completely visible. During the Scottish Enlightenment James Hutton, widely recognised as the 'Father of Modern Geology', developed theories for what is now called deep time, identifying the mutable and changing nature of our planet and anticipating the Gaia hypothesis. When I was born we were only just beginning to understand that all land was once one large, huge, land mass and that this land has separated, drifted over millennia to form the continents and islands we have today. The backbone of the planet, the underwater mountain ridge that circumscribes the globe had not yet been charted. The fault line near the cottage is reputed to be the best example of a fault line in the UK.

Our cottage garden had rich fertile ground formed from Devonian sandstone that led down to a steep bank bordering the river. I loved to dig in the earth for snail shells, for stones, for signs of life. I spent happy hours in the garden alongside my mother. My mother swam in the river and left me in the pram in the garden. In the summer there was the shelter of leaves, the hum of bees and the smells of flowers. Nearby is Silver Glen, a glen formed by the maximum downward movement of the fault. The silver that the glen contained was revealed and in 1776 one of the members of the renowned Scottish Erskine family opened a mine. The mine produced best quality silver and made the area's fortune. Silver, malleable, shining, reflective must by moonlight have glistened in the glen for centuries, undisturbed. I was given a silver spoon and a silver napkin ring as baby gifts. Mummy complained that as a toddler I buried my wet pants in the garden with a silver spoon.

In a photo I lie on a rug in the garden and our dog, Happy, has come to join me. I wear a summer hat and there are roses, mature trees and an evening light. I appear content, part of river and earth that surrounds me. In the River Devon now they pan for gold. The allure of gleaming rocks an almost primal drive. The gravel of the river and the stones I played with in the garden contained the story of our molten merging and reforming world.

Morag and Happy in the garden at Path End

Muckhart Mill

I hear the eagles call, a high shrill sounding to each other over the hills. I toddle along the lane with my mother, while my sister is at school. We are going to the mill farmhouse and pause to stare over a bridge where a burn joins the river with a roar. The mill wheel is no longer active. We stare into the merging brown currents that tumble together. Waves are solid shapes moulded from the force of each perpetual hypnotic repeating and colliding movement. Frothy white tops fall into eddies, flatten into slow bubbles as the two rivers rush on together away down the glen.

There is only the Mill and our cottage in this part of the scattered hamlet that forms the Yetts of Muckhart. Richard Elmhirst, the farmer, greets my mother and me at the farm gate with Shakespeare's words from Richard III "now is the winter of our discontent made glorious summer". Something about his bearing, the way he delivered the lines, the way he presented the milk in the churn on this bright sunny morning carried such a portent the moment made a lifelong impression on me. I was given the sense of something universal beyond the warm breath from the cow's nostrils, the sound of the hens clucking. I cannot have been more than three or four at that time. Only decades later, when I was giving a talk at Dartington Hall, would I come to fully understand how much these early years of connection with our remarkable neighbours had influenced me.

Richard stayed and taught in Dartington for many years, he was engaged with the creative arts, especially drama, and also involved with progressive rural developments. In 1946, five years before I was born, Richard married Morna Haggard, and they moved to Muckhart Mill, this smallholding in Perthshire bringing the imbued values from Dartington with them. I was born in the cottage next door to the Mill in 1951.

Someone who lived here decades later wrote an article on the exceptional comfort and security this hamlet represented, a place of retreat, meditation and engagement with the land. I think the nature of this place, the refuge it presented after the Second World War, with all the separation and loss that entailed, is what both my parents and the Elmhirsts were seeking when they made their homes here.

My parents rented the cottage and moved here with my older sister in 1949 when my father took up the position of Personnel Manager at Patons and Baldwins, a wool company in nearby Alloa. My parents were from Glasgow and the Elmhirsts arrived here by way of England and North America, none of them related to families who had farmed here for generations. There was the romanticism of the arts and crafts movement, a valuing of rural life and a conscious embracing of the notion of freedom and of allowing imaginative play, and a sense of hope that a different approach to life and in particular to child care might produce more peaceful and ecologically aware human beings.

I was always a free-range child, the deeply inculcated

knowledge of allowing children the opportunity to choose their activities and explore their environs was embedded in my upbringing. I played with my sister Sheila and the Elmhirstchildren when they were not at school, was at home with my mother when she helped Morna give birth to her youngest daughter and much of the time I was happy playing alone. We explored barns, fields, woods and burns, fed animals and understood how the body functions.

My mother joins Morna for a chat. I stay on the warm and dusty kitchen floor. There is a kettle bubbling on the stove and I like the warm cooking smells, the sense of activity, the sound of the women's voices and the bread crust I have been given to chew. A dog sniffs at my crust then settles in his basket. Cats curl around me, I am in a sleepy state and do not understand the meaning of the words the women speak. I do understand the sense of deep peace after a period of great disturbance. I have the sense of families reforming, the idea of new beginnings and the feeling of hope, although I have as yet no words to form this understanding. The muted hum hypnotises me and I fall asleep.

How much a young child can understand of the conversations around them is unclear, I grew up hearing Joyce (my mother) and Morna discussing literature, drama, and politics from an early age. Joyce was writing and submitted a story, which among great excitement was read on Home Service Radio. Morna then submitted a story of her own that was also selected. It seemed to me to be a valid way of life to write stories for others' pleasure. Joyce was a great teller of stories, rolling her "rrrs" and reading characters in different voices and emotional keys when reading us stories, and as a child I was enraptured.

Joyce's work as a Social Worker in Glasgow and my father Howard's work as a Personnel Manager instilled in them both a strong sense of social justice and equality. Discussions were animated and active. I do have one memory of sitting at the kitchen table in the cottage where I was born and hearing discussion about the effect, impact and aftermath of the Jewish holocaust. The shocking facts of man's inhumanity to man, woman and child were not hidden from me. Indeed, in the nineteen fifties there was an active movement to ensure these issues were openly discussed and not held as previously in secrecy and denial.

Somehow before we moved to the nearby town of Dollar, in Clackmannanshire, all these values were already absorbed in my being. Embracing diversity; rural care and animal welfare; awareness of seasons and plants; growing our own food; rearing chickens kindly and killing them quickly to eat, and generating our own power.

Generating personal power too in the freedom to run and explore, to connect with the earth, with dark skies and infinity of stars. Freedom of choice; joy in language, culture, drama, self- expression; and a deeply connected bond to place were my heritage. All this before I was four. Many would come crashing down by the time I was six.

Tigh na Feile

When I was two years old, Sheila, my sister, started school. Each morning the three of us, my mother, sister and I, would walk up the lane to the main road for Sheila to catch the school bus to the nearby town of Dollar, then Mummy and I would walk back home. The lane was lined with mature deciduous trees, mainly beech, some oak. I would cuddle up to the trunks of the trees, caressing the bark, I would slide my arms as far round the trunks as I could to give each tree a hug. The trees were so solid and permanent they felt like my companions, silent sentinels to the day.

For the next year or two I had my mother to myself for most of the school term days. Sometimes she sang or talked to me, sometimes we baked in the kitchen. Often, she liked me to amuse myself while she was busy with household chores. On rainy days I played in my sister's bedroom and waited to play with Sheila when she came home. On fair weather days I explored outside and enjoyed playing with moss or a bird's feather or stones, making up universes from the universes within each thing.

My father, Howard, was posted to the Middle East for the latter part of the Second World War, and returned to Scotland late in 1946. In his letters home written during the war,

Howard made it clear he did not want my mother to work. In his thirties then, Howard would have been eleven when the law changed to give women equal voting rights in 1928. I think, like many men of that generation, throughout his life he had some internal conflict about women's emancipation, probably founded in the conflict between his parents.

Howard's mother, my Nanny, embraced women's emancipation. She spent some years in London working with her boss when Howard, the youngest of five, was still a young teenager. Howard's sister, my Aunt Katie, had been expected to give up her higher education to look after the household - her father, Howard and his two brothers. Katie never fully got over her resentment for this loss of opportunity while her older sister, Jean, continued her studies at Glasgow University, and her younger brothers were also able to continue their education.

My Grandfather worked all his life to support his family but it is possible in the years of the depression he may not have earned sufficient to support a family of five. Grandfather Carleton died just after the end of the war, before Sheila and I were born. He was Treasurer and Secretary of the Glasgow Masonic Burns Club, their letter of condolence in 1947 describes him as a dear friend. Like his Uncle before him, Carleton played church organ for over twenty years in Glasgow and was clearly a loved and respected man. There was a concert grand piano in the living room of their spacious flat in Glasgow. The whole family, Jean and Katie and their brothers Carleton, Ian and Howard - the youngest - gathered round the piano to play and sing together ever since they were children. Nanny, the youngest of ten children, was vivacious and energetic. I have somehow formed the impression that in the 1930's my Grandfather Carleton's more settled life was not quite enough for my spirited Nanny.

Howard's quick wit and humour combined with his gentleness and strength, was very popular at work and at home. He had an excellent ear for music, when he was a teenager Katie bought him his first trumpet. The trumpet went to war with Howard and kept him very socially active and popular between military Signals missions. Being close to his sister, he'd shared in Katie's resentment and did not appreciate the impact on him and on his father of an absent mother and perhaps blamed the loss of his mother on her having a career. When Howard returned from war my mother, like many other women, left the job she loved in Glasgow to be with her husband and to have a family. My sister was born in 1948 in Glasgow. Shortly after this my parents moved to Path End.

Howard and Joyce, Glasgow

Despite my mother's love for Howard, and her apparent acceptance of his views, my sister and I were aware of her gnawing sense of frustration at her isolation and disempowerment.

My mother went to Glasgow University and worked in Personnel for Hoover in Glasgow during the war. She would sometimes erupt in angry clattering in the kitchen. Outside in the garden she was happy, inside in the winter in dark cottage rooms she was too contained. Nevertheless, my parents were enjoying the romanticism of their situation. Consciously rebuilding a relationship after the years of separation during the war they were aiming to build a different future for their children.

Howard became Chairman to the Dollar Burns Club. My mother kept a typed copy of the talk Howard gave for the

Burns Night celebration when I was six months old. It is a well-written humorous speech that focuses on the virtues of Robbie Burns' wife. My father admires Burns' love for his wife, Bonnie Jean. In the speech my father refers to the weaker sex (women) and recounts Bonnie Jean's challenging life with her swain Robbie Burns. While his life and career accelerated, Jean was at home nursing her first set of twins by him, pre-marriage. These were followed by a second set post marriage who both sadly died. Jean and Robbie continued to have seven more children and Jean also cared for the child of one of Burns' 'paramours'.

My father's talk recounts Burns' job specification for a wife, made in a letter to Alex Cunningham in 1792: "The scale of good wifeship I divide into ten parts: Good nature, four; Good Sense, two; Wit, one; Personal charms – namely a sweet face, eloquent eyes, fine limbs, graceful carriage, one; …divide the remaining two degrees as you please"

His talk ends with proposing a toast praising Jean saying her "rare combination of character, devotion and womanhood entitle Jean to a place of honour in our thoughts tonight besides the man she loved and helped". Perhaps my mother kept this talk to show Howard's attempts (in which she probably had some influence) to aid the male only Burns club to recognise the importance of the role women play, yet his humorous asides stubbornly adhere to the values of his time.

Burns roamed the Ochils and his poetry was deeply embedded in the landscape. Perhaps Howard was inspired by Burn's poem, Braving Winter's Storms:

"Where braving angry winter's storms. The lofty Ochils rise, Far in their shade my Peggy's charms First blest my wondering eyes;

As one who by some savage stream A lonely gem surveys,

Astonish'd, doubly marks its beam With art's most polished blaze."

Path End was a wonderful place to heal and to reconnect after the disruption of war. Our cottage was rented and hard work to maintain. My parents began to look for their own home. Clackmannanshire local authority, aiming to attract young professional families to the area, were offering low fixed rate mortgages as a post-war incentive for new build houses in Dollar. My parents bought a plot and over the next year Sheila and I frequently visited the site with my mother and saw the new house gradually emerge from the piles of blocks and sacks of cement.

Mummy took keen pleasure in the modern clean lines of the fifties designs and was an active participant in the design of the build. Pouring over the drawings at home and choosing where to place windows to make best use of the light, the design of the new kitchen and utility room with up to date facilities, she enjoyed long discussions with the architect and builders while I played with wood or sand, or ate the sweets I'd been given as a rare treat to keep me quiet. The influence of seeing a house emerge from drawings to final build would prove to be the foundations to my future career in interior design. The transition to moving into this new house was so gradual it was almost a natural process.

My parents named the house Tigh Na Feile, Scottish Gaelic for 'house of welcome', and filled it with modern elegant furniture, a bookcase, laminate kitchen surfaces, pastel lemons and blues, an upright piano - Sheila was learning to play the piano and she showed me Middle C on the keyboard and how to stretch my little fingers - a dining table and vases of flowers. We settled in with barely a backward glance.

Other families were also moving in to this new development and we soon made friends with our new community. My best friend was Carole and we loved playing together in the local park, chatting and sliding or swinging. Carole showed me how to jump off the swing, but when I jumped I mistimed it, fell and fractured my wrist. A "green stick fracture" the doctor called it when my arm was placed in a sling and left to heal.

Our lives became more social in every way. There was great excitement when Aunt Katie, my father's sister, and Uncle Peter came to stay. Mummy would become very activated, almost frantic, preparing food and putting the house in order so we knew an event was about to begin. Aunt Katie's voice could be heard before the front door opened and from the moment of their arrival until their departure everything would change. Out would come Daddy's trumpet, and with Katie sitting at the piano and singing, Peter with his double bass and our friend and neighbour Walter, with his saxophone, the adults would settle in for a night of free jazz and reminiscence while Sheila and I were quickly sent to bed, able to listen comfortably from the top of the stairs.

Katie had been a member of the Rhythm Sisters and her repertoire was extensive and memorable. "Howard you've got a bit rusty" she would remonstrate with my father and chivvying Peter and Walter into action they would soon be jamming a spirited medley. The Rhythm Sisters played with Ambrose and his Orchestra, and their rendition of "Who's been polishing the sun?" was used recently in the film, the

Kings Speech. I have old recordings of some of their sessions and when I play them and hear their voices and the music they are still full of life.

Mummy described herself as entirely unmusical and eventually she would become irritated by the complete take-over of her home and husband, with herself in a solely hostess role. After everyone left there would be an active reclaiming of territory, with Mummy shaking out cushions and putting coffee tables back where they should be, tutting as she did so and the home would subside to a quieter more settled and orderly place - for a while.

Dollar Academy

My environment became more fixed, solid and concrete almost without my noticing. Carole and I were free to roam and play without adult supervision or intervention, and it was not until I went to school that the full nature of the restriction I was now to be subject to became clear to me. When it did so, it was a massive shock.

Dollar Academy, a Scottish independent school, was founded in 1818 with funds from benefactor and successful trader John McNabb, who was born in Dollar. William Henry Playfair, who designed much of Edinburgh's 19th century buildings, was the architect commissioned for the design. At the centre of the Academy was a large and imposing Doric façade. Doric, a classic Greek design of tall fluted columns dated to the 6th century BCE and represented the preferred male order. The building was dramatic in its setting at the hill foot of the Ochils and was surrounded by acres of grounds in which pipers regularly rehearsed. It was a dramatic and awe-inspiring setting for a young child's journey into Education.

I was a small shy child, my neck craned constantly upward, up to the crown of the hills of my birth that seemed to cradle these enormous polished stone buildings, up to the top of the columns many times higher than me and up to the whispering gallery of the domed ceiling in the library. We walked to school entering the campus by the central gateway and walking towards the main building then round the corner to the slightly less imposing prep school buildings. The prep school classrooms were set out in the Victorian style - desks in serried rows with a blackboard and teacher and cane at the front. My sister appeared to enjoy school, she was popular with the teacher and with friends and seemed confident in her ability. I was terrified.

There was no view from the tall windows whose sills were above my eye level and neighbouring walls largely blocked any view of the sky. We wore uncomfortable uniforms with large navy-blue knickers and prickly socks both of which were always sliding down. We were not allowed to speak, move or wriggle in our chairs, or interrupt the teacher. This made a small child's bladder control very difficult. I would feel an urgent rising need to pee, but unable to interrupt the teacher I would try with all my might to hold on until the break. All too often I did not manage and suffered the desperate and humiliating warm outpouring of urine and saturated knickers. The teacher was absolutely furious with me and marched me off to the toilets to find dry clothes. Sometimes she would march me into my sister's class to get my sister to walk me home. My sister, mortified with embarrassment, chastised me all the way home and when we got home my mother, equally embarrassed would shout at me too. I soon developed the bladder capacity of a camel and rarely used school toilets at all.

It was an interminably long day for a four-year-old, and was unpunctuated by much in the way of play or pleasure time. My recurring embarrassment made me a source of ridicule for the other children. I was also struggling with this method of teaching. I knew I was different to my sister and to other children in the way I learnt and thought but I had no language with which to articulate this and soon learnt the best way to cope was to keep my voice quiet. My day dreaming capacity developed and I was imaginatively absent from the classroom for much of the day.

My early education was not entirely without creative activity. My mother saved the first cards I made - an Easter card with a broken shell and emerging fluffy chicken stuck on the front and with 'Morag' written painstakingly on a line someone else has ruled in, another card where I have tried to write xxxx's for Mummy and drew instead zig zags and crossed them out. This kind of messiness and difficulty in being neat, never getting it quite right, was a source of pain for me always and humorous or irritating for others.

I became very spatially aware. This may have already developed for me in my free-range infant exploration, but something about the confinement of the classroom amongst all the limitless space I knew to be just outside enhanced or focused this ability. To this day I can remember the orientation of the desks and blackboard in the two different classrooms I was in. Birds orientate spatially for migration with magnetism and with visual clues, including the height of the sun and the position of rivers and stars. Somehow, I have retained some of this primal capacity.

Ian Hamilton Finlay, the Scottish concrete poet and artist, was sent to Dollar Academy from the Bahamas when he was six years old and studied there for most of the 1930s. In a 2004 poll conducted by Scotland on Sunday a panel of artists voted his work Little Sparta to be the most important work of

Scottish art (above the Glasgow School of Art). An article in The Guardian marking his death in 2006 mentions that he left school at 13, that his studies at art college were curtailed by the second world war and described how "the improbable roots (of all he achieved) lay in the only semblance of education Ian received: wartime service in the Royal Army Service Corps". I think this commentator is unaware of the fundamental impact the early education that Ian received at Dollar Academy is likely to have had.

In the 19th century the Academy had a strong emphasis on horticulture and pupils were allocated their own plots. It is likely that in the 20th century some of those values still underpinned the academic experience. As a boarder Ian must have often walked the mature planted acres of the campus, which included ponds and several mature sequoias while trying to explore and understand the conflict between learning, control, creativity and freedom. Ian's work in landscape and space, with text and installation and nature relates, I believe, directly to this experience.

Often seen as a metaphor for the conflict between artist and establishment, Little Sparta, his major work, is seen as a riposte to Edinburgh's classic Greek influences. The writer's view does not appear to fully recognise the impact for Ian, as for me, of encountering a Doric façade with its educational constraints in the Ochils at Dollar Academy at a tender age. The contrast of this encounter with another culture stays with a child, as it has stayed with me.

Road to the Isles 1

Over two years of my life has been spent in and around the highlands and islands of the west coast of Scotland. The time has accreted throughout my life from my earliest holidays with my family to my most recent visits.

Our early family holidays were filled with a sense of freedom and adventure. The car was loaded with all supplies needed for what was the norm then and what is now called wild camping. We children were often very car-sick, my father remembered the places we had to stop for us to either be sick or to gulp in lungs-full of air to recover as we neared the coast. The road got thinner and thinner with signs for passing places and poles to indicate the edge of the road and the height of the snow. Drivers of the occasional other cars we passed waved in camaraderie, black faced sheep lay in the road and on the verge in small groups round sharp bends, mountains sheered up on our right and the sea and lochs opened on our left.

We found a deserted bay with beaches of silver sand and simply pulled the car off the road onto the firm and springy turf. Sheila and I ran down to the sea to explore while the tent was erected and sandwiches produced. Long light days of play followed, collecting shells and pebbles from the shoreline, paddling and swimming, creating hollows for our imaginary boats in the sand. Mummy read her book while Daddy snoozed with a knotted handkerchief to protect his bald head. The sea was cold and we emerged with chattering teeth to be wrapped in towels and given what Mummy called "chitteringbites", a sweet biscuit, or a sandwich, and curl up thus comforted on the soft smooth and giving sand.

I was three when we went to the then deserted island of Tiree. Its long white beaches curved round the bay framed by sand dunes ideal for shelter from the wind and to roll and hide in. Huge long breakers rolled in to surf and Sheila and I shrieked as we played in the waves. Dolphins were leaping through some of the deeper waves, and though at my height I could not easily see them, I felt their presence. I vividly remember one large wave, twice my height suddenly completely immersing me. I looked up and saw fronds of seaweed floating in the sea above me. Everything went into extreme slow motion; I had time to observe the vivid colours of the different weeds and the golden light of the obscured sun. At that moment I was completely unafraid, just fascinated by this unexpected Gaia baptism. My family remember my father wading in to save me followed by my spluttering emergence from the sea. All I recall is that timeless moment of complete calm.

Sheila and Morag in Tiree

The Isle of Arran had been a favourite for my mother's family and she also spent childhood holidays there. As children we stayed on a croft and were allowed to bottle feed the lambs, whose strong suckling at the bottle was quite able to pull it from my small handed grasp. It was often rainy and we ran from the croft in our swimsuits to the beach, the sea seemed warmer when it rained and we were wet before we entered the water.

Many of my ancestors came from the isle of Bute. Bute and Arran, along with Isla Jura, Mull and several smaller islands are known as the Western Isles. Warmer and softer islands than the inner and Outer Hebrides. Their rich fertile land and location sheltered by the Mull of Kintyre led to millennia of settlement.

Isle of Arran

The name McKirdy is an ancient Scottish surname in the isles of Bute, Arran and other western isles. The fifth and fourth generations of my father's mother came from this line. The name is derived from the Albanichs, a tribe who held these islands prior to the 400 years of Scandinavian occupation. In 880 the Western Isles were overrun by the Scandinavians (Vikings) and held by the King of Norway until 1265. There is a sense of homecoming during my visits to these islands, and a sense of great continuity and peace as though political troubles rarely intrude on the daily life of the people here.

Children take their cue from their parents and my parents were at home on the road to the isles. My father had been stationed in the Shetlands with the Signals Regiment during the Second World War and had driven all the highland routes.

He formed a habit of free- wheeling down every long hill to save fuel, both due to rationing and because there were not many service stations in the highlands. We travelled miles on almost empty tanks of petrol, holding our breath on the down slopes and willing the car as far up the ensuing hill as possible before Daddy put the car in gear. My mother's father had made a living selling the knitwear from the highlands and islands. We visited and formed bonds with people all over the region, the remote roads and Gaelic place names were second nature to both our parents and therefore we girls also felt comfortably at home.

When we moved to England, we continued to spend our holidays on the road to the isles. The long drive to Scotland would be broken, staying with our Grandparents in Glasgow. Then the adventure would begin. When we got to the Kyle of Lochalsh we knew we were truly on our way. In the nineteen fifties there was no bridge to Skye and as with other parts of the route small ferries were employed to join up the single-track roads separated by sea. Often managed by one or two people the ferries carried very few cars and slowly crossed the stretch the water as though from here on we would have all the time in the world. We would stop for a picnic beside a bay, eating salted hardboiled eggs and seeing the range of mountains open out before us. Sea and sky appeared to meet, lochans scattered everywhere reflected the colours of the hillside - bracken, heather, gorse, turf and rock - merging in the living painting that continued to unfold forever.

Once our friends rented a caravan on Ardnamurchan, the remote, wild and wonderful peninsula which includes the most westerly point on mainland Britain, Corrachadh Mor. We drove up to join them, and to our surprise arrived in the aftermath of a media storm. Our friends' children had been caught out by the incoming tide while they were exploring the white beaches and coves. As the tide came closer and closer to the edge they began to climb the inaccessible cliffs and managed to scramble to a small cave higher up where, trembling, they sat and waited to see if the tide would come up that high. Fortunately, it stopped a few feet before the ledge they were on. They stayed there all night while their frantic parents, the coast guard and rescue parties hunted for them. The children scrambled down once the tide had receded and were picked up from the beach.

Peter, one of the children described it to me, "We were so cold - we were all trembling and we only had a few sweets to eat. When the sea came up to the ledge the waves were roaring and pounding the cliff and we just clung together. We couldn't hear anything over the sound of the sea."

Somewhat more impressed by the attention they had from press and television crews and the newspaper reports I said, "Oh, it sounds so exciting. I wish I had been with you".

"You would not have liked it!" came Peter's firm reply.

The experience did not put us children, nor our parents, off continuing our free exploration. We had many happy days exploring caves and rock-pools, constant attention now being given to the tide and the presence of the sea. The sound at night as the waves rhythmically crashed on the shore was our lullaby and stayed with us as a memory when we once more headed south, away from our spiritual home to our practical one.

Hillfoots Way

"We have something to tell you." My sister and I waited expectantly. We were sitting at the kitchen table. I was leaning forward on the pine chair, my hands spread on the lemon yellow Formica table top. I was five and due to begin the second year at Dollar Academy in September.

"What is it Mummy?" Sheila, squatting on her knees on her chair, asked impatiently.

Mummy smiled conspiratorially at Daddy who nodded, "we're having a baby," she smiled.

"Will it be a boy or a girl?" Sheila asked.

"We don't know," Daddy replied, "which would you prefer?"

"A brother," Sheila could not contain her excitement, "a new baby brother. Can I tell my friends? When will he arrive?"

"We don't know yet if it will be a boy or not," Mummy reminded her smiling and seeming pleased by Sheila's excitement. "January is when the baby is due."

I stayed quiet and thoughtful. Over the next few weeks, gender was the main topic of discussion among our family and friends.

"I can't wait to have a brother," Sheila announced.

"It will be lovely to have a boy in the family," said Lila

Galloway, our friend, neighbour and wife to our Doctor.

"Aye well sure don't we always want a boy?" stated Mrs Boyd as she washed and stacked the dishes on the draining board.

"Oh I don't really know," said my Grandmother, mother to two girls.

"Och, I think a boy will be just the ticket," Aunt Jenny, my father's secretary and our family friend, ruffled my hair, "would ye no like a brother Morag?"

Eventually, somewhat stung by the evident value being placed on a boy and the effect on my own position as an "also-ran daughter" becoming clear to me I found my voice. "I want a sister," I declared to all who asked and to all who would hear. Definitely, defiantly I wanted a sister for me.

What wasn't discussed in front of the children, and what seemed inexplicable to my five-year old self, was Daddy's increasing absence from home. Maybe I was told Daddy was away at work, but he did not usually stay away from home for weeks and more at a time. Maybe the conversation went something like this.

"We can't really afford another child, we're only just managing on my salary."

"I know but we'll find a way."

"No I've applied for a job in England and I've been invited for an interview. The salaries are double what I can get in Scotland and there are no prospects here."

"You've done what? Without discussing it with me? Howard how could you?"

"The new company have made me an offer. It's too good to refuse."

"I don't want to leave Scotland. We have all our friends and family here."

"I know but Scotland is in such a poor state after the war. We need to think of the opportunities for our family. Don't worry. I'll go on ahead, start work and find us somewhere to live. You can have the baby here and come to England when the baby is a few weeks old."

This prolonged negotiation was accompanied by my father's absences and silences and my mother's distress and frustration, tears and slamming of doors. I was undoubtedly aware of the atmosphere without understanding the cause, and I missed my father.

I vividly recall the day of my brother's birth. Daddy was away and Mummy must have been in labour overnight because Lila Galloway gave us breakfast and saw us off to school. We were not told to expect the baby. Sheila and I walked to school with John, Lila's son and my friend, who was in the same class with me. John and I sat on the same row, near the front of our new class. Sheila and I didn't go home for lunch, but John did. When he came back after lunch, he bounced up to me, "You have a baby brother," he said.

"I do not," I replied crossly.

"Yes - you have - I've seen him," said John, whose father had delivered the baby.

I burst into tears, "I'm having a sister." I could not be consoled.

We walked home together after school and I rushed into the house.

"Hello Morag," Dr Galloway greeted me in his gruff and gentle scots voice, "would you like to go upstairs and meet your baby brother?"

I was shown up to my parents' bedroom and there was my

mother with the baby in her arms and my father sitting on the bed beside her. "Is it true?" I asked.

"Yes dear," said Mummy. "This is your brother, Alan."

As I write today it is my brother's sixtieth birthday. Only relatively recently have I come to fully understand how much the upheaval in my life at this time was unfairly blamed by my five-year old self on my brother. The absence of my father, my mother's depression, the loss of our beloved home in Scotland, the loss of culture, family, friends and security was accompanied by the arrival of an unsettled and therefore demanding baby.

What his arrival also did was illuminate for me the gender division in the UK in the fifties, highlighted again by the universal joy that accompanied his birth. When I was in my thirties my father said to me, "you always thought we favoured Alan because he was a boy, but we didn't. We loved you just the same."

The fact is that the expectations on, and the priority for, a boy were vastly different to that of a girl. My father mended my brother's bike, built dens with him and generally treated him quite differently to his daughters throughout his life. My mother too treated him differently, despite her wish for emancipation for herself and her daughters, she was inevitably rooted in her time. It made me very aware of and resistant to the unfairness of this division from an early age.

"Oh what a dear wee sweet boy," said Mrs Boyd.

"A grand son," said Grandpa holding him up proudly for all to see.

"How's your lovely wee brother?" asked the teacher.

"A boy how wonderful!" was the general opinion.

"Will you be having him christened?" asked Aunt Jenny.

Neither my sister or I had been christened, but it was clearly thought important for the boy. Mummy wanted to ensure we had the same status. And so it was that when my brother was four weeks old, and I was five and my sister eight, we were all christened in the Church of Scotland. I remember the ceremony and looking forward to eating the enticing looking marzipan fruit, a little yellow banana and a red cherry, that turned out not to taste as good as they looked.

Two weeks later Mummy, with Alan in her arms, our cat Sooty in a basket, and Sheila and I boarded the bus in Dollar. Daddy, with no paternity leave, had already returned to England. We left the Hilllfoots villages of the Ochils - Muckhart, Tillicoultry, Dollar and all – and began our long journey south. Many of our friends had come to say goodbye. We looked out from the rear window as the cheerily waving group diminished in size and we pulled ever further away from home.

When we arrived in Glasgow from Dollar, we were all exhausted. Our Grandparents had prepared a welcoming meal and I fell asleep at the dining table as our mother caught up on news. My Grandfather's treat for us was segments of bitter orange around a plate with brown sugar in the centre to dip them. The sweet sharp taste is still a source of comfort to me.

"Don't let the cat out," Mummy told Grandpa.

The atmosphere next morning was tense. We had a long journey to make by train to England and my mother had to prepare our baby brother, myself and my sister, as well as get the luggage together, say our goodbyes and be in good time for the train. It must have been hard for my Grandparents, my aunt with her husband and son had already emigrated to

Australia, and with our move to England they were losing both young families.

Sooty meowed and howled at the door in the kitchen that led, by way of steep steps down to the garden. Mummy was upstairs and only I saw Grandpa open the door. "Ach well, don't be long," he scolded Sooty and the cat without a backwards glance shot out of the door.

Just before we left, Mummy, Grandpa and I were all in the garden calling and crying out for Sooty. There was no sign of the cat.

"Don't worry we'll look after him when he comes in," Grandpa said.

"Cats find their way home," Mummy told me.

I imagined Sooty trying to find his way home across the Ochil Hills as we steamed steadily south on the train. We never saw him again.

Scarsdale

From my earliest years my mother described me as "fey", the Scottish word that describes being able to see into the future or being marked by an other-worldly air. "Morag's away with the fairies" she would say. I was not sure what she meant but I was away in a world of my own. Not talking to fairies or angels, just communing with something otherworld I sensed rooted in the nature that surrounded me.

I had a strong imaginary world. Our neighbours in Scotland still recall the impact of my childhood imagination. One day their son John came home in tears. I'd left him in charge of the care of my imaginary elephant. I was away on holiday and without me he was unable to find and to feed my imagined creature.

My christening into the Church of Scotland, aged five, was not a spiritual experience. Rooted in the physical world I remember the cool of the stone, the feel of the pews and the simplicity of the Presbyterian building. It stayed with me as a very human experience of community and belonging. My spiritual experiences were more those of being a connected part of the ecology that embraced me.

It was when I was seven that I had my first vivid spiritual

encounter. I was standing on the pavement of Station Road on my way home from school and just like the shaft of sunlight piercing the clouds, I had this sudden certainty that there was a god. It was such a comforting knowledge, and somewhat like hearing a divine voice in the brain, that I was rooted to the spot for a moment and had that clarity of vision when time slows right down and you are absolutely in a moment that will stay with you forever.

When we moved from Scotland to England, I became deeply unhappy. The memorable long journey to England by steam train was etched in our minds. Our friend, Mrs Bain, packed a parcel containing little surprises for Sheila and I. We were allowed to open one at each station, when the train stopped. The huge engine with its shiny name plate stood panting at the platform while Sheila and I excitedly opened crayons or a colouring book. The rhythmic sound of the engine ch-ch-chuh and the wheels going over the tracks accompanied us as we travelled on, the whistle blew and we cheered as we passed the border between Scotland and England. The restaurant car had heavy silver cutlery and we were served teacakes and cups of tea in cups and saucers with tongs for holding sugar lumps. The journey was an adventure and exhausting. We were all relieved and happy to see Daddy there to meet us at Birmingham station. He drove us to our new and unfamiliar home.

I was given a Brownie 127 camera for my birthday and have taken most of the photos in the film I find from this time. In one there is a large empty Jerry can beside me that Daddy has pulled out of the garage, my brother Alan is sitting on the Jerry can, Great Aunt Jessie is in a deck chair and Nanny, Daddy's mother who developed dementia, is sitting in the canvas director's chair. The can and the director's chair both carry an air of the Second World War, I remember how the hollow metal can resounded when scraped along the floor, and the way the director's chair with its thick canvas folded up to be put away.

Another is a photo of me, I am holding my doll tightly, with one hand at her back, the other across what would be her heart. She is closely wrapped in a shawl and she is held the way I wanted to be held, safely, securely with loving attention. I look warily at the camera, my eyes have shadows below them and although I am smiling my eyes are sad and questioning. My brother Alan is a year old I am nearly seven. Nothing is in its place or as it should be. My mother hates Scarsdale, the three-storey house we now live in, and she finds it hard to run. I like my room at the top of the house, painted red and yellow with sloping ceilings, and I spend a lot of time in the garden. The rest of the Edwardian house is dark and has a heavy atmosphere. There is a line of bells with room names on them in the hall that used to be rung for service. In the photo I am sitting on a glazed porch at the back of the house and wearing the summer dress of my hated new Warwick Preparatory School. I try to look after my brother but I can't seem to do anything right. Mummy screams at me when I carry him down three steep flights of stairs and when I carry him in from the garden, a wasp sting in the sole of his foot. When I throw my attachment "silkie" onto the fire to please Mummy, who is always moaning about my need for this "filthy rag", she barely notices. Watching it going up in flames I am consumed by regret for my wasted gesture.

I was six when I went to Warwick Preparatory School with my sister, Sheila. Wearing our grey uniforms and little bowler hats, the two of us walked up Station Road to Knowle and Dorridge station and took the steam train to Warwick. Steam trains represent separation and loss for me. This small steam train with separate enclosed carriages carried me daily away from home. It was quite usual in those days for children to travel some distance to school unaccompanied, but my already unhappy school experiences were compounded by the effect of distancing this journey had. Not for me the nostalgia of the smell of the engine and the sound of the whistle, more a sense of claustrophobia and of being trapped in the little carriages with their dirty antimacassars well above my head on the seat.

When we reached Warwick we walked up the hill past the Castle to the school. I was so unhappy at the Prep School my memories of the school itself are blocked; yet the memories of the journey to school are quite clear. I remember walking up Station Road past the Edwardian and Victorian houses with their tree lined gardens. I remember waiting in the station, and Sheila and I both remember my getting locked in the toilet and Sheila having to get the station master to open it for me. I remember saving my pocket money week after week until I could finally buy for five shillings the little blue accordion with red wooden handles I had seen every day in the window of the newsagent we passed on our way up the hill to the school. The idea of the freedom of music sustained me through what seemed interminable days of misery.

Sheila remembers how we were bullied at the school. Mocked by teachers and pupils for our difference, our Scottish accents and for the openness typical of a Scot's communication and very different from the English reserve. Two English girls, Rosemary and Margaret, lived near us and

Sheila became friends with Rosemary. I was expected to be friends with Margaret, who was the same age as me, but we did not connect, I was feeling unconscionably lonely and isolated. It became so bad ultimately I had school refusal and hid in the garden at home.

"Come on Morag," Sheila said crossly.

"I'm not coming," I replied and ran down the garden.

"We'll miss the train," Sheila shouted. "Well I'm going then."

Some hours later Mummy found me hiding. "is that you Morag, are you all right?"

Mummy was busy with my baby brother and was not happy herself. She was probably suffering from post-natal depression and she did not like the house my father had chosen for us, nor the English suburbia we were living in. Until now, she had not realised I was terribly unhappy too. I wept and she comforted me.

Soon afterwards I was moved to a small private primary school within walking distance of home. Now I was the older child in charge of a younger child called David on our way to and from school. Our walk took about half an hour out towards countryside. We passed banks of snowdrops, hazel catkins, horses, and we chatted happily all the way. At the school I was welcomed, well treated and I thrived.

Perhaps before this change of school I'd been praying for change and this may account for the moment of clarity and faith alone on my way home. What is sure is from that moment my memory is unblocked and I can remember a great deal about this school even though I was only there for two years.

Once a private house, the school had two large bright classrooms on the first floor. After my first three years of schooling in large independent and public schools with severe rules and hundreds of pupils, this was a small school with about forty pupils. With just two classes teaching was flexible for ability and age. At playtime we went out into a field adjoining the house for free play. This was reminiscent of my early free-range years. We found grass snakes and slow worms, we drew, we played and we learned fast.

Reading came quite early. Following my sister's lead I traced the form of the letters with my finger. I remember each book in the bookcase, the sliding glass door holding small hardback treasures, many adorned with our colouring in. When I was six, I had a hardback copy of Doctor Dolittle. The blue fabric was comfortable to hold and the thick pages of cream cartridge paper a pleasure to turn. I read the book by torchlight under the bedclothes, absorbing every word. I vividly remember my intense pleasure when I finished the book. I rushed downstairs to tell my mother I had finished it, but she was not impressed – I don't think she believed me. I still believe we can talk to animals. For years after losing our cat Sooty in Glasgow I would imagine him returning to our home in Dollar looking for us, years later a similar tale about two dogs and a cat based on real events confirmed for me this was a possibility. Mummy promised me a cat, instead we got a dog for Sheila, a lovely Staffordshire bull terrier called Beau, and years later I would take animal matters into my own hands. Ever since this first book, I have been a voracious reader, devouring books, losing myself in words.

Writing, however, is an altogether different story, a sorrier tale. My mother's writing was swift, spiky and illegible so she was not able to help me in my struggles. These had begun in earnest at Dollar Academy where I was taught to write in italics. I was shown wonderful script that I never learned to emulate, my italics flowing or rather stuttering and blotching at different angles all over the page. In England at the Warwick School, I was taught a cursive joined up writing script, which I also failed to master.

At the new smaller school, I was allowed to develop at my own pace and my drawings were appreciated. I received personal attention, was listened to and my work was greeted with respect and approval. The teachers valued me, told my despairing parents I was very bright and reassured them I would easily pass the eleven plus, a test for grammar school streaming that my sister was soon to take but that for me was in the distant future. Only later did I come to realise that the price of finding a school that was right for me, together with this change in life for my sister, led to our inevitable and irrevocable separation. Our close days together were over.

Knowle and Dorridge

I settled in to my new school, everything changed and I started to feel much happier. Still missing my friend Carole from Scotland, my new best friend Pippa was a joy to be with. The youngest of eight daughters she was an active tomboy and together we climbed trees, jumped from walls and rode her horse bare back in the paddock.

When I called for Pippa one or other of her sisters would greet me at the door giggling. "Oh no More Rags today thank you," she would say, and others sisters would appear to share in the hilarity. This good-natured ribbing was very different from the contemptuous name calling and bullying I'd been subjected to in Warwick and I was accepted even with my Scottish accent and name. Gradually my accent began to disappear and I developed flattened nasal Birmingham tones. This development horrified my mother, who was trained in elocution and proud of her public speaking ability. "Oh no Morag, it's not Sco-ish – it's Scottish" she would tell me, accentuating the open vowels of an 'a' or an 'o' and the accents of a 't'.

Pippa's father was a clothes manufacturer in Birmingham. Several times Pippa and I were taken to the factory and allowed to explore. There were huge bundles of fabrics of many different colours and patterns. We played with the samples, felt the quality of different cottons and other materials and took off-cuts home to make clothes for our dolls. Rooms full of women at sewing machines and the clatter of talking and stitching filled the entire building. Outside brick walls several stories high filled the street, the sound of the machines echoing from the open windows and the chatter and banter of the women as the needles flashed in front of them and reams of fabric were expertly and rapidly pulled under the foot of the tread and cast onto a growing bundle in a basket beside each stool.

My Grandfather Carleton Smyth worked for the Singer Sewing Machine Company in Glasgow all his life. His father, a watchmaker from Ireland, had died from tuberculosis when Carleton was just eleven years old. As the oldest son, Carleton became the family's main wage earner, starting work at Singer's newly built factory when he just fourteen and retiring in his seventies. A BBC radio documentary on the world wide significance of the development of the Singer sewing machine in the 20th Century explored Singer's influence through its designs and engineering. The new Singer factory in Glasgow was a huge building and a major employer in Glasgow. My grandfather, starting work there when it was first built, must have seen its inception and development and grown with it over the years. During the Second World War it became a munitions factory and was heavily bombed. Many workers living in homes nearby died.

Moving from the rural highlands to Birmingham gave me a belated taste of the industrial revolution and introduced me to industry and commerce. My father worked as Personnel Manager for Phosphor Bronze a metallurgy operation that eventually became part of the huge Rio Tinto Zinc (RTZ) organisation.

My mother's grandparents were Jewish and as immigrants they had moved to Birmingham from Warsaw before settling in Glasgow, where my grandfather - the youngest of thirteen children - was born. In common with many others they were given the surname of Friend as the immigration officers found the Polish names too difficult to spell and used the nomenclature of "Friend" as the name of the person who vouched for them.

In my Grandfather Isaac's Jewish family marriage outside of the faith was forbidden and by marrying my highland grandmother he was now dead to them. He was cut out of the family estate and all contact with his family was stopped. He never saw his father or older brothers again. My mother remembers, after her Jewish grandfather died, being taken to see her Jewish grandmother when she was about eight. Mum says there was warmth between them despite the separation and they met occasionally until she died. The younger brothers stayed in touch with my Grandfather, and, to his delight, left small portions of the estate to him when they died.

Isaac also went into the textile industry. He was a textile designer and had owned a carpet factory in Glasgow. Unfortunately this burnt down during the Depression years and, without insurance, Grandpa once again had to start from scratch. He made a living buying Shetland and Fair Isle knitwear from the knitters in the highlands and selling the garments to businesses, shops and people all over the world.

I grew up with a rich colour and design textile palette and

the fabrics I was now encountering in Birmingham, silk, cotton, linen, printed designs and weaves were like little jewels. I saved all the off cuts I was given from Pippa's father's factory and if I didn't make something with them, I saved them as treasures.

Daddy used to call Knowle and Dorridge 'Bowl and Porridge' and I don't think he was any fonder of the area than Mummy was. They both missed Glasgow and the Ochills. They made good friends - I have some black and white photos of Mummy and Daddy dancing together in classic fifties style at a works dance - but it was not the same as the community culture we all shared in Scotland. Suburban isolation and closed doors were the norm in Bowl and Porridge.

Just a year later RTZ took over Phosphor Bronze my father's role was made redundant and no sooner had I finally settled in we were once more on the move.

Netherlee

Sheila and I sometimes stayed with our Grandparents in their home in Netherlee, a suburb of Glasgow. They lived in a three-story house filled with dark wood furniture and long heavy drapes to the tall windows. The noises on the street outside were unfamiliar and I would wake to the sound of the milk float, or of doors slamming and people shouting. We slept in a room on the third floor and the house seemed very tall, its ground floor having a flight of steep steps down to the back garden. Our Grandparents welcomed us with a meal and were always delighted to see us.

Grandma was from Blackford in Perthshire. A place steeped in history on the other side of the hill from Dollar. Local legend describes how Queen Helen, wife of the Caledonian King Magnus, was accidentally drowned at the ford of the Allan River. The village at the foot of Gleneagles became known as Blackford as a result. A sizeable community had been established by the turn of the 18th century but was destroyed by Jacobite forces in 1716. According to the Blackfordhistorical society the communities in the area "were all burnt to the ground to deny food and shelter to the troops of the Duke of Argyll". By 1799 the village had been rebuilt. My Grandmother's family, the Sharps, are first recorded here in 1790.

Grandma's father, John Munro, was the schoolmaster at Blackford. In a historic account of Blackford, dated 1799, and written by the Reverend Mr John Stevenson, he states the "schoolmaster has the highest legal salary" and the "usual branches of education are taught so cheap as to render education affordable to all". I doubt that by the time my great grandfather was schoolmaster at Blackford he was the highest paid man in the village, but undoubtedly it was a position of some status and those values of 'education for all' are deep in my genes. Sadly John Munro died when Grandma was very young, leaving Daniel and Elizabeth Sharp's daughter a young widow with three children to support.

The Sharp family funded the bereaved children's education at John Watson's Institution in Glasgow. I have a school photo that unrolls to reveal an enormous number of unhappy children, my grandmother and my great aunt among them, as lonely wee girls. They studied at the Institution, recently converted from a work-house to a school, and thus Grandma became a Glasgow girl.

Grandma and Mummy used to visit Blackford quite regularly. Distant cousins are still alive and what was the Sharps brewery is now home to the famous Highland Spring Water that is exported to fifty countries all over the world. As they say on their website "what makes Highland Spring so wonderfully pure and fresh is its turbulent journey through the rocks and glens of the Scottish Highlands to its final destination deep within the Ochil Hills".

Grandma's beauty caught my Grandfather's eye when he was a young textile designer, his dark haired and passionate nature so different from her kind and gentle approach.

Yet the love that grew between them was strong and they withstood the opposition of his family and married and had two daughters.

What I particularly loved about my grandparents is that they listened to, and supported, my interests from an early age. They saw art as a useful career. They knew I loved ballet and took my sister and me to see Swan Lake and Coppelia, and bought me a much-treasured jewellery box with a dancer on the lid. One visit I wrote to my parents in Dorridge and told them I was going to change my name and be a dancer. I did go to ballet classes when I returned to England, but I was too awkward and tall to be a dancer, though I was full of expression and was given a bronze medal for mime. I kept my given name, when I suggested in the letter home that I change it I was - I think – trying to address the bullying around my name that I had encountered in England.

Both Grandparents had started in life from scratch, without family backing, and - with their wits and with the history and culture that could not be taken from them -built a life and home for themselves and their two daughters, and in turn their grandchildren. Grandpa's business buying Shetland and Fair Isle knitwear and selling to businesses, shops and people all over the world continued until he died. He visited the knitters at their homes and knew many of them personally. When my mother and aunt were children he was away for long periods visiting the isles and sent postcards to his daughters from his travels.

We used to get letters from the knitters even after his death. He brought a spinning wheel with him when he moved to join us in England and kept it in his workroom above the coach house. He was a clever man and loved to read and to expound on politics, quote from Robbie Burns and debate current times. As my grandmother was withdrawn so my grandfather was expansive.

When he moved to join us in England Grandpa always made his presence felt. Sometimes he loudly erupted into favourite catch phrases in a Scottish accent, "Ay Pieces of Eight, Pieces of Eight", sometimes he wore his skull cap and sang or muttered prayers. He was very deaf and played his radio and television at full volume, which drove Mum to distraction. "Morag, are you cooking bacon?" he called out angrily to me from his flat upstairs, and I had to admit that I was.

At festive times, such as Easter and Passover, we children were invited up to our Grandparents' flat and given special festive food, delicious matzos and olives. Candles were lit and Grandpa in his skullcap chanted in Hebrew. For many years I was somewhat confused between resurrection (Christian Easter tradition) and Passover (Jewish celebration of the Jews release from slavery in Egypt) thinking Passover had more to do with passing over – dying - than with a celebration of freedom. Now I believe all spring festive observances are to do with fertility and renewal.

My Grandparents had survived dislocation and loss and they helped me to survive mine. Their move to join us in England healed a great part of the loss I felt when we left Scotland. My Grandmother's sister stayed in Glasgow and we kept family connections in that cosmopolitan city until that generation had all died.

Howard's Way

Hi Dad

It is thirty years since we talked face to face, though you are always with me. I thought of you the other day when someone described me as enigmatic and I realised this reminded me of you. How Mum used to complain that you didn't talk to her. You just didn't see the point of discussing the minutiae of a day, or how you felt about things, your communication was in your music and in the way you acted and responded to people.

I remember such loving things about you. Although you never spoke of love and only held me if it was high up on your shoulders coming down a hill or to carry me when I twisted my ankle, what I knew from you always was warm humorous loving kindness and a responsiveness to my needs.

I was seven when you and I went to see your mother, my Nanny, Katie Munro, in her final hours in her nursing home in Kent to say our goodbyes. I remember it was late and dark, we must have set off from Warwickshire after you finished work. I was dozing in the car when you - knowing the night shift would be on duty, and frustrated by the winding unsigned lanes and being unable to find Nanny's home – unexpectedly decided to stop at a factory we passed to ask the way. The gatekeeper told us to go on in and ask the workers for directions. At the time it seemed entirely natural to me that one of the workers would rush up to you, shake you warmly by the hand "Hello Mr Smyth. How nice to see you here," and make us welcome, giving us directions and refreshment. He'd worked with you in Scotland years previously. We found our way to see dear Nanny, tiny in her big white bed, and she knew we were there.

I grew used to the high regard and warmth from those who knew you. If someone was ill you would visit them in hospital, if they had family needs you visited them at home. People would always speak fondly of you, and your humane approach to what was then called personnel management underpinned your career. I recognise the values that you embraced. You had a warm spiritual energy and shared that with me. You and I went to a few services in Darley Dale Methodist chapel when I was between eight and ten. Knowing that your father had played the organ in a Church of Scotland in Glasgow for thirty years I realise a spiritual Christian faith was natural to you, but we didn't find an alternative to the Scottish church in England and our attendances soon waned – I suspect you were quietly supporting my quest for answers about religion.

When we moved to Derbyshire I really struggled with the new accent and my school-mates' affectionate language such as "Eee bah gum" or "Ay oop dook". I developed a speech impediment, keeping my teeth together and turning my sss's into schhs. I was often in tears. "Why are you so sensitive?" you asked. Now I could answer "changing schools four times in five years may have something to do with it". But you were right, although I did not have words to describe it at the time - I was born sensitive, and it was something my family struggled to understand.

Your quick wit, ready use of puns and ability to turn potential conflict into humour and shared laughter was exceptional. Of course, that was one of the things that would infuriate Mum when she was trying to make a serious point or when your humour verged on the innuendo. "Oh Howard" she would say, knowing she would get no further with the point she was making. You sometimes used that humour in a collusive way so we children would share in the joke at Mum's expense. But we all adored you, Mum in particular – many years after you died you were still the only man for her.

I shared some of Mum's frustration about your gender bias and somewhat dismissive approach to women. You would deny this and after all it was simply the norm in your generation of men. As Mum said, you were much more for women's emancipation than many men. You were also fiercely stubborn, and clearly had some resistance from your own past and upbringing. I guess like most women my age we were always apologising to some degree for our liberation to our fathers. In our family you wryly conceded the revolution for women in the sixties.

I was jealous of the attention you gave to Alan, building dens with him or helping him to create one of the many 'Heath Robinson' constructions you made, your risky electrics feeding the wonky standard lamp, or the interesting combination of varied unrelated engineering parts that held the lawnmower together. I was particularly upset that you supported Alan's guitar playing when you had refused to buy me one unless I learnt to play the piano. I was also furious when you reversed over my bicycle, buckling its front wheel and never recognised how much that bike had meant to me.

Perhaps I was angry because you often did recognise my needs. I realise now that far from being a purely absent or partisan dad, you and I often had time together where you did give me time and attention. My memories of time alone with you mostly centre on being in the car. At weekends you sometimes worked in Sheffield on a Saturday. I took a lift with you to go in and shop and we talked amicably and sang on the route through Chatsworth Park to the city centre. Once or twice we stopped at a pub on the way home and you bought me a small shandy or a lager and lime, reminding me not to tell Mum.

You taught me to drive, patiently taking me through the basics in Matlock Station car park, then buying a series of old cars to learn on. We went on weekend drives together to Derby or into the dales. The clutch of an old Standard gave way at the traffic lights in Derby. Another time something fell off the back of an old Hillman Minx in the dales. These experiences also taught me your deep knowledge of mapping and orienteering, from your service with the Signals Regiment, and how to stay calm in a crisis with practical survival strategies probably learnt from your many years driving in the Highlands of Scotland. You were so pleased when I passed my driving test first time, just after my eighteenth birthday, you bought me a Triumph Herald and with it supported my liberation. I heard you telling Mum what a good driver you thought I was. Shortly after that I drove your car, and you and Mum, to Edinburgh when a reaction to a bee-sting incapacitated your leg. Thanks to your trust and support I became a confident driver and shared your pleasure in driving.

Before I passed my test, I grew selfishly used to your

coming out at short notice late at night to collect me from some pub or disco in town or to take me back to my flat in Chesterfield once I started art college. I remember one awkward conversation where you enquired in an oblique way about birth control and I told you I was on the pill. We never discussed it again. I think your life as the youngest of five - the older siblings all involved in jazz music or being students at university - your own teenage years, and the values of your home, enabled you and in turn me to be liberal, joyful and unafraid.

As Chair of the West Derbyshire Liberal Association, I remember you and Mum hosting garden parties attended by Jo Grimond and later the infamous Jeremy Thorpe. The garden full of people holding glasses and having spirited discussions. And I remember you always in the garden at weekends, up to your thighs in waders in the lake, pulling out mud and old bulrushes, or in the woods taking out dead branches, planting new trees and in the orchard harvesting the fruit. I particularly loved the way you created a Christmas tree out of pieces of other variable trees, yew branches and conifers would be hauled in and tied together to fill one of the tall Georgian windows in the sitting room.

Best of all was Hogmanay, because it was your birthday on New Year's Day, and with the Scots preference to celebrate New Year's Eve over Christmas, we would hold a party in your honour. Our friends came from the village and from much further afield if they could get there. Wearing your kilt you would provide music, dancing, games and your liberal hand with the home-made punch (and it did have a punch) and scotch ensured the party went with a swing and even Mum let her hair down. Next day we had a family meal to celebrate your birthday and to share a 'hair of the dog'.

How sad I was long after we all left home when you and Mum decided to sell Ladygrove house.

Mum was finding it hard to cope, "the upkeep is a huge amount of work and we are just rattling around in there" she said. "Where do you want to go next?" I asked you. "Heaven" you replied, my not realising how prophetic your words were, you maybe realising how frail you were slowly becoming.

Not long after you moved Mum rang me on my birthday "Dad's got cancer" she said. You were the one who remembered to wish me a happy birthday. And when I got up to Derbyshire you were the one who said, "I'm sorry this has to happen for you now". Always thinking of others over yourself. We know now that the carcinogenic fluid used to clean your trumpet caused the cancer of the oesophagus with which you were diagnosed, but we didn't know that then. How brave you were as you undertook all the unsuccessful interventions on offer. Maintaining your sense of humour to the end. We all found it hard to face the loss of our big strong father. Once I came into the hospital to find you on the floor of the bathroom unable to get up and another time at home, turning off the bath tap you were unable to reach, you thanked me and said you had had your "three score years and ten", but it was only by a month.

Mum and Alan left your hospital bedside to get a cuppa and so it was that I was alone with you when you died, able to tell you we all loved you and to hold your hand as you sighed out your last breath.

And now I often feel your presence, in my son when he smiles, in the rhythm of our lives and in the freedom and zest for life you gave us. I hear your voice sometimes, "I'll take it from here" when Mum had her major stroke, and "be ready for anything" before I heard the news my brother and his partner separated. And I am always grateful for your love, commitment and all that jazz.

Katie and Howard at Ladygrove

Ladygrove

Ladygrove House

Dad was excited when he first took us to see Ladygrove House. He had learnt from his mistake in not showing Mum the house in Dorridge, which she hated, before he bought it and he was sure we would love the house he'd found for us in Derbyshire.

We did. We ran around the empty rooms, claiming them and calling out at each new surprise we found.

Ladygrove House is a large detached Georgian house with six double bedrooms in grounds of three acres. It occupies a commanding position at the head of the main road in the village of Two Dales in the White Peak of Derbyshire. The name Thomas Dakeyne 1796 is carved in a capstone over the front door and the drive sweeps round, past a coach house to the front of the house which faces a large rolling lawn leading to a small lake. I was overawed by the enormous sense of space. The high ceilings, tall windows, large hall and landing led to graciously proportioned rooms which were an extraordinary contrast to the dark Edwardian house we were leaving. Many large country estates had become defunct and too expensive to run after the First World War and in a similar way after the Second World War large country houses in rural locations became briefly affordable to the middle class. We were not wealthy, but the income from Daddy's new job as Personnel Manager for Sheffield Steel Rolling Mills, combined with family funds made the £6,000 price manageable. My Grandparents in Glasgow were increasingly finding life difficult and were missing us a great deal. The plan was for them to join us and to move into a self-contained flat within this spacious home, enabling us to become custodians of this beautiful family home for twenty-eight years.

As a family we were delighted to move into a home that was surrounded by hills - if not the mountains of Scotland, the Peaks of Derbyshire had their own beauty - and we had a wild landscaped garden to explore and recover, complete with running stream, small lake, orchard and walled vegetable garden, overrun with overgrowth. There were also the foundations of a rose terrace, a wood, and secret paths through the whole garden with a high stone wall that enclosed the boundary.

The garden was paradise for me as a child. Able to resume my free range ways almost every day I explored the garden in all weathers, learning about nature and seeing worlds within worlds in the life of ponds and woods and trees. The only thing that scared me was ants - their intelligent highways made me uneasy – but spiders, bees, water boatmen, shrimps and centipedes were all a source of fascination and wonder. The lake was more of a large pond, but its shape echoed the three dams in the hills above, having one long thin body of water and two smaller ones. I spent hours at the intersection between the brook and the stream that fed the ponds. A path led to a bridge and side gate to the road that led to the mill. Below the bridge there was a little beach formed from the roots of a yew tree that had a firm base on which to stand and fish with a jam jar or to just gaze into the life that teemed in the water.

There were large established rhododendron bushes that provided ideal den spaces, under the spread of tall dark canopies of rhododendrons' glossy green leaves. Francis Darwin, Charles Darwin's uncle, bought Sydnope Hall, uphill from Ladygrove, from the Dakeyne family and instigated the laying out of grounds that by 1874 were, according to Horticulture and Cottage Gardener "full of natural beauties and attractions". This included the importation of rhododendrons. Since their introduction to the UK from Turkey in 1763 rhododendrons had become immensely popular and by the 19th century James Smith Nurseries of Darley Dale were proud of their one million rhododendrons. Eighty-six years after Francis' work on Sydnope Hall, I was a child building dens in Ladygrove's garden.

Walking out from the back gate and following the stream led first to a large mill that in 1789 Daniel Dakeyne bought as an unfinished cotton mill from a local farmer, and converted to a flax-spinning mill. Daniel and his wife Hannah had eight sons and one daughter. Three of his elder sons, John, Thomas and Daniel, were partners in the enterprise, and it was this Thomas Dakeyne who laid the capstone at Ladygrove House in 1796.

Two of the younger brothers Edward and James, were accomplished engineers and in 1794 their father patented a machine his sons had designed to prepare flax for spinning called the Equalinium. Unfortunately, by 1800 the huge investment made by the company and partners had become overwhelming and in 1801 – just five years later - Daniel, his sons and families were bankrupt and destitute. The tradition of engineering and design was everywhere in the dales, buildings with large fine cut stone blocks often dominated the villages and not far away - in Cromford - Arkwright built his famous spinning jenny. The ideas and imagination fostered by the industrial revolution aided by the water power in the peak district led to rapid developments in design and engineering. By 1826 Edward and James Dakeyne somehow made enough money to buy the mill back and to build a three-storey flax mill alongside the cotton mill. In order to get enough water pressure to power the two mills they built a series of three dams in Sydnope Valley, rising to 96 feet. To cope with the increase in water pressure they developed a revolutionary water pressure powered disc engine, patented in 1830 as the 'Dakeyne hydraulic disc engine'. Sydnope Brook flowed from the dams to the mill, and from there into the garden of Ladygrove House.

By the time I walked past the mill as a child, it was largely empty, used by an agricultural feed supplier, there were no sounds of pumps of engines, just the occasional lorry loading up with supplies, but the dams were still there. The dams were steep sided and deep and the path through the woods held an air of mystery and wildness. Untouched fallen trees bridged the paths and there were boggy watery swamps and beech tree groves. Rhododendrons grew everywhere and our dog, Beau, loved scrambling through them.

Charles Darwin visited Sydnope Hall and in 1858 he wrote to his friend W.D. Fox of his memorable visit to Sydnope, citing "the cross from wild Boar and common pig at Sydnope was wilder than the wild Boar". At least three generations of Darwins were all keen naturalists and explorers. Francis' father (Charles' grandfather), Erasmus, was an abolitionist and free thinker who wrote The Botanic Garden and Zoonomia, containing a system of pathology and theory of survival of the fittest that Charles Darwin read and commented on prior to developing his own Theory of Evolution. I saw no wild or tame pigs, just badgers and foxes, on my walks but I did like to identify plants and trees.

A solitary Scots Pine crowned a limestone cliff above the dams, its stunted growth and lopsided flag-like branches were visible for miles, and we called it Flag Tree. An expedition up here was quite tricky, navigating cliffs and steep hills. The slopes and valleys and woodland of the White Peak meet enclosed gritstone upland and - where they do - a diverse range of acidic soil types, ideal for the cultivation of heathers and rhododendrons, exists.

I loved to climb trees and an oak tree that framed the lawn had two low branches, easy for a child to reach, one branch formed the seat and one the backrest of my arboreal sofa. An avaricious reader I reclined in my tree with a book and was lost to the world. I read the Little Princess, the Secret Garden and Anne of Green Gables and related strongly to lonely and isolated little girls. I was completely connecting with the environment in which I now lived, but it was harder to connect with the people.

I was sent to buy the warm bread fresh from the ovens in the bakery down the road in the village. As I walked home, chewing on an irresistible crust from the loaf, two village children walked towards me. "Hello" I said, mouth half full of half chewed bread. The boy who was younger than me started to reply but his older sister clapped her hand over his mouth and they walked silently past me as I stared in disbelief. We were considered strangers in the village for some years to come.

Given the option by my parents, I chose to go to the local Darley Dale County Primary school rather than the nearby public school for girls - I felt I'd had my fill of those. There was a footpath across the fields to get to the school and Ladygrove stayed in sight for half of the way as I slowly climbed the hill with my satchel on my back. I was the sort of child who - having set off perfectly prepared - would arrive at school with one plait unravelling or with one welly boot remaining, the other having been lost in a boggy spot on my way to school.

In the morning the children would stand in lines in front of their classroom doors in the open playground of the school. One day the Headmaster called me out in front of the whole school. "Morag meet Morag" he said loudly with a laugh and we two Morags greeted each other uncomfortably with a half-smile before returning to our class lines, both probably becoming used to a lifetime of teasing and humiliation for our Scottish name. To make friends I became a bit of the classroom clown and was soon being chastised by the teacher, who in front of the class used a ruler to hit me hard on the knuckles of my hand and who made me stand in the corner, my back to the class where I hoped they could not see my tears and bright red cheeks of shame.

I did make friends and we went on outings and excursions, once a three-day trip to Cheddar Gorge. Learning that my friend Tamsin had a cat with kittens we hatched a plot and one day Tamsin brought a beautiful short-haired grey kitten to school for me. I carried it all the way home in my satchel and presented it as a fait accompli to my mother, who could not say no to this small girl with her self-made and long-awaited cat reunion. We called him Mini, French for cat, to go with our dog, Beau. Beau, a Staffordshire mix, viewed Mini with interest and soon accepted him into the family and Mini had many happy years curled up with Beau or exploring the garden with me.

Beau and Mini

I was chosen to sing at a school concert. I was to be one of the babes in Babes in the Wood and to sing "one little robin in the cherry tree" a popular song of the time. All went well in the rehearsals. The village hall was full and when the pianist began my cue I started singing a full octave higher than I had in rehearsals. This came out as something of a forced squeak and I looked out into the audience and saw my parents wincing as I gamely struggled on. This marked the end of my performance ambitions.

I loved to dance. I put Bizet's Carmen or Tchaikovsky's Nutcracker Suite on the record player in the big sitting room at Ladygrove, turned up the volume and twirled in my stocking feet to my heart's content on the wooden tiled floor. The little sitting room, with French windows that opened onto a terrace, was turned into our playroom. I could spread out large paper, lie on my tummy on the floor and paint with no fear of being in trouble for the mess. As a young teenager I was allowed to paint a mural on the entire wall of this room based on the wonderful illustrations by Joan Kiddell-Monroe for 'the Dragon Fish' by Pearl S Buck.

The sitting room and the dining room were elegant rooms with long curtains to their tall windows. What we called the big sitting room had a huge mirror over the large stone fireplace. At festive times the room was filled with light, candles, trees and decorations made from silver sprayed fir cones, teasels and dried honesty. A crackling log fire, the dog asleep on the hearth, feast treats and decanters reflecting the flames on the side tables are what I remember, with the sounds of the piano being played by my father, or sister or brother coming from the hall when I think of the anticipation of our Christmas celebrations.

There was central heating, the old cast iron radiators held some heat, which was fortunate for the severe winters of the 60's hit Derbyshire particularly hard. One year we built an enormous snowball, like a huge boulder, from the snow on the lawn and there is a photograph of me sitting on it on the ice on the lake, while my brother Alan stands on the slope in front of me. My hands were blue with cold and we trooped into the kitchen for a welcome bowl of hot soup.

Alan and Morag in the garden at Ladygrove House

The kitchen was the hub of the house. It was always warm, the sounds of the Aga coals being raked echoed through the house twice a day. Here my memories centre round the kitchen table, leaning back on two legs of the pine chairs and waiting for my mother to spread the brownie into the tin so that I could lick out the bowl. I chewed orange peel, pith and all – to the horror of my mother and sister – or cut off charcoal crusts of toast while we talked, laughed, argued and generally connected as a family here more than anywhere else in the house.

On a shelf above the Aga several old jugs and plates were displayed, including a Copeland plate, which - being cracked, chipped and repaired - had been left in the house.

I imagine Thomas Dakeyne having discussions with his family in this kitchen. Maybe even meeting here with Francis and his nephew Charles Darwin. The Darwin and Wedgewood families are interrelated. Grandfather Erasmus regretted that a good education for women was not generally available in Britain and proposed that young women should be educated in schools with subjects to include physical exercise, botany, chemistry and experimental philosophy, and that women should familiarise themselves with the arts and manufacture through visits to sites like Coalbrookdale - where this Copeland plate would have been made - and Wedgwood's potteries.

When we first arrived at Ladygygrove photos show us as a family dwarfed by the house. But the house became part of us, and our history, and we became part of the history of the house. To this day when I catch up with old friends from these days the first thing they refer to is Ladygrove House. They have their own memories of visits, camp-outs, sleepovers and parties. It is an imposing house that speaks of status and wealth - parksandgardens.org now describes it as "an attractive hillside house and gardens" - it has a warm unchangeable architecture of perfect proportions. If friends knew the house and where I lived before they knew me, our friendship was coloured by this impression. If friends knew me, and then the house, they were taken aback and often in awe of where I lived. It became impossible to separate my identity from that of the house. I had a fluid position within the English class system and I became familiar with aspects of the working, middle and upper classes through living at Ladygrove House. The years here gave me space and time to develop my creative imagination unhindered by

forced activities or social constraint and offered opportunities
- encouraged by my parents - to explore my ideas through art.
Whether through painting and dancing, or playing music and
building constructions, I was never confined to a small piece
of paper or restricted room. I could have big dreams.

Thomas Dakeyne, 1796

   This Copeland plate cracked, chipped, repaired
   displayed on the shelf above the Aga
   treasured in the Georgian kitchen
   where the Dakeynes possibly
   met Darwin and Wedgwood and certainly
   knew of their endeavours. When free thinkers,
   abolitionists cast their thoughts in clay,
   transferred images of exotic flowers
   in gold and blue symbols from the colonies.
   Maybe they had discussions round
   the kitchen table, Rhododendrons in a vase,
   soup bubbling on the hob.
   And trying to understand nature
   children, like us, brought tadpoles,
   moths to the light.

Kay (cousin) and Morag, kitchen Ladygrove House

Bakewell

Passing the eleven plus exam appeared to have been straightforward for me, and I started at Lady Manners Grammar School in Bakewell when I was eleven. There was a walk down the road in Two Dales to the main road from Matlock, where we caught the school bus to Bakewell. In the first year, I mainly sat on my own, often feeling motion sickness in the stuffy swaying Silver Service bus, especially if I tried to read. The bus was slow, stopping often to pick up pupils and reaching the school forty minutes later, just in time for the bell. The school was arranged on three sides around a quadrangle with open roofed corridors leading to the classrooms. Most of my friends from primary school had gone to schools in Matlock and the new classmates came with friends from their schools around the Peak District villages.

I felt pretty invisible and imprisoned. My free-range days were evidently over and I escaped into my imaginary world. Gazing out of the window, occasionally tuning in to a snatch of history – Henry the VIII again – or trying to make sense of Physics. Where did electricity come from I wanted to know. Nobody gave me an answer, "it just is" I was told. My Physics teacher told me he had a Scottish doll called Morag, only it was a boy. Ha-ha laughed the class as I sank further into incomprehension, boredom and loneliness. It would be another twenty years before I realised nobody else knew where electricity came from either. The school reminded me of my painful experience at Warwick Preparatory School, the kind of school that would have prepared me for an environment like this. Teachers wore graduation robes and often carried a stick. I was there, but absent, and became quite accomplished at reading comics or books on the back row. I liked Art, Biology and English. I hated Maths and simply could not do multiplication tables at all. The first year crawled by, with my becoming increasingly introverted and shy.

Bakewell is a pretty market town and an important centre for the Peak District. The River Wye runs through it and roads from Sheffield and Derby lead there. Bakewell is famous for a certain almond dessert. Girls from Lady Manners School were inevitably known as Bakewell Tarts. The school established by Lady Manners from Haddon Hall, initially for poor boys from Bakewell, became in 1896 the first endowed school to admit both boys and girls. The current school buildings were built in the 1930s, had a mix of day and boarder pupils and with its motto, *Pour Y Parvenir* (strive to attain) and Peacock badge emblazoned on our obligatory blazers and berets, there was something of the feel of a public school about it all. The hall at the centre of the school was the fulcrum and the only large interior space for the pupils.

At the beginning of the second year we waited after assembly in the hall while our names were called out one by one to decide into which of three class streams we were to be placed. The top stream was L for Latin, the L indicated you would be in the top sets and would study Latin. The middle stream was

G for German and the bottom stream - for the least intelligent - was F for French. My sister was in the L stream and I was disappointed when my name was not called out for L. The L pupils filed out of the hall and I waited again. I was not called for the G stream either. By the time those pupils filed out and the rest of us knew they had been selected for the F stream I was in tears and absolutely mortified. My parents were equally upset when they heard the news and promptly made an appointment to discuss the decision with the headmaster. They came back with the news that the teachers felt I would be overwhelmed in a higher class as I was clearly struggling with so many subjects. By the age of twelve sciences other than Biology, languages other than French, and Geography had all been dropped from my education. The seeds for a rebel were sown.

"You are here to pass your O levels", the Form Teacher announced sternly. I was unimpressed, my parents believed in education over exam results and the GCE's were many years hence.

"Morag I want you in the top set for French", said Winnie Wheeler, one of two assistant principals, her hair always pulled back into a tight bun at the nape of her neck. Unfortunately timetable clashes with other options proved unmanageable and I chose to move down a set.

"Mo Rag don't run!" Mr Pontin, the other assistant principal (known as Ponty) yelled down the open corridors, his robe flying in the breeze. He taught Maths but he didn't want me in his top set and I was placed in the middle set where I could continue my back seat reading.

I had been noticed. It turned out I wasn't invisible after all, just discounted. Luckily my friend, Jennie, had also been discounted and together we formed rebel's corner. Cut our hair, wore jewellery, rolled up our skirt waistbands to shorten our skirts and chuckled over the preposterousness of life. Susan, a friend who lived in Two Dales and was a year younger than me, had now started at the school so I had company on the bus too. Life was easing up, it was 1963 and the Beatles were on the radio. We loved them.

Jennie's Dad was a manager at Sheffield City Hall and Jennie invited me to go with her to see the Beatles there. The crowds when we arrived were enormous, but Jennie's Dad ushered us in, and to our seats on the front rows. Wow! We were surrounded by hordes of screaming fans and we were standing and screaming too and the Beatles were on stage right in front of us. Love Love Me Do. Oh I do I do. If ever a moment is seared on the memory it is the sight of those four young men singing their hearts out to us, inaudible under the screams, beautiful in every way.

Jennie unexpectedly brought me a photo while I was writing this memoir. It is taken on a school trip to Fountains Abbey. My packed lunch and flask are spread out before me beside my green tartan bag. The photo is black and white but I clearly remember the bag, the school summer dress and jumper I am wearing, as well as the pleasure of sitting on grass strewn with daisies and of not being behind the uncomfortable imprisoning school desk.

We did not get out much. Once a year Mr Wooley, the art teacher, would walk us out of school and down to "the dip". Mr Wooley had been in a Japanese prisoner of war camp and I suspect he had been given the job of art teacher as a safe sinecure. Art, then as now, was not important to the school curriculum. A gentle natured man, he had curly longish ginger hair and a slight palsy. He would set us tasks that were unvaried through each year. Painting with the poster paints we had to mix from powder with varying degrees of failure. And in the summer term he gave us the outside 'drawing from life' experience. With our drawing boards and paper we would troop down to "the dip", a valley half a mile from school but already out into the Peak District, and draw the farmsteads, stone walls and rivers. Most of all we would sit quietly ruminating and chatting and enjoying being out in the world.

Our other annual excursion to "the dip" was for cross-country. I was never the sporting type and there was a point on the route, just after the dip where you could sit out of sight behind a tree and wait to re-join the runners on their return. In a similar way I was left back for hockey and could wait out most matches somewhere near the back of the field with knees purple with cold and lips frozen, hacking at the grass with my stick until just once or twice the ball briefly came my way and I would be struck at with sticks leaving purple bruises to match my knees. "You should be brilliant at hurdles" the PE teacher told me, commenting on the length of my legs, but I was only good at the long jump.

What I loved was English. I was often top in the top set. So much so that I amazed myself by winning a prize one speech day – a book about Marie Curie which was fascinating and helped me to see that women could study science. My English teachers loved me too. Mr Day and Christine Wragg waded through my awful handwriting and gave me great feedback on my essays. One term we wrote a serial and I was called to read mine out to the class every week. I wrote poems and I was writing a children's book by the time I was fourteen.

When it came to my failing the English Literature GCE the teachers were so astonished they wanted to query the result for me. I shrugged my shoulders, knowing exam markers would not have the same patience with my script and simply took the exam again, this time gaining a B.

Most of my diary entries for school in 1966, when I was fifteen, read "school not much". My entry for the 1st November reads "Another day of boredom at school. What a life". Then on the 2nd November a school careers fair was held in the hall. Companies and organisations set up their information on tables and we were invited to have a look round. We were expected to be staying on to take A levels and not to be leaving school, the idea was to inspire us for the future and I was inspired. Two young men from Chesterfield College of Art and Design took time to show me the Foundation Course and to talk me through my options. Until then I had not known that Art College might be open to me. Or that I could leave school at sixteen, and I would turn sixteen during the school summer holidays. A rainbow lit up in my mind. Taking my details they promised to arrange an interview for me and advised me on my portfolio. I could not stop smiling. Freedom was in sight. My diary for the 2nd November: "Not much in the morning. Careers convention in the afternoon and evening. Very Good. Decided. Hope to get admitted to art college next year".

Of course, my parents were very unsure about the idea. They thought it was just a flash in the pan and watched me go off for interview in Chesterfield, not taking it too seriously and not expecting me to get in. The tutors were interested in my varied portfolio. As well as the school drawings portfolio, I included my sketchbooks and designs, as well as my personal photos. I was offered a place and I accepted.

My parents still didn't really believe I would leave school. "Wait and see what your O level exam results are", they said. I had gained a B for my mock O level exam and my Maths teacher had dismissed my results, "I don't know how you managed that" she said contemptuously. When I sat in the walled vegetable garden revising I decided not to bother to attempt to repeat the result. I failed that exam, got low grades in Biology and higher grades in Art, Religious Instruction and English Grammar, and I failed English Literature.

Freedom beckoned, I had had enough of school and I left Lady Manners before the process turned me into a well-baked tart. My mother was supportive and persuaded my father. I joyfully enrolled on the Foundation Course in Art and Design, at Chesterfield College of Art, aged just sixteen. Life had begun.

Part Two Design and Romanticism
1967 – 1983

The Cottage, painting by Martin Hursthouse

Hasland

Chesterfield College of Art was up a hill in Hasland and looked over industrial chimneys in the valley below. A thick black smoke that occurred during the process of creating smokeless fuel filled the air when the wind was in the right direction and left black particles stuck to our clothes. The small campus was built from a series of single storey structures that had been quickly built from thin materials post war. Each building had a separate discipline, the ceramics studios and kilns, the drawing studios and the design and print studios. The offices were in the central Penmore House on whose land the studios were built.

To get there I had to take one bus to Matlock, another to Chesterfield, and walk up the steep hill to college carrying my work. I quickly set about learning to drive. Chesterfield was known for its drawing expertise and the failings of my limited art education quickly became apparent - my early life drawings revealed a stilted and lumpen hand. Charcoal was better, more freeing and I slowly began to improve. I remember my father's shock when he saw my portfolio. "Oh" he said, "I didn't realise you would be drawing nudes". Mother, who'd been the one to take me regularly to galleries and museums had more sang-froid and shrugged her shoulders with a smile.

The foundation course consisted of six weeks block study in each discipline, print making, ceramics, drawing, photography, sculpture, fashion design and graphic design as well as general studies and three weekly evening classes, including life drawing. This was followed by a similar one-year pre-diploma course. The uninterrupted six weeks were a great way of immersing ourselves in the subject and rapidly seeing a process through from initial sketches and concepts to the completion of a pot or sculpture or dress or fabric design. I still have some of my early pots and photos and I clearly remember my first dress design, a turquoise broderie anglaise wrap over dress that would be fashionable today.

Sculpture was taught at the foot of the hill, in the ground floor of a disused mill in Lordsmill Street. Ken Burgess taught us to mix plaster and apply in layers to frames to build organic forms. We got very messy and experimental, building sculptures as tall as ourselves, with holes Hepworth style. One six-week session we were encouraged to use alternative materials and I built a two metre tall sculpture from grey rectangular plastic pipes with a water filled triangular base. This sculpture was selected with others to be exhibited at the Arts Tower in Sheffield. The 78m tall building had recently been opened to great acclaim and housed the Arts Departments of the University of Sheffield. Robert Smith, the project architect, is quoted as saying he was influenced by the work of Mies van der Rohe, and the tall tower had a water feature at the foot which my sculpture inadvertently echoed.

We had to take the selected sculptures to Sheffield ourselves, and my friend Debbie and I set off in her Mini with one of the sculptures precariously attached to the roof rack. Half way there the Yorkshire winds threatened to dislodge the roof rack, sculpture et al. But we limped up to the Arts Tower and carried the sculptures into the lobby only to find we had to get to the exhibition area at the top of tower via a Paternoster lift. These lifts are walk on and walk off open platforms that never stop slowly moving. Walking on with a two metre high sculpture was again not an easy feat, but somehow we managed it and my sculpture was on proud display for several weeks. The exhibition area had a wonderful 360 degree view of Sheffield from its twentieth floor and in windy conditions you could feel the sway of the building which gave a slightly disorientating feeling. The top floors of the refurbished building now house the University of Sheffield's Architecture Department. English Heritage has called it the most elegant tower block of its period. I'm sorry to say we dismantled my sculpture to bring it home when the exhibition ended.

We formed a group of four close friends: Debbie had long black hair and sensual Italian looks. She wore a pink leather coat and was confident in her sexuality. Sally was blonde, always stylish and striking, and wore a bright red pvc coat. Gerry had long straight dark brown hair down to her waist and looked like Mona Lisa. And then there was me - lanky, thin, long legged and awkward - lucky for me that Twiggy looks had hit the height of fashion. We four walked arm in arm down the hill from Hasland, filling the pavement and loudly singing Martha and the Vandellas' Dancing in the Street. "Calling out around the World, are you ready for a brand new beat?"

I was hyper excitable that first year, like a bottle of champagne that had been corked up for too long. The release from tedium and my entry into a creative education experience was exciting. I was anxious and lacking in confidence, partly to cover this up and partly because of my excitable nature, I could not stop talking. Most of my tutors found this exhausting and disruptive, but the General Studies tutors liked it. Part of the course included many visits to galleries and museums. It was 1967 and British Design was at an all-time high. Modernism was moving on to Post Modernism and every exhibition was full of the new and what are now design classics, from the angle poise lamp to the mini, and of sculpted shapes using new technologies and vivid colours - Pop Art, Op Art, Kinetic Art and Minimalism were all presented to us with the shock of the new. I bought a stunning slinky sexy black dress from Biba, but that was a step too far for my mother and she made me send it back. But there was no putting the cork back in this unstoppable bottle. Things really had changed from black and white to colour.

General Studies was fascinating. I received a brief tour of science, the theory of relativity, and an introduction to ecology. We were given the prognosis for population growth, pollution and global warming and became early eco pioneers. We had drama and literature. We did performance art and happenings. My first poem to be published was in the college paper. I gained an A level in one year of evening study in art history. My lecturers undertook an IQ assessment with me and confirmed that I did have a high IQ despite my poor academic performance. This was reassuring, but could not replace the confidence I had lost in myself. Two of the tutors suggested towards the end of the second year that I try Transcendental Meditation, a gift that would prove to have lifelong benefits.

In the first year I had trouble organising myself and was often late and missed the bus. My 'Honey' diary from 1968 is full of social activity, shopping, parties, pubs, folk clubs, bands, and of course hormone mood swings and boys. Early in the second term at the College I became very low and eventually it was diagnosed that I'd contracted Glandular Fever, which was often referred to as the "kissing disease". This further affected my self-confidence and I was very sensitive to criticism. My end of year report refers to my disruptive behaviour and lack of application and talent and so does my diary, where - when I actually managed to engage with the work - I put entries in the diary "worked!" with an exclamation mark or after feedback from a crit "hopeless".

A couple of things upset the Principal when I crossed his path. A group of us decided to support our fellow students in other colleges protesting about war, some thirty colleges a month were protesting with 'sit-ins'. When we proposed holding our own sit-in we were amazed by the strength of his anger and anxiety, and we realised our power. Another time, a friend was discovered - by her mother - with some dope. Her mother called the police and threw the dope on the fire. The police interviewed the friend and in a panic she said she'd got the dope from me, which was entirely untrue. I was innocently whistling my way into college when I was suddenly called into the Principal's office. He explained what had happened and that he'd had a discussion with the Police. I was astonished and my heart hit my boots. I think he realised my surprise was genuine. He warned me to be careful about the company I kept, and said that on this occasion he would not inform my mother, who he knew to be a magistrate.

At the end of the first year I went to visit my friend Eva

on the beautiful island of Gotland in Sweden. We met when we were fourteen on an exchange visit and had become good friends. Eva lived in the exquisite town of Visby and most days we would cycle to the beach or walk round the old town. I had the great good fortune to experience both classic Swedish design, very much with the feel of a Carl Larsson painting and - especially in Stockholm - contemporary Swedish design. This experience profoundly influenced my approach to design ethics, material choices and fabric. Eva told me recently that it was her mother who chose the now classic contemporary Danish designed furniture that so impressed me in their apartment.

I scraped through the first year and things began to improve in the second year. I was still disorganised, but my life became easier to manage. I was more engaged with my studies and my confidence was slowly improving - I was enjoying the course. Sheila left home to go to University and my brother - having completed a first year at Lady Manners School, and like me encountering difficulty - had been sent to Fettes Boarding School in Edinburgh. Sheila and I were very against the idea of sending Alan away and pleaded with our parents to no avail. Alan, having been persuaded by my father with a new camera and promises of exciting times, went off quite cheerfully. He realised later in life how my negative experiences had impacted on our parents' anxiety for their son and their decision for his education. I gained the impression that while it didn't matter too much for me, as a girl, they were disappointed by my failings and for their son sought a better education. At the time my father earned £3,353 per annum and that proved enough to pay the mortgage for Ladygrove House, support Sheila at University, me at Art College and

Alan's school fees at Fettes and to live comfortably if not luxuriously.

Fifty years ago two men walked on the moon for the first time, we watched in awe on television, there was a long wait for their fragile craft to come back into view and begin their safe return to earth. This was just after my eighteenth birthday and I passed my driving test at the same time. My journeys would not be quite as adventurous. The bangers I learnt to drive in being no longer road worthy, my parents bought me a Triumph Herald and I drove to college every day, no longer having to take the buses. I gave a lift to two fellow students and we climbed the steep hairpin bends of Sydnope Hill to the Moor across the Pennines. One wintry day in the second term my lack of experience in driving on ice became apparent when I changed down a gear, as usual, to navigate a bend on the moor only to find myself, car and all occupants sliding off the road, over the verge and rolling into the deep ditch.

"Sorry guys, we're going to crash", I said as we left the road and everything went into slow motion, a vivid series of still photos like shutter stop processed the calamity. We ended up upside down in the ditch. Miraculously we all crawled out of the windows unharmed. A lorry came along in the opposite direction, the driver looked down at my flipped car in disbelief, "I cannot understand how you all got out", he said. Neither could we, we'd no seat belts and no protection, but thankfully we did all get out unscathed, and the lorry driver took us home.

We put on a couple of plays, The Caretaker by Pinter and Lysistrata, the Greek classic by Aristophanes, where the Greek women withheld sexual favours from their men until they agreed to end the Peloponnesian war. We updated the script to provide a contemporary focus and I was given the lead role. Before the performance a fellow actor and friend, Jenny, and I went to the shop for some 'Dutch courage'. We bought the cheapest thing, which was cooking sherry and consumed it in the park. Jenny said I should take twice as much as her as she was half my height, with the predictable result that by the time we were due to perform I was in no fit state to do anything. The performance was postponed to the following evening, the story went round, and by the time we came to put on the play the auditorium was full and people were standing all round the walls. Some of the audience were so shocked by the explicit content they left part way through, but at the end we got a standing ovation.

When I completed the second year in 1969 I was offered work experience in interior design in a prestigious design practice on Sloane Street in the centre of London. Billy McCarty worked for David Hicks prior to opening his own practice - his clients included the Vidal Sassoon Salons, Kenneth Tynan and the Marquess of Londonderry. Now I was in the heart of swinging London. I was living in Bywater Mews, just off Kings Road at a friend's flat. Billy took me with him to visit an apartment in Mayfair that he was designing. Images of his work featured in Architectural Digest tend to show the rich fabric designs and patterns he used. Once he designed his own wallpaper collection "Noble Savage". But this apartment was entirely minimalist, cream shades and silk and linen textures. A huge room with a low king size bed and long drapes. Billy showed me how the fabrics should hang and we measured for a further room he'd been commissioned to design. He was a beautiful gay man with long sensitive hands and a thoughtful approach to design. I was sad to learn he died in 1991 (in America) from AIDS.

It was at that practice I learnt a whole new vocabulary of swearing and ever since I have been able to drop well-chosen expletives into conversation where appropriate, and sometimes when not. The job only lasted for a few weeks, but I stayed on in London until the end of summer, working as a waitress and meeting up with Debbie and Gerry, who were also in town, for the night life. Gerry took me to Covent Garden in the early hours one morning. The still functioning market was full of men shouting, moving flowers and vegetables, and setting up their stalls. The atmosphere was vivid, active and exciting. We had a cooked breakfast in one of the pubs at 6am. I think of the liveliness and heart of that experience when I visit the sanitised place it has become.

When I returned to Chesterfield at the end of the summer my friends were waiting to meet me at the station. I'd decided to undertake a Diploma in Environmental Design, specialising in Interior Design, at the same college and I was ready for my next academic adventure.

Newbold Road

Four of us shared the attic flat on the top floor of a Victorian house on Newbold Road in Chesterfield. The landlady told us she was happy to have girls, the previous male student tenants having reputedly left the flat in a mess. She would unfortunately be a disappointed woman by the end of our year. The sloping roofs reminded me of the bedroom I had as a child in Warwickshire and the views over Chesterfield's rooftops to the railway line and the hills enhanced the sense of liberation, of not being caged. We shared bedrooms, clothes, beans on toast, music, parties, personal stories and the strains of being eighteen. Having spent the summer in London, I was the only one who'd lived away from home before and we revelled in our newfound freedom.

Anne, my flat mate, and I were the only two girls on the new Environmental Design course at the Art College. My mother, seeing my interest in architecture, had once said to me "you should marry an architect dear". The idea of a woman becoming an architect was so remote that in the sixties less than 1% of students of architecture were women. This new course was designed to embrace the ecological and environmental challenges that were becoming evident. While traditional architecture still focused more on structure and not on people, this course asked us to consider who we were designing for and what materials and processes we were using. The flat filled up with our portfolios, sketches, sketch models and maquettes, and with heated debates with fellow students as we learnt how to develop a brief.

Norman Potter was our principal lecturer and our first task was to design our new studio at the top of an old Flour Mill in Lordsmill Street. The ground floor was the sculpture studios, filled with plaster dust and the sounds of hammering, music and shouts to each other above the din. There was a woodworking studio led by a traditional craftsman who closely supervised our use of circular and band saws, sanders and drills. We presented him with new challenges and he was in constant anxiety about these two girls with long beads and long hair. We had no experience of, or access to, what would now be called craft design and technology, girls not being allowed to study this at school. This was a new experience for him, he and all the wonderful tools were also a new experience for us.

My design for the new studio proposed using the defunct railway lines outside the mill and I designed studios inside railway carriages. My tutors liked the concept but with no budget for railway carriages we set to and built a studio for ourselves with low partitions between drawing boards, utilising the light from the large leaky skylights on the top floor, and creating a library and meeting space for us all to share. I was in the first year of a new course that had begun the previous year. There were fewer than twenty students on the course with a teaching team of three. In those days education was free and our fees were paid by Derbyshire County Council.

Tanya Harrod's obituary for Norman Potter, designer, craftsman, writer and poet was published in 1995 by the Independent and begins "The designer Norman Potter liked to quote Rilke's command 'Hold to the difficult' alternating it with the sombre maxim of his fellow poet and friend (and one time lover) Denise Levertov, 'We are living our whole lives in a state of emergency'. His presence was uplifting, even electrifying. He was a free spirit of great charm, wit and integrity, a Christian anarchist with deeply ingrained habits of dissent, whose thinking like the layout of his typed lectures and letters, tended to be ranged left and open-ended".

Tanya continues "During the Second World War he spent a month in Chelmsford Prison (aged 16) for refusing to carry an identity card. This was followed by six months in Wandsworth and Wormwood Scrubs after an unsuccessful attempt to initiate a moral debate on the nature of war with a military tribunal.... He thereafter saw himself as outside the class system and duty bound to question any kind of institution. In solitary confinement for non- cooperation he scratched some lines by W. H. Auden into the plaster with a bent pin 'look shining / at new styles of architecture, a change of heart'."

Potter established a design workshop in Corsham and at the end of the 1950s he went to teach in the Interior Design School at the Royal College of Art. Tanya exploring his "bringing in a modernist monoculture and methodological underpinnings with Bauhaus precedents" to the Royal College, describes how he "demanded a whole hearted commitment from his students. Those able to take the heat and fire found themselves embarked on an invigorating, far reaching, occasionally unsettling dialogue with their tutor".

That is a precise description of the journey on which I found I had embarked. I embraced the passion and poetry of design that Norman taught. I began the course in 1969, the same year that Norman Potter's seminal work, 'What is a Designer: education and practice', was published. After teaching at the Royal College Norman had developed a construction school at the West of England School of Art and Design, beginning what Potter described as a "long, long struggle against the grain of English design education". In 1968 he resigned from Bristol and left to join the disaffected students at Hornsea and Guildford. When those student protests were shut down he was welcomed in Chesterfield, and no wonder our college principal in Chesterfield had been so alarmed when the previous year we staged our own sit- in, in solidarity with Hornsea, we students discovered our own power. For a largely undocumented and undisturbed three years Norman developed his ideas and experimented with new teaching practice on the Environmental Design course at Chesterfield. We few students had the full force of his extraordinary commitment to merging making with thinking, and design with ethics and meaning. Small wonder then that this experience informed my approach to design for life. Norman left teaching at Chesterfield in 1972 and returned to Bristol to inform the development of the renowned Bristol School of Construction in 1975.

In the first year we had to design a chair, using pipe bending technology. I painstakingly drew in pencil, using a flexicurve to guide the pencil and imperial measurements. My chair design used one long tube bending over to form the seat frame and back. Norman Potter and Jim Woods looked over my shoulder pensively at my drawing. "Mmmm" said Norman.

"Not bad. You need to redraw the design in metric as this is the new measuring system". I was not an experienced nor particularly competent draftswoman and the re-drafting was a slow and painful process, but it taught me a memorable and important lesson about design system changes. When I'd finished Norman and Jim exchanged glances and produced a book with photos of the famous Marcel Breuer Bauhaus chair. I had never heard of it, and was not aware of having ever seen the design before. My design was remarkably similar, with just a higher ply back and bent ply seat to lay claim to the idea as my own.

Paula Taylor, a rare female lecturer, was an important first mentor for me. She was seen as mannish, and was probably gay. She brought a feminist perspective to male debates, adding her animated and challenging points to the discussion, and afterwards joining us outside where we smoked our roll ups and she smoked her mini cigars. Paula taught part time, and at the end of our first year she was appointed to a full time lecturing position in Nottingham. She invited me to transfer with her to Nottingham, but I chose to stay in Chesterfield.

Norman often lived on his boat in Falmouth and in the second year he invited us to redesign his boat. We had to build a scale model of the boat made from vacuum formed plastic with a fibre glass hull and then model the interior we designed. The end of project crits were always a tense affair. We lined our boats up with their accompanying drawings. The tutor team considered each design carefully and asked questions about our design approach. Two of my male colleagues produced stunning drawings and models for which they received high praise in a self-satisfied way. When all the students had left for lunch in the Feathers, a pub across the road, I was tidying up my own attempts and feeling somewhat crestfallen when I heard Norman, Jim and Mike Rowbotham discussing the designs in the library area. "Of course," said Norman, "Morag's design is much the best design, it is just not so well presented". The others murmured assent and unseen I skipped out of the studio elated.

In that same year we were invited to mount an exhibition in the House of Lords. British design was becoming internationally famous and sought after, and the exhibition aimed to celebrate British design and to express the relevance for the British economy. The workshops were frantic with activity as we sanded and prepared screens, created signs and individually laid letters from 'Letraset' with which to elaborate the board contents. We had a 'live project' with a true deadline and this focussed all our minds, working late into the night to complete each screen. When we arrived in London even the tutors were nervous as we set up our exhibition in the main foyer. One or two of the Lords came round to see what we were doing and to chat to us. This was when there were hereditary Lords and little security. It was a fascinating insight into the workings of Westminster, and when we finally finished the exhibition set up we walked along the Thames, exhausted and satisfied with the results. "You know," Mike Rowbotham told me when we met years later "none of us had mounted a full exhibition before. We were flying by the seat of our pants but it worked brilliantly". Mike and Jim joined Norman when he went to Bristol and ultimately the course at Chesterfield ended just a few years after it had begun.

I used to wonder if I'd missed an opportunity to go to an art college with a higher reputation. Chesterfield was known for sculpture, ceramics and drawing, but not for design. Art courses were not awarded degree status for decades to come, and the reputation of the college was therefore important in gaining credence for the Diploma awarded. Instinctively and intuitively I chose to stay in Chesterfield with the 'heat and the fire' of a Norman Potter course, only appreciating years later that I had purely fortuitously gained an extraordinary design education of Royal College of Art standards.

Angela Carter said that women went through a revolution in the sixties. Men caught up much later. At first men thought the newly available contraceptive pill would give them more sexual freedom, not understanding the way this fully liberated women. None of we four flat mates were virgins by the time we moved into the flat. Birth control was not discussed. My mother, a keen advocate of the pioneer Marie Stopes and her birth control clinics, had been open in her discussions with my sister and me. My father rather sheepishly broached the subject once when he was giving me a lift home. "Oh it's all right Dad, I'm on the pill", I told him breezily, and nothing further was said. This did underplay my anxiety about the high doses of oestrogen in the early pills and the dire warnings in the press, but I preferred the pill to the very rubbery condoms. Maybe it would have been better to discuss these things, but it was controversial and we all felt embarrassed and a degree of shame. Two of my flat mates and a fellow student had babies during their courses, one baby was adopted, one baby's 'single mother' fought to keep her son and one pregnancy resulted in an early marriage before the baby was born.

One or two friends had very difficult abortion experiences. Denise Levertov became pregnant to Norman Potter and went through emotional turmoil in 1946. Levertov's biography by Donna Hollenberg, A Poet's Revolution: The Life of Denise Levertov, describes her letters to her previous lover, Stephen Peet, in which she explained that while her relationship with Norman was more exciting sexually she missed the emotional connection she had enjoyed with Stephen. Ultimately Levertov effectively waited for Norman to decide whether or not she should have an abortion. Levertov reflected in an essay she wrote in the 1990s on the pivotal effect of the abortion at this turbulent time in her life. Her biographer relates Levertov's behaviour and "muddle" during and after the war to the so-called "lost girls" phenomenon described by Andrew Sinclair as "independent and adventurous young women" who were "wayward and lonely and courageous". This was ascribed to the effects of war and living in the present with no thought for the future, while post war the ideology of domesticity that denigrated careers for women was the norm. The social split and mores right through to the mid and late 1970s were explicit and designed to control reproduction and keep women constrained. Women having sex was bad, women having sex out of wedlock was a mortal sin, and women getting pregnant out of marriage was a disaster. Men having sex was a natural need and to be applauded, except for homosexual sex which was a criminal sin. Women who "got into trouble" had only themselves to blame. Levertov wrote brilliant poetry resulting from her trauma and found her own way to emancipation, ultimately becoming a Professor at Stanford University. Norman married Levertov's friend, Caroline, and remained friends with Denise Levertov for many years.

This was twenty years before I met Norman, and I knew

nothing of his personal life. However, the strains of this cultural hypocrisy and double standard for gender were becoming evident in society and the cracks that were showing were an essential part of the revolution in the sixties, helped by new and reliable birth control.

Our fellow male students oscillated between emotional inarticulateness, treating us as honorary men, or lewd and inappropriate comments and conduct. Without exception they viewed themselves as superior in every way and casual contempt was a norm to be ignored. Nevertheless, they protected us from the ready predatory men on the street whose overtures ranged from loud cat calling about our miniskirts to appalling propositions to actual stalking.

One dark night on our way home to the flat in Newbold Road my boyfriend and I found ourselves facing a drunken man wielding a machete. We ran and took cover in a phone box, pretending in loud voices to be calling the police. Luckily the man ran off and, terrified, we ran the last few hundred yards to the door for the flat.

Peter Sutcliffe, the serial killer dubbed the Yorkshire Ripper, is believed to have been responsible for the murder of Barbara Mayo, a student teacher from Chesterfield whose body was found near Mansfield in 1970. Sutcliffe's proved series of murders date from 1975. Sutcliffe recently confessed to another brutal assault he committed on a fourteen year old girl and an article in the Birmingham Mail suggests his killings began much earlier than those proved. Professor Celia Kitzinger, in an article in the New Internationalist in 1990, writes "Germaine Greer once commented that 'women have very little idea of how much men hate them'. For it is painful to confront the extent of men's hatred. But only when both men and women acknowledge its existence, its extent and its pervasiveness, can we act to end it".

As I write, there is press coverage of Harvey Weinstein's history of sexual abuse with a questioning of how this could go unchallenged for so long in the film industry. A hashtag 'metoo' movement on Facebook is gathering momentum, showing the ubiquity of the experience, nine of ten women are said to have experienced sexual abuse from men. At the same time there are press reports of an unprecedented protest by female students at Banaras Hindu University following an overt sexual assault by two men on a female student in which the University security staff had been apparently complicit. The report describes how the commonplace acceptance of female sexual abuse in India is known as 'eve-teasing'. One student is reported as saying, "Every girl at the University has been eve-teased, molested, from the moment she set foot on campus". We did not have a phrase such as 'eve-teasing' in the sixties, but it was impossible to get sexual violence taken seriously and male aggression was commonly accepted or excused. All my fellow female students dealt with this in various ways. Rape happened frequently and was never reported or even spoken about. I was not raped but I was sexually abused by schoolboys as a child, had several experiences of molestation and exposure, and at least two horrible lecherous masturbatory advances from old men before I was eighteen. I tried to support friends who had been raped and once tried to report a rape to the police, without being taken seriously. The book 'Our bodies, ourselves' invited women to claim their own sexual pleasure and their right to their own informed choice. Published in the late sixties, as the second wave of feminism got under way, the book was seen as revolutionary and influential in changing the myth of female passivity in sexual relationships. The third wave of feminism is confronting and challenging the longevity of these hard to shift gendered attitudes now.

This culture did not stop us having a brilliant night-life. From blues and soul clubs in Sheffield, Chesterfield pubs with live acts such as Family and Pink Floyd, folk clubs and Joe Cocker playing the college dance, we had a ball. Northern soul was embryonic then, but the tradition of live music and dance was well established and readily available for the cost of a pint.

During rag week we decided to rescue an upright piano that was being thrown out of one of the pubs. In fancy dress we pushed it round the streets raising funds by playing requests. Ultimately, since we had not got as far as planning how to dispose of the rescued piano, we tried to take it up to our flat. We could not get it up the final flight of stairs, of course, and it remained stuck on the first-floor landing until our landlady eventually made us take it outside, and sadly it was dismantled in the garden.

All who spent time there fondly remember Flat Seven. One of our close friends Mac's family held a surprise seventieth birthday party for him recently. He is a wonderful photographer and I was given some classic black and white photos he took from this era. The group of us had not met for over twenty years and it was a joy to reminisce and share our memories. The house, along with all others on that part of Newbold Road, has long since been demolished. It was a new bold time indeed and is remembered in our dreams.

Snake Pass

I was frequently in Manchester where my boyfriend Stuart was studying engineering whilst a student in Chesterfield. We first met towards the end of the second year at a party hosted by one of the tutors. Maybe the summer heat and end of term celebration affected us, something magnetic attracted us and over the following months we fell deeply in love. Neither of us was 'Derbyshire born and bred', both misfits, we were used to being different. Stuart's tall good looks came partly from his Polish father, a refugee who married Stuart's mother Marion and settled in Chesterfield after the Second World War. He died when Stuart was a teenager and by the time we met, Marion was living with his step-father Leon in their terraced house in John Street. Like all the adjoining parallel streets of brick built terraced houses this led onto a road that bordered huge gas storage tanks that dominated the horizon.

Stuart was cooking me a steak in the tiny kitchen. This brunch was a weekend treat we got into, the house was usually empty on a Saturday. His mother Marion walked in the door.

"So this is who has been keeping my son busy," she said to me and gave me a big hug. "I thought I'd better introduce myself, because he never will." With this warm welcome our relationship received her blessing and while she would always hold me responsible for encouraging Stuart to return to College and therefore leave her, she always recognised and supported the love between us.

Stuart began studying engineering in Manchester the following year and at weekends I drove over Snake Pass, a pass through the high hills of the Pennines, the shortest route between Chesterfield and Manchester, in all weathers and down into the city suburbs of Didsbury and Whalley Range. During the December vacation I got a job in Boots in Manchester and stayed with Stuart and his friend Gareth in their flat in College Road. On the first floor, the flat had a large living room with tall windows, a battered carpet, an assortment of old chairs and a record player. There was always a blue fug of smoke in the room and various people coming and going, sitting chatting, getting stoned, listening to music or just generally chilling out.

Gareth was a fearless square shaped Welsh man with a booming Harry Secombe laugh. He took us to Yates Wine Lodge in the city centre. We leant on the long bar that stretched away in the distance and scraped our shoes on the floor which was covered with a thick layer of sawdust. The whole place had something of a Victorian music hall, almost Dickensian feel. Openly transvestite people and flamboyantly dressed men filled the enormous space with a hubbub of sound. Gareth introduced us to some young girls he was trying to help. Not more than fifteen they had been groomed into addiction and prostitution to fund their habit. Their heavy black eyeliner and spiky hair acted as a hard shield to disguise their vulnerability. Sensing they were safe with Gareth they came back to the flat with us and would sometimes come along and hang out in, what was for them, a safe space. I think they saw me as something of a naïve social worker, but they gradually shared some of their stories and I became aware of the hard unforgiving underworld of the drugs and sex slave culture.

Open house Sundays in the flat, when people would come and play guitar, sing, and share ideas, were often rainy and I remember Rainy Days, Dream Away, "lay back and groove on a rainy day" from Electric Ladyland by Jimi Hendrix playing on the record player while the rain poured down the window panes. One friend, John, brought a very long poem to read one day. He was a wired, skinny and witty guy and, curling up in one of the larger chairs, he said "I don't know how this is going to be, but I'm just going to read it so here goes - this is 'Miriam and the Banjellane.". I was sitting next to him and, while the chat in the room went on and off in a desultory way around us, I was transported to a fantasy fairy story world of size changing magic. John's reading and rhythm were captivating, hypnotic. "That was really good - I loved it, you must get it published," I told him. "Well," he said "you'd better look after it for me then," and he passed the tightly typed sheets of paper to me. "I will," I promised.

John Cooper Clarke, for this was the poet's full name, later became rapidly famous for his punk poems. Punk overtook the hippy peace movement with its powerful challenge to the establishment. Unfortunately, John disappeared into addiction for many years. When he re- emerged to iconic acclaim, I went to one of his gigs and was struck by how physically like the character of Banjellane in his story poem he is. But the story was a fairy story, written in hippy days. He never replied to my attempts to return the manuscript to him, I keep it safe for him still.

Stuart and I became engaged, we bought an antique silver and amethyst ring in the flea markets in Manchester and announced our engagement to my parents when we went home to Ladygrove at Christmas. Sheila and her boyfriend Roger were also engaged to marry and after a family supper we were in the sitting room discussing our plans.

"I know," said Sheila "let's make it a double wedding!" And with laughter we called our parents in to share the idea.

Our parents had a quiet registry office wedding in Glasgow during the Second World War and were surprised by our combined wish to have a church wedding and a big splash. They generously agreed to our plan and Mum spent the next few months working hard to arrange and organise everything. Sheila and I were fairly oblivious to how much work was involved and responded rather haphazardly to her requests for guest lists and dress fittings. We chose identical dresses in cream satin with a simple classic line, made by a local dressmaker, and flower headbands.

All revolutions have their conflicts, outbursts and collateral damage, and the sexual revolution of the sixties caused havoc in many homes. One set of very firm rules, such as no sex before marriage, was being replaced - second wave feminism was well underway - and the generation who'd lived by those rules often found the change difficult. There was a conflict of emotions for Mum. She was menopausal and hormonal and her passionate nature led to explosive outbursts. In my teens I tended to avoid the conflict by absenting myself, hiding in the woods or in the airing cupboard in the bathroom, where nobody ever found me. Sheila and Mum clashed head on and Sheila, as the eldest, often bore the brunt of challenging convention. Pre-marital sex, smoking cannabis, smoking cigarettes, what we wore, or staying out all night, all brought forth the full fury for our anxious and frustrated mother.

We were all living busy lives - I was self-absorbed and unaware of how it had been for my intelligent mother. She was still caring for her elderly parents, my grandmother was becoming increasingly frail, but Mum was finally free to return to work and she was in demand both as a magistrate and working as a staff trainer. However, this put a strain on her relationship with our father - he was often absent, late home or away. Mum was alone in the house when we were at college and University and I think now the explosive arguments with our father were a symptom of their struggle. I even made entries in my diary about how frustrated I was with the situation, "Mum in a good mood – excellent day!"

We didn't know, but things had come to a head for them shortly before our wedding. Just as we were celebrating our union and young love, our parents unknown to us, had been on the point of separating. It was a closely guarded secret that was only revealed to me years later. I sometimes think had I known, I would have understood better the feelings of insecurity I suffered in my late teens. Maybe I would have made different decisions about my own life and not been determined to marry for security. Mum was protecting us from this reality about relationships, even though I felt the undercurrents I tried to reconcile romanticism and hope.

In some way our dual wedding was a coming together again for the whole family. Mum and Dad were in very good spirits, Mum in her element organising the social arrangements and Dad in his as host. Even though it was only three days after my twentieth birthday when I married Stuart my parents somehow respected and accepted the bond between us and seemed happy about supporting the match.

Shortly before the wedding I was getting ready, alone in my bedroom. Mum was busy with Sheila and with guests, some of whom were staying with us. I was trying to sort out my ever- straight hair, my friend had set it for me earlier that morning, and I was combing it out when Dad tapped on the door. He came in with a couple of glasses containing some scotch. "I thought you might need this" he said, and raised his glass in a toast to me. It was thoughtful of him, in the hectic busy household, to think of me and to come and see if I was all right. He looked wonderful in his kilt and he told me I looked beautiful. I felt reassured and prepared and ready as Dad, Sheila and I set off in the car for the church.

St Helen's Church in Darley Dale has a yew tree, reputed to be two thousand years old, and a history that stretches back to the twelfth century. The church was packed and my knees shook as I walked down the aisle, Dad holding each of his daughters, one on each arm. We'd been able to change some of the traditional service and we chose not to say obey. This idea that we were not owned by father or by husband was still quite novel in 1971. We two couples made our vows separately and the atmosphere was intense and moving. We turned to face the joyful congregation of our family and friends.

Morag on her wedding day, Ladygrove garden

Our extended family and friends had come from Scotland,

Canada and all over England and the reception was in a marquee on the lawn at Ladygrove House, a rare and happy opportunity for us all to catch up. Champagne flowed, toasts were made, music played, and the fun went on until early the next morning. Sheila and Roger were the first to leave. Stuart and I were having an extended camping honeymoon in Scotland. By the time we came to leave we were exhausted and in no state to find the first campsite. Dad paid for our first night in a hotel in Sheffield. Married life had begun, and with it I felt free and safe, as though potential storms had been averted and we had come through to a harbour where I somehow entered into adult life.

A year after our wedding my Grandmother had a series of strokes and was moved into a cottage hospital in Bakewell. I drove across Snake Pass to see her, having been warned she would not recognise me. As I entered the ward I saw her, at the end of a row of beds, and she saw me. I waved and she tried to sit up.

"Hello Morag" she said, clearly recognising me and delighted to see me. My sweet Highland Grandma had always been delighted by my freedom. She was particularly pleased for me when I passed my driving test and she enjoyed hearing about my work. Before her strokes I'd been her confidant when, either as a sign of dementia or of the effect of transient ischemic attacks, she would be entirely in the past for a period of time and would call me by the name of her school friend. Once Mum had to run down the village road to collect her when she went for an unexpected stroll in her dressing gown and Mum spotted her from the window.

"Don't end up like me, Morag" she said as I left, and I promised her I would not.

She died a few weeks later. My parents were away on holiday and Stuart and I were the first to hear the news from Grandpa when we arrived at Ladygrove. I went to see her at the funeral parlour, her tiny body still, her face yellowish and soul gone.

I loved my Grandmother. I loved sitting with her and playing Ludo or Pelmanism (the card game matching pairs) for hours on end. I loved her quiet wit and the way her bright eyes took in everything around her without taking an active role or overt interest. A kind and thoughtful person, she had a very different nature to the spirited outgoing energy of her husband and daughters. Grandma had more of the gentle courteous highland ways. She would always secretly pass an extra biscuit or a penny or two to me when my Grand'pa wasn't looking.

Grandma's grandfather's headstone in Blackford, Perthshire reads 'In affectionate remembrance of Daniel Sharp, brewer, and of his wife Elizabeth Connal'. In keeping with Scottish naming traditions Grandma was given the names of her Grandmother, Elizabeth Connal. My Grandpa's affectionate nickname for her was Con. She'd been ill for many years and their two characters could not have been more different, nevertheless he loved her dearly, went every day on the bus to Bakewell to see her while she was in hospital, and was devastated by her loss. Her death at eighty-four gave me a reminder that life was short.

Elizabeth Connal Munro

Road to the Isles 2

Assynt, Highlands of Scotland

During the Easter holidays, the year before we were married, Stuart and I decided to hitch to Scotland. With very little money and not much in the way of a plan we stood at the junction to the M1 and stuck out our thumbs. Soon enough a lorry stopped that could take us all the way north to Carlisle. For the next part of the journey a car took us as far as Lochearnhead where we pitched camp by the loch-side for the night. It was cold and when we woke in the morning there was an inch of snow on the ground.

After breakfast and striking camp, we lifted our rucksacks and felt our adventure had begun. Stuart in his white sheepskin flying jacket and me in my blue jeans and boots, were confident and exhilarated by the sight of snow on the hills. In what is now known as Loch Lomond and the Trossachs national park a lorry driver picked us up on his way back to Oban. He had delivered fish to England on his regular run, and the faint smell of fish accompanied us all the way there. On arrival we got foot passenger tickets on the ferry to the Isle of Mull. As we stood taking stock on the jetty of the small port of Craignure a local man approached us. "Are ye just visiting?" he asked. We explained we'd just arrived after hitching up from England. "Aye come on then, I'll buy ye a drink" he said and took us into the nearest bar where he bought us each a beer and a whisky chaser. We thanked him for his kindness, he did not stay long to chat, just wished us a lovely stay on the island and left us to it. We emerged later with a warm feeling for highland and island hospitality and found our way to our campsite as the sun set over the beautiful bay.

Away from the trappings of work and studies, flats, friends and family we luxuriated in our romantic isolation. We shared long walks and talks and hopes and dreams. My dream was to run my own interior design practice and to design and build our own home, Stuart's was to escape the confines of the industrial midlands and to develop his career, he was studying electronic engineering. When it rained we snuggled into our tent, made love and, wrapped in our sleeping bags, we slept and read and made love again. By the time we left the island we'd made a long-term commitment to each other.

Our first lift home took us as far as Glasgow, where we found ourselves camped on the outskirts of Glasgow Zoo, hearing the lions roar startlingly nearby. This was the first of our many visits together to the Highlands of Scotland, and the thread of these journeys would become firmly woven into our lives together.

We married the following summer, three days after my twentieth birthday. For our honeymoon we set off in our Anglia van for five weeks in the highlands and headed up to the North Coast. The north of Scotland still forms one of Europe's last great wilderness areas. Leaving behind the wild and remote Rannoch Moor, we journeyed to Sutherland, with its extraordinary mountains and stunning views round each bend of what were then single lane switchback roads, our journey the experience of freedom.

Durness, on the way to Cape Wrath - the most north-westerly point of the Scottish mainland, is a remote village of scattered crofts and houses. We camped in the hamlet of Balnakeil, to the west of Durness. This glorious beach curves round the bay in a wide honey coloured arc, framing the sea that is sometimes steel grey, sometimes Mediterranean blue, often sky silver, with rolling sand dunes and mounds of mattress grass. We spent days walking and exploring, relishing the daily finds of mother of pearl or cowrie shells, hare bells and white heather, deer antlers or polished stones. I walked the tide line, head bowed over, looking for the day's treasures. We had the beach to ourselves most days and alone at night, the stars in the black sky swept over us like a diamond-studded blanket. Sometimes two otters joined us and played together with large strips of seaweed, chattering and chasing each other on the beach and into the shallows, paying us no attention - like us they were oblivious in their joy of the moment and each other.

I heard recently that the hyper-charged pheromone stage of love lasts for a maximum of two years. Scientists now scan the brain to try and understand the synapses fired by the body chemistry that we know as love. We were engrossed in each other, the merging and connecting, the coming together and leaving, the changes that bring the body to life have more in common with the sea soaking into the sand as the tide comes and goes. We walked barefoot together and each night as we slept on the ground we connected in a fundamental way with each other, and with our elemental connection to our planet.

We could sometimes barely breathe for the sheer beauty of the light interplay between sky and sea and the exquisite quality of presence in the landscape. Near to where we camped the erosion of sand dunes recently exposed the body of a young Viking boy on the ancient broch on Faraid Head. On Sangobeg beach the body of a Pictish boy has been discovered. The remains of the church are 13th century and its history dates back to the Culdean monks. Nearby the embryonic craft village of Balnakeil, housed in a collection of disused MoD buildings, a group of young people had set up their craft studios including the ceramic artist Lotte Glob.

John Lennon spent his childhood holidays in Durness and came back in 1969 with his wife, Yoko, and their children. Some years before I visited Durness I had, through repeated listening, become word perfect on the songs from the Beatles' Rubber Soul album. The track 'In my life' is based on a poem John wrote about Durness.

"There are places I'll remember all my life, though some have changed…. All these places have their moments, with lovers and friends I still can recall. Some are dead and some are living, in my life I loved them all." There is no better tribute to this beautiful memorable place.

Cakor Pass and Cheshire

There would be another year of driving over Snake Pass for me, while I finished my course, before I could join Stuart in Manchester full time. At the end of my final year we decided to use the summer as an opportunity to travel and we set off in our Ford Anglia van to explore Europe.

At the top of Cakor Pass, in what was then Yugoslavia, we met another young British couple of similar age coming in the opposite direction. They were also driving an Anglia van and we stopped to talk. The top of the Pass felt like the top of the world, views stretched out for miles in all directions. Cakor Pass at 1,849m high put Snake Pass, 510m high, into perspective.

The Second World War had left its mark but we believed peace had come to Europe. We were warmly welcomed in Greece, and stayed for some time on the beautiful island of Thassos where there were no hotels and just donkeys for company, package tours being in their infancy. In Sarajevo, Yugoslavia we had sensed some unease and suspicion, but were more aware of the undeveloped landscape with horses and carts still being the main form of transport. There was no hint that Cakor Pass would be mined, become impassable, and would be closed to traffic during and after the Balkan

War. Nor that it would later still become a major route for migrants trying to enter Europe on foot during the war in Syria. There were no other vehicles, just the sound of the wind, the call of some birds and the quiet conversation of four young British travellers, to accompany a great sense of peace.

After our summer in Europe Stuart and I moved to a flat in Marple Bridge, a commuter village with a regular bus service into Manchester centre. My first job was with Kitchen Queen in Cheetham Hill, a diverse area of Manchester city, home to a Jewish community and Strangeways Prison.

I remember standing at a bus stop in the rain one wintry evening on Cheetham Hill and crying. Is this what all my studies were for? To work for a fitted kitchen company and draw kitchen plans? Perhaps I should have been more proud. The four page pull out advertisement in the Manchester Evening News in November 1972 celebrates the opening of "Britain's First International Fitted Furniture Centre", and describes "The secret is in the planning: Planning, design and installation are all part of the Kitchen Queen service and for everyone thinking of a complete face lift... the Kitchen Queen Design team will take care of everything from start to finish... highly skilled and experienced designers are standing by". Twelve months of planning had gone into the new 40,000 square feet Kitchen Queen showrooms and brothers Neville and Joel Johnson were right to be proud of their new domain. This was the first showroom of its type in the UK and the forerunner of the now common place fitted kitchen and bedroom industry.

I found it hard to adjust to working life. I missed my fellow students and the freedom and energy of art college. Planning kitchens, although complex and interesting, did not offer the option of developing a design brief of my own. Fitted kitchens were still being developed, British companies like Hygena were still using imperial measurements and German companies like Poggenpohl and Neff were leading the way in developing a standardised modular system with integrated appliances. I soon found my feet and enjoyed working with my colleagues and with customers, surveying their homes, discussing their needs and drawing up designs.

The range of kitchens available was rapidly increasing and we were at the forefront of what would become a massive industry. I was visiting homes with kitchens that were almost outhouses, lean-tos containing broken fifties units, leaking taps, grease filled corners and twin tub washing machines. I enjoyed overseeing the development from a place of drudgery and isolated domestic work being transformed into warm, modern streamlined 'hearts of the home' that are the norm today. We were busy and popular and 'Kitchen Queen' was a success.

One of my colleagues told me about some purpose built flats on Bramhall Lane in Stockport that offered part ownership, part rent. There was a waiting list, but somehow we managed to be accepted for one and soon proudly moved into our first home of our own. Now we lived much nearer to my work and to Stuart's college, he was now in his final year. Life improved for us - the flat had clean modern lines and was spacious and comfortable. Our friends came to stay or for meals, and by 1973 we were living the young and upwardly mobile life before the term 'yuppie' was invented.

Unfortunately, the inflation rate was beginning to increase rapidly, it was hard to make ends meet. Unrest in working people increased and it was a grey and difficult time. Miners were paid 2.3% below the recommended wage and became militant in their demands for an increase. The Conservative government responded with increasingly draconian austerity measures, beginning with electricity restrictions and culminating at the end of the year with the three-day working week. At another bus stop I flinched when a passer-by spat at the black man waiting next to me for the bus. I hated the way people were becoming increasingly insular and isolationist, huddled down into their dreary raincoats as though we were going back in time.

I realised I could not stay at Kitchen Queen. I saw a job advertised in the Manchester Guardian for the manager of an Interior Design studio in Altrincham, Cheshire and applied for and was offered the post. The studio for Roger Davies Design International was on Goose Green, a prestigious area of Altrincham that has now been converted into a shopping village. In 1973 there was an open square with a mixture of old cottages. Roger Davies' studio occupied a commanding position with a large front window proudly displaying a Charles Eames chair and footstool. Inside there was a large drawing board and an extensive range of samples of fabrics and flooring designs. My role was to manage the showroom, survey clients' homes, draw up designs with sample or mood boards and sketches of how the finished design would look. I would coordinate the work of fitters and makers and, in a similar way to Kitchen Queen, see the work through to completion.

Roger had a great eye for modernism and formalism and the ranges stocked were at the height of contemporary fashion, Liberty, Sanderson, Osborne and Little, Wemyss Weavers among them. Salesmen would arrive with sample books of gold leaf and silk slub wall coverings or luxurious bathroom fittings with hand painted tiles. Roger would come and go, he was rarely in the studio for the whole day. I often had long periods of time to myself. It was deliberately stylish and not the kind of place that encouraged people to just drop in from the street.

One of Roger's clients wanted an entirely black office, with black wall panelling, black desk and black fitted cupboards and bookshelves. This was extremely difficult to render in a colour perspective and I struggled with shadows and greytones to give any sense of the feeling of the room, ultimately relying on the mood board to show the effect. Another client had an extravagant bathroom design with roll top bath and free-standing washstand with gold taps. These were not designs I would have chosen but I learnt about meeting the client requirements and about the range of high quality very expensive products required by the wealthy people of Cheshire and Manchester. I went out to the clients' homes for the finishing touches, hang pinch-pleated curtains, add cushions and accessories, and ensure the client was happy with the finished result.

Roger treated me in a different way to the way he treated his girlfriend. When she called in to see him he would smirk when he took misogynistic pleasure in getting her to clean the toilet, and after she left complain to me about how demanding she was. In turn she would call in when Roger was out and complain to me about how neglectful Roger was to her. It seemed to me she was a trophy girlfriend and I felt sorry for her. With me he was professional and attentive, discussing designs and fabric or wall covering options and focusing entirely on the work. It was clear design was his first love.

My difficulty with time continued to haunt me. When I left Kitchen Queen my colleagues gave me a pendant watch together with some humorous commentary on helping my time keeping in my future role. I took the train from Stockport to Altrincham and I remember running on to the bridge on Stockport station and watching the train pull away below me with tears of frustration in my eyes. I was responsible for opening the studio and I'm afraid I was often late. Roger's girlfriend told him she had found the studio closed and he had words with me, but he was tolerant and I tried hard to improve my time keeping.

Stuart had found a job in electronic engineering when he finished his course, but neither of us were particularly enjoying our work.

"I'm just so fed up of designing rooms for people with loads of money and no design sense," I told Stuart.

He too was disappointed in how his work was progressing and despite our modern flat, our two incomes and the flash seventies culture, we both knew it was not for us. When Sheila and Roger suggested a move, we were ready and willing and we packed up and left Manchester with barely a second glance.

Somerset

The Bath Festival of Blues '69 was the finale of the Bath Festival and held on Bath's small Recreation grounds. The programme lists among many others Nice, Led Zeppelin, John Mayall and Fleetwood Mac, and the foreword by Sir Michael Tippett says "Of course Folk and Blues should be big and splendid with lots of bands and lots of people. We expect them from all over the country". And we did go to Bath from all over the country.

Stuart and I set off in my Mini, armed with our orange programmes, sleeping bags and not much else. According to press reports of the time, describing it as a "blues bombshell", over twenty thousand of us attended this ground-breaking festival, to the astonishment of the people of Bath. The fantastic line up had attracted us and we were not disappointed. Reading the online comments of others who attended the event, we share memories of a glorious summer day and warm evening, a chilled, relaxed, intimate atmosphere at what was for many of us a first festival experience. We were treated to the finest live performances. The songs were being performed prior to being recorded and ultimately became tracks for albums that now feature in listings for the best albums of all time.

The buildings around the recreation ground formed a sort

of amphitheatre that amplified and echoed the sounds back from the small stage. From Nice with their pipers to Led Zeppelin, the whole impact was to be completely immersed in these new sounds, mesmerised, and to experience a fundamental change in music performance. Robert Plant from Led Zeppelin adjusted his playing to accommodate the echoes round the ground. Some commentators speculate this pre-album performance influenced the rhythm ultimately used on a "Whole lotta love" when the recording was made later that year. Fleetwood Mac with Peter Green were unforgettable, powerful and astonishing.

Somehow, we knew we were on the verge of something new and momentous, part of what is now known as the counter culture revolution. We were sharing this with long haired, like- minded young people and could see we were part of a movement, seeking a different way to live. When we returned to Chesterfield we were buzzing with this new experience – so different from Sheffield's soul clubs, like the MoJo run by Pete Stringfellow. I loved soul, I loved dancing, and I enjoyed the clubs, but the experience of this new sound was extraordinary, liberating, the combination of poetry in song and emotion in electric guitar was a powerful new form of communication. Michael Eavis was also in the audience and, inspired by this festival experience, he decided to start the now internationally famous Glastonbury Festival.

The following year we attended a second event in Somerset, the Bath Festival of Blues and Progressive Music, at the Bath and West Showground, Shepton Mallet. Described as a 'counter culture era music festival' (and not as well-known now as the famous Isle of Wight Festival where Bob Dylan played), in many ways these two Bath Festivals had programmes that were more representative of current and future directions in music and culture.

The Somerset lanes were choked with traffic as 150,000 of us converged on the show ground site, attracted by headline acts Pink Floyd and Led Zeppelin. There were insufficient plans in place to manage the enormous crowds, and the poor security meant the event had many programme delays and changes. However, we had come better prepared for a longer stay with tent and provisions. There were many logistical difficulties getting basic needs met, long queues for toilets and for food, lack of cover from the rain, all precursors to the difficulties facing the festival movement of the seventies. My paisley cotton kaftan was a warm enough layer to protect me from most of the cold wind on the site, that and the adrenaline and dancing kept me warm. Fairport Convention are reported to have recruited a Hells Angels motorbike convoy to help them get on to the site. With the programme times ever shifting we relaxed, got stoned and went along with the flow, as Fairport sang 'who knows where the time goes?' and warmed us up on the Saturday afternoon.

Led Zeppelin considered their appearances at the Bath Festivals to be a turning point for their popularity in the UK. The sheer sexual and spiritual energy in their performance has rarely been surpassed and became intrinsic with the fundamental cultural shift we, this coming of age post war generation, were living through.

Pink Floyd finally appeared at 3am and their performance of their new "Atom Heart Mother" album, complete with Gilmour's first outing for his famous Fender Stratocaster, stunned us with 'Set the controls for the heart of the sun' and had us dance the night away into dawn. We all took cover from a horrendous downpour on the Sunday, and Moody Blues failed to play because the stage was too dangerously wet.

This festival was the true precursor to what would become the Glastonbury Festival, now the largest music festival in the world. I imagine Eavis, who was again at this second festival, was thinking how much better this event would be if it were held in the sheltered and beautiful bowl of his farm's valley in the Mendips, and he would be right. He held the first festival on his own farm that autumn and, although it would be some years before he achieved such an amazing line up, it was the beginning of this change.

Like many others who attended Glastonbury Festival over the years, we fell in love with Somerset. The hedge lined lanes, the curved fields, clean air and expansive views from the top of the Mendips, and the slow gentle approach to life was a complete antidote to the urban living we were experiencing in Chesterfield, Sheffield and Manchester. It is not clear whether the solitary cow on the album cover of Atom Heart Mother was influenced by the Somerset experience but for many of us, the germ of the idea grew. E.F Schumacher's "Small is Beautiful: A Study of Economics as if People Mattered" was published in 1973.

When Sheila, my sister, invited us to join her and her husband Roger in their house conversion venture in Somerset we were delighted. The idea was to sell the house they were in and for us to buy a property together to renovate. Four years after attending the second festival, we moved to Somerset in the summer of 1974 to share their small house until it was sold and we could start a bigger project.

I got a job at the Bristol Evening Post selling advertising. The newspaper was moving from old premises to new purpose-built accommodation on Temple Way in Bristol. The imposing brutalist building with its bronze brick walls and multi-layered roof was impressive, but I would soon come to feel the building suffered from sick building syndrome. Many of the open plan office workers got headaches and unexplained symptoms of nausea, I was never quite sure whether this was due to the blanket of bright fluorescent lighting or the air conditioning. I was travelling by bus to Bristol, a long and sometimes nauseous bus journey in itself, and was not at my best, but my colleagues were great fun and soon became good friends.

Unfortunately, the sale of my sister's house took much longer than we hoped and the pressures of sharing took its toll on us all. Stuart and I realised we wanted to stay in the area, but really would prefer a home of our own. Shortly after our move to Somerset my Grandfather died, leaving each of his grandchildren £500. This was almost sufficient for a deposit on a house. Stuart managed to get a job in Wells, in electronic engineering. For me it was harder to find design jobs in Bristol and it would be six months before an interview with an architect's practice in Blagdon led to my finding my dream job, and becoming an architect's assistant - my dream being to combine interior design with architecture.

I loved my drive to work across the Mendips, with their limestone hills, cave systems and dry-stone walls - they had many of the elements of the Peak District, but in a more gentle and warm climate and without the dramatic peaks. There was also something about the area that reminded me of the Ochils, my birthplace. On my way home one day I called in to the Waldegrave Arms in Chewton Mendip. It was a friendly pub and, chatting to the Landlord, I mentioned we were house hunting. He told me about an empty cottage and I drove by - just to have a look.

I followed his directions up a lane called The Folly to the top of the hill and found the cottage tucked away from the main road. It was love at first sight. The small, detached cottage had all the picture postcard romance of the rural idyll. I climbed out of the car, wandered into the garden and gazed across the views of the Mendip Plateau, and knew I had found home. The gardener for the Waldegrave Estate had lived here for many years and the small garden had a cared for feel, full of roses – bare when I first saw them - and a rich dark earth in the overgrown vegetable patch. The field at the back of The Cottage was bordered by a high stone wall, a boundary to Lord Waldegrave's garden.

Chewton Mendip was still an estate village. The houses, mainly cottages, were all owned by Lord Waldegrave, a hereditary title, and were occupied by families who worked for the estate. They had uniform maroon paint to their wooden doors and window frames. The Cottage turned out to be the first property to be sold from the Waldegrave Estate. A prolonged learning curve for the Estate Manager and myself ensued. I negotiated a mortgage from the local authority - the derelict state of the property had precluded receiving a standard mortgage. I drew up plans and negotiated to include part of the field at the back of The Cottage in the purchase, to facilitate parking and access. Finally the sale was concluded and The Cottage was ours. 'The Good Life', the iconic BBC comedy drama for a simple life of self-sufficiency, first screened in April 1975 and in May 1975 Stuart and I moved in to The Cottage in pursuit of our own good life.

A steep spiral stone staircase, hidden behind a door in the corner of the main room, connected the one and a half rooms downstairs to those upstairs. Alongside was a large open fireplace and on the left a window seat overlooking the garden and the plain. The floor was dry - small tightly fitted quarry tiles with almost no space for grout acted as a damp proof membrane – and the eighteen inch thick stone walls gave the cottage an insulated and protected feel. To begin with we had no water and no power and brought only sleeping bags, a bucket, cups, a bottle of champagne and some roses for our first night in our new home.

Almost immediately Hilda, our new neighbour, appeared to introduce herself. She had lived in the village all her life and was garrulous to the extent that people often avoided getting into conversation with her. But with us she was warm and welcoming, offering a cup of tea and clearly pleased that the cottage was no longer empty. Hilda was surprisingly open to us despite our being outsiders. She had worked for much of her life for Lord and Lady Waldegrave as a maid. Her husband Doug still worked on the Estate, and the house they lived in was one of four council houses that had been purpose built to accommodate redundant miners who were employed to work on the estate when the local mine closed. They were built between wars on the same field at the back of The Cottage, with Hilda and Doug's property bordering the drive to our cottage and the field. They shared the view across the Mendip Plain at the front and had long gardens.

Soon enough we got power and water but it would be the following year before we had a phone, radio or television. We had a copy of Richard Mabey's 'Food for Free' and I walked the lanes picking rose hips, elderflowers and berries, and bought demi johns in which to ferment wine. I double dug the garden and planted broccoli and runner beans. We had our stereo and we lived the dream, blasting out Pink Floyd's 'Shine on You Crazy Diamond' through enormous speakers across the fields and dreaming of things to come.

The Cottage, 1975

The Folly

Without a phone I took to writing to my parents fairly regularly. My mother saved those letters and as a result I have quite a full account of our first, very busy, eighteen months in our new home. Prior to moving to The Cottage, we'd barely had a weekend to ourselves for a year. This pattern continued for our first year in The Cottage. Many of our friends and family visited, braving the discomfort of an outside toilet, no outside lights, no hot water, sleeping on floors with basic facilities and no heating. Something about the sheer romance of it all appealed to them as much as it did to us. My parents thought we were brave, Stuart's mother said he had always promised her a cottage in the country. Our friends brought gifts, fabric for curtains, food, fuel for the fire. We had parties and singing and memorable meals cooked on our basic Baby Belling. One friend of a friend was heard to say, with horror, "They don't even have a proper cooker".

All was not wine and roses however. I suffered from a seemingly endless series of bugs, cold, flu, streaming nose and bronchitis. After a year of this I found myself crying at the GP's surgery. Luckily, he took me seriously and signed me up for an allergen research project being run from Bristol. It turned out I was highly allergic to dust, feathers and dust mites and the last thing I should be doing was being exposed to all the ancient lime dust from stripping the plaster walls, and dust mites from the pulled up floors. I shouldn't even be doing my own dusting and vacuum cleaning, not that there was a lot of that. I was offered a series of injections designed to build immunity. After several months my symptoms had massively decreased and I never suffered to the same degree from my allergies again. Sadly the funding for this project and the expertise were subsequently cut from NHS provision, and this treatment is not available now.

I loved my work at the architects' practice. I was learning every day, undertaking surveys, planning drawings and drafting development layouts where, unlike interior design, I had to consider such things as contours, road widths and drainage maps. There was a small cheerful team and we worked in a light, purpose designed studio upstairs in a converted barn. My drawing ability slowly improved and I learnt the difference between designers' and architects' approaches. John Chamberlain FRIBA, whose practice it was, also taught at the University of Bath and was a surprisingly patient and supportive boss, understanding that it would take me some months to gain confidence, and ensuring the team offered guidance and advice. We went for lunches in the local pubs and got supplies from the one post office and shop in the village. Therefore it was all the more of a shock when six months after starting there, and two months after moving in to The Cottage, I was made redundant.

I was devastated. Real grief accompanied my tears as I drove home. I think John was genuinely sad about his decision and he paid me off with a month's wages - being last in and first out I had no employment rights. All my dreams about designers and architects were shattered and I had to face the reality of the brutal side of architecture. It was a cost saving pragmatic decision for John, and my learning curve was probably not profitable for him. Also, I was the easiest to dispose of, and the only woman in the office (apart from two administrators, one of whom was John's wife). Stuart was earning and we decided not to panic while I looked for another job. We had such confidence in this that we bought an Austin Healey Sprite with some of the redundancy money so that we now had two cars. This would enable me to find a job, my experience with the bus to Bristol having shown me the woeful inadequacy of rural bus services.

We bought a kitten, her long fluffy white hair and blue eyes melted my heart and she was my constant companion. We called her Muckhart, after my birthplace. Her name was quickly and permanently abbreviated to Mucky when she emerged from exploring the fireplace covered in grey soot. I began painting and sketching. I delighted in new discoveries in the garden each month as lupins succeeded irises and carnations followed. I drew garden plans and planting schemes.

I set up my drawing board in the bedroom and drew the designs for a two-storey extension to The Cottage, and applied for planning permission and building regulation approval. I also applied for a grant that had been made available through the local authority to support the conversion work.

Our confidence in work opportunities paid off and I managed to get a job with one of the largest employers in the area, Foster Yeoman, a huge quarrying company. I was to be Assistant to John Yeoman's PA, Anne. I was made very welcome and soon became good friends with Anne, who patiently took me through the clerical and administration practices. The office buildings seemed so small in the enormous space. The huge stone trucks were completely dwarfed by the quarry cliffs. The sheer scale of the quarry gave me a whole new understanding of stone extraction, from the warning sirens before the blasts, to seeing in the distance the dust from cliff edges being blown away. Lorries were queuing to load the limestone that would be taken by rail for roads and buildings all over the world.

My ambitions in design were unresolved and I kept job hunting. I applied for and got a job with a company called Solar Home Improvements. It was to be managing a new showroom in Bristol for what I believed would be an exciting approach to ecological design. The first few months were training in Bridgwater and I began to realise it was nothing more than a glorified double-glazing company and that ecological considerations did not underpin the values of the company.

We got another kitten to keep Mucky company while we were working – a beautiful short-haired tortoiseshell who we called Minnie. We spent our first Christmas at The Cottage and were given a tree from the Waldegrave Estate. To most of the village we were still strangers, interlopers, but we were made welcome, treated affably and questioned in the village shop, the hot bed for all the community gossip, about ourselves.

By the end of our first six months in The Cottage I'd had three jobs, and four in our first eighteen months in Somerset. Nothing was resolved for me career wise, but we were happy. One thing that strikes me in the letters is my sense of empowerment and confidence that I would always find work. I describe my determination to navigate and create a career for myself. I'd reviewed what I wanted to do with my life and I'd set the wheels in motion. By March 1976 the job at Solar Home had become untenable for me and I left and began my self-employed career.

I took a freelance job selling fitted kitchens to bring in a small income and made a proposal to Jollys of Bath, part of the House of Fraser Group, for my providing an in-house interior design consultancy. I had a series of meetings with the management of the store to discuss my proposal.

I acknowledged my wish to write, and I applied for and was offered a place on a degree course in Creative Writing at the University of the West of England. I applied for a grant, and asked my mother to find and post the evidence of my qualifications to the local authority to support my case. When my initial application for a grant was refused I appealed. But when I went for appeal the committee advised me that because I had received a grant of £50 per year for my Diploma at Art College their policy was not to give a second grant within a certain period of time. I received a letter from the Principal of my old art college, wishing me well and referring to "my undoubted talents". I read local author Geoffrey Ashe's book on becoming a writer in which he suggested the best way to do so was to live a full life. So with some sadness I declined the offer of a place at University and put my writing ambitions on hold to focus on my design career.

Jollys accepted my proposal for a design consultancy. The local authority approved my plans for The Cottage, and I received the offer of a grant towards the cost of the building work. The die was cast and decisions made. In late summer my parents brought down a caravan to park at the back of The Cottage for Stuart and I to move into while work on gutting the cottage and laying the foundations for the extension began.

I designed stationery and information for my design consultancy. The launch received some local media attention, and as a result I received a congratulations note from John Chamberlain and his wife. They referred to their having every confidence in my abilities and wishing me success with the venture.

Given the challenges facing young people now in the 21st century, I am astonished at my youthful bravery and by the opportunities open to me, and by the clarity with which I carved out my path. I put some of this down to my design education, writing my own brief, planning a structure. I think my regular meditation practice also helped. I clearly remember a meditation sitting in the cottage where I felt the barrier between the two hemispheres of my brain being pulled out, like removing a metal plate, and the connections between the hemispheres opening, healing and recovering. I recommended meditation in one letter to my Mum, quoted from Khalil Gibran, and I signed some of the letters "with love and peace".

I was basking in love: with Stuart, with our cats and our dogs - our family now numbered two cats and two dogs, Ben and Sunshine, who we adopted from friends and family - with the cottage and our garden and the nature of the village and Somerset, and life itself.

The lane The Cottage is on is called The Folly - reputedly because there is no water supply. The source of the River Chew rises at the foot of The Folly, but any water goes underground on the hill, except in a storm when the lane becomes a stream. I was naive, I did not know about over extending ourselves. My mother was worried for us, but I was not. I had complete faith in my and Stuart's abilities to realise our dreams, and I set out on my self-employed path with determination and confidence.

Ben, Mucky and Sunshine, The Cottage garden

Bath

I was twenty-five when I started Homestyle, my interior design consultancy based at Jollys on Milsom Street in Bath. "Mo's grand designs on living at just £10 a room", read the headline for the article in the Western Daily Press that announced the opening in 1976. Youth culture was prevalent and with it, the idea that if you'd not made it by the time you were thirty it would be too late. My idea was that design would be available for everyone and not just for the wealthy few. I believed in designing 'from the inside out' and wanted to integrate interior needs with exterior building design. To make a living I would be employed direct by the client but would also receive commission on any products, carpets, curtains, wall coverings that I sold for Jollys. I wanted to make a name for myself as a designer and I had the ingrained ideology of social practice. This was an unusual combination, especially for Bath - a city that was designed to be self-consciously stylish.

Morag, Homestyle, press photo Jollys of Bath

I filled my Escort van with my samples library and Jollys

gave me the use of a room on the furnishings floor to meet with clients and discuss their needs. I sometimes wonder if the BBC sit-com "Are you being served" was based directly on Jollys, a store then still proud of being the supplier of Queen Mary's hats. The sales staff viewed me with suspicion accorded an outsider, but were kind to me and genuinely interested in what I was doing. I did have competition, some staff did not want to risk losing commission for their own sales and the window dresser tried to poach a couple of clients for his own embryonic design ambition.

One of these was Sheikh A from Saudi Arabia. He owned a large estate in south Somerset and met me at the entrance to the enormous country house to show me around. A fountain was being installed in the large entrance hall. A twin staircase curved round either side of the vestibule leading to spacious first floor rooms with beautiful views. He was evidently very comfortable in the company of western women and introduced me to his mistress who was from Somerset - she lived in the house, and moved out temporarily when A's family visited. Sheikh A was happy to discuss his needs with me and I surveyed several of the rooms and drew up designs and sample boards.

I was proud when I presented him with my initial sketch designs based on silk slub fabrics and rich pile carpets in a neutral palette. He nodded knowledgeably and when I'd finished my presentation he explained to me that because he lived in a desert country, he and his family preferred bright colours and vivid designs and not the sand shades I was showing him. I'd not considered the cultural dimension and was grateful for his patience and for the clarity with which he explained. I reworked the designs in rich turquoises and golds and he was delighted with the results.

A couple of years later I had an unannounced visit from Customs and Excise. They appeared to be investigating the Sheikh's financial dealings and to half expect me to have a Rolls Royce parked at the back of the cottage. Their main concern was VAT, for which I was not registered having too small a turnover to qualify. The investigators realised I was genuine and wished me well as they left. Sheikh A did have a Rolls Royce parked in his drive, as well as a chauffeur and a maid. Soon after the investigation the estate was sold.

My clients often lived in beautiful properties in small villages - I designed for farmhouses and historic cottages, as well as for city apartments and council houses. I returned home to our cottage to draw up my designs in what was effectively a building site. At times I would be building a wardrobe or plastering the walls while Stuart was fitting the plumbing and building the extension. We did not have the budget of my clients and we were fitting in the building work around the demands of our careers. It was a strain, but it was also a pleasure and I was happy, finding it a privilege to see these beautiful homes and loving the work we were doing on our own home. Frequently Stuart and I were both very tired, and the conversion work was a day-to-day strain. A friend once told me I had big ideas but then I expected others to help to see the ideas through, and this was true. I expected people to share my vision and see what was possible, and they often did, but I was always undercapitalised and over committed.

My writing was still driving me and one spring I took a few months off to write a novel about cats. I'd ambitions for a Paul Gallico type of work, and I engrossed myself in the developing story. So much so that Stuart told me he felt he'd lost me to my writing. I had no keyboard skills and my dear friend Di painstakingly typed it all out for me from my handwritten draft, a labour of love especially since she was also the mother of young children. When it was complete I sent the printed manuscript off with high hopes. It was returned to me three times and I again gave up thoughts of being a writer and returned to my design practice. Di went on to become a writer herself and years later she achieved a Master's degree in creative writing.

In 1979 the International Wool Secretariat ran a competition to source the best of British Design. My design for a low budget scheme using pure wool products was one of six selected and chosen for a major exhibition in London. This received extensive media coverage and my work was featured in a cover article Best of British Design in Homes and Gardens and in several other design articles and journals. My private practice took off - I began to get an increasing number of interior architecture commissions and decided to focus on these. I left Jollys and Homestyle and set up my own practice. The manager asked at a subsequent store meeting whether the fall in sales had anything to do with my departure. The fall in sales probably had more to do with the structural problems in the economy - inflation was running at double figures and Margaret Thatcher had been appointed Prime Minister.

The cracks in my relationship with Stuart began to show. We had different ideologies. Stuart was a supporter of Thatcher. I was not. Stuart was enjoying his career travels and expansion.

I wanted to create a home and have children. Stuart did not. We had frequent rows and we grew apart. The pressures on the economy put interest rates through the roof and the financial pressures were hard to manage. I'd not chosen the best time to set out in my own right.

According to the newspaper report 15,000 people attended the NoRad 1980 exhibition in Midsomer Norton, held in a school and aiming to exhibit local companies. I was pleased to have the opportunity to showcase my work locally. I arrived early and set up a design room set with walls and furniture and samples and drawings of my designs. When I left that evening it looked perfect. My neighbour exhibitor was a fabric shop – they'd not yet arrived but there was plenty of space for their exhibit. When I returned the next morning the shop had deliberately set their racks of fabrics in front of my room set blocking both visual and physical access. The woman involved was not available. I spoke with the managers of the show but basically I had to put up with the sabotage. It was distressing and it helped me to understand the difference between a professional event, with help and support, and the realities of having my own practice without backing. It showed me a side of the business that I really had no time for, and the realities of a 'me first' culture.

I had work, interiors and extension designs, but not enough income to manage the true costs.

A magazine journalist visited me at home and asked to see my standard designs. When I told her there are no standard designs, they are all individually tailored, she was amazed.

"How do you manage?" she asked.

"Not very well I'm afraid," I replied.

Friends who knew Stuart and I were struggling tried to mediate for us with no success. They gave us immense support. We were treated to a weekend in Paris. Stuart was uncommunicative and unresponsive and I came back lonelier than when we went.

My mother said a wedding photograph of me taken by the lake at Ladygrove reminded her of Ophelia. There is some echo in the photo to John Everett Millais's painting of Elizabeth Siddall as the drowned Ophelia. Elizabeth posed for Millais in a bath dressed in a vintage silver dress and became ill as a result. The tragic drowned heroine, the heroic artist, the healing power of nature, were all inherent features of Romanticism and aimed to be an antidote to the Industrial Revolution. New Romanticism and the New Age movement had similar features. I was a romantic. Stuart's mother used to say she couldn't wait for me to lose my rose coloured spectacles. And when I did it was, for me, a catastrophe.

"Just tell me the truth. I think you're having an affair", I confronted Stuart. He denied it. "If you don't tell me I'm going to see a psychotherapist, because if you are not I think I must be going mad." Mad with fury, rage and loss.

Finally he told me he was, and I left home. I stayed with friends and, broken hearted, wept on their shoulders. I read Khalil Gibran's Prophet again and trusted the idea 'the more sorrow carves into your being the more joy it can contain'. Stuart and I recognised we still loved each other and we decided to try again.

I was amazed and moved by how much support we had for our relationship from friends and parents. I realised I was far from the only person to go through this particular rite of passage. I believed in honesty and openness, truth. Many believed that discretion was the better part. My old ideas of right and wrong began to fragment and eventually I was able to reconnect with Stuart and he with me. We began a new and different relationship.

It would be many years before I came to understand that I had been attempting to rebuild the lost 'idyll' of my birthplace. Even though the similarities between The Cottage and Path End where I'd been born were staring me in the face, the deeper underlying drive to reconnect the part of myself I'd left behind in Scotland had not been visible and was unconscious. This separation and loss probably led to my lifelong passion for working things out, identifying issues and designing solutions.

Unfortunately, neither my relationship nor my first design plan for my own practice had worked out and, with great sorrow, I gave up the idea of owning my own design studio and having children and I started job hunting. I was still angry, disappointed and determined to carve out a path of my own. Fighting to recover my self-esteem I scanned the paper and spotted the advertisement from a Kitchen Distributor in Bristol - the pay was good and there was a company car. I applied.

Bristol

"I don't want a woman for this job," Mike Walker said, almost as soon as I arrived for the interview.

I sighed, another man who thought my name was that of a boy's. I stood in front of him in my new Mondi shirt and skirt. "Why not?" I asked. "I can do the job," and sat down and told him how. To my delight Mike decided to employ me.

All the sales representatives for the distribution company named HMW (Mike's initials) had company cars and their own regions. Mine was to be Dorset, Somerset and parts of Hampshire and Avon. Demand for integrated kitchen appliances was rapidly increasing and Mike's company, based in Bristol, held the agency for Bosch and Franke. Over time I managed to persuade Mike to give me equal pay and an equal car with those of my male colleagues, and I received a VW Passat rather than the Renault Clio he initially had in mind for me.

I loved the freedom of being on the road. This was before mobile phones and the internet intruded into every minute of the day. For long periods of driving and planning there was no interruption to thinking. I raced down an empty rural road listening to music, Dire Straits "Money for Nothing" on full volume, or classical radio as I queued in traffic in the city.

I enjoyed getting to know the region in all weathers. Mike took to calling me 'his secret weapon' and I would change from my driving shoes into my stilettos as I went into the showrooms to sell the managers our wares.

One day when I'd collected a new Passat in Bristol I slowly glided to a halt on a minor road in Dorset miles away from anywhere. Luckily I got a lift to a nearby garage and rang the office. "Are you sure it is overheating?" they asked. "Yes" I replied, "the gauge is red and a light has come on on the dashboard".

The garage soon identified that I had in fact run out of fuel and had been looking at the wrong gauge. Women were still being mocked for their 'inferior' driving skills and, embarrassed by my claims to equality, I shamefully decided not to admit my basic error to the company. Mike, however, rang the garage and found out, and to my chagrin told everyone and always remembered, as he reminded me when I saw him recently.

For the most part, after a few months, I no longer had to defend my gender to my colleagues or to customers and sales were soaring. One colleague told me he did not believe in women working as this "took jobs away from the men. But you're all right," he said, implying that unlike his wife - because I didn't have children - I was allowed to work. At events I did occasionally get "hit on" by predatory men and lewd remarks were common, but I was supported and protected by our small team.

Mike had hit on the right products at the right time and the business grew rapidly. Good at sharing the success of his business with his staff, he took us to the European trade fairs and when sales figures exceeded expectations he paid bonuses and booked treats for the staff. One time taking us to the Munich Beer Festival, and another time chartering a plane and flying us with our partners to Switzerland where we visited Geneva and a salt mine, and stayed in a Porsche Hotel.

Mike was passionate about Porsche and raced and rallied in Porsche events. One day when snow blocked the roads in Chewton Mendip I rang in to say I couldn't get to work. Mike, always unstoppable, drove from his own snowed in village to mine, where he collected me and gave me a memorable rally drive on minor roads in deep snow to Bristol. One of his fellow rally drivers told me almost all accidents are caused by excessive speed and rally drivers take highly calculated risks. I could see Mike's mind working as he swung the back end of the Porsche round bends and drove forward, finding the grip and accelerating away into the straight.

It took me time to adjust to this new life and there were times when I would park up in a lay by and cry. I was grieving the loss of my romantic notions and design ambitions. But I began to really enjoy being part of a team, achieving shared goals. It was great to have a decent income and to be free of the uncertainty that goes with being self-employed. I enjoyed the power dressing and power driving and the boom time of the early 1980s. The office staff increased to manage demand and the warehouse in Kingswood in Bristol filled with stock. The office 'home' team supported us staff – answering queries, fielding customers and sorting out orders.

Once, a home economist they had booked for a microwave demonstration at a showroom in Dorset was taken ill. Microwave ovens were still viewed with suspicion by the public and these demonstrations were designed to educate and overcome the fear. The office rang to ask me, because I was a woman, to handle the demonstration.

About thirty people crammed into the showroom. I told them my domestic science education at school had been full of culinary disasters, such as flat and chewy chocolate eclairs. I explained, that as I couldn't cook, if I could use a microwave oven anyone could. I talked about how they worked and demonstrated baked potatoes and simple recipes. Somehow the event was a success and the office invited me to do more, but I declined – I could design a kitchen very ably, but not yet cook in one.

Our customers, as managers of showrooms, often had difficult or challenging customers themselves. I would find myself despatched to a penthouse flat overlooking Poole harbour or to a beautiful farmhouse in the New Forest to show someone how to use a new lever tap or compact sink, and sometimes just to reassure an obsessive housewife they were cleaning the product correctly, and calm her over-cleaning behaviour. The magazines showed such perfect images that sometimes new owners had to learn to relax in their own homes. Although more involved in showroom design than in domestic design, I still enjoyed seeing the designs in practice and my European experience kept my design knowledge up to date.

Mike and I were on the M5 in his Porsche on the way home from a major trade exhibition at the National Exhibition Centre. These three-day events were exhausting and adrenalin filled, fuelled largely by gin. "Watch out for the police car" I said to Mike, we were cruising in the middle lane at about 90 miles per hour. "What police car?" Mike replied glancing to his right and then seeing the police car that had come alongside us in the fast lane. It was keeping pace with us and the policemen were staring at Mike, who smiled, waved and pulled back. Fortunately the police car sped on - I doubt that Mike would have passed a breathalyser test had they pulled us over.

When I was in Bournemouth, I liked to take a lunch break overlooking the sea. The wide- open horizon invited rest and contemplation. I'd not entirely given up on my dream of having a family. Once in a deep meditation I had a very clear vision of a beautiful child with dark hair and blue eyes who spoke to me. "Don't worry. I'm coming" he said. Thereafter I'd been reconciled and wrote and told my friends that somehow it would all work out. I trusted that one day my son would come. Meanwhile I was enjoying my career, my freedom, and my travels. I'd rediscovered my sexuality and my self-esteem.

The extension to the cottage had been completed and, while there was always work to be done, we had a habitable home ready to receive new life. My own kitchen, still part finished, was much simpler than the glamorous ones I was involved with designing. I loved my big kitchen table by the inglenook fire, the glow of the old quarry tiles in the night-light and the views through the windows across the fields when we relaxed with a glass of wine at the end of a busy day and were fully rooted at home. Stuart sensed that I was potentially moving away from him. The tables had turned and now I was the one who was away, and he missed me. One day he announced he had changed his mind and he would like a child.

Soon after our holiday in Scotland I had my pregnancy confirmed. There was very limited maternity provision and I knew I would not want to be managing the stress of driving and a demanding job while heavily pregnant. We decided to manage on one income and I handed in my notice.

"Don't wear anything too dressy," Stuart said. I chose jeans and a loose top. Mike collected us and drove us to Bath where a surprise leaving party had been planned for me. A boat complete with jazz band and dinner service had been booked for the whole team and we had a wonderful evening cruising the River Avon and reminiscing on our adventures together. Sharing stories and laughs I knew I would miss the camaraderie of the team. The company was changing. Stuart and my lives were changing. New life was entering. The river shone with the reflections and I climbed out of the boat feeling joyful to have shared with them this part of my journey and happily expectant for the future.

Road to the Isles 3

Stac Pollaidh, North West Highlands of Scotland

We expanded our experience of the Highlands, returning often for holidays in our years together. Achnahaird, with its views and closeness to the extraordinary Sutherland mountains - Suilven and Stac Pollaidh, became one of our favourites. The camp site had toilets but very little else in the way of facilities, and rolled down to enormous sand dunes that led directly to the beach. The dunes protected our little tent from the sea winds and our hidden location allowed us to feel as alone together as we had at Durness. One night, hearing a noise among our kitchen things, I peered out and found a Scottish wild cat staring back at me.

We toured islands - Lewis with the Lewisian gneiss coming through the peat. "Like the bare bones of the planet", Stuart said. Harris, where the Gaelic speakers changed to speaking in English to welcome us when we entered the hotel bar to shelter from a storm. Skye, where a kindly farmer fixed our MG's broken spring with the metal strap from a farm gate. We explored the Scottish mainland from Ross and Cromarty to Inverness and Caithness, often driving back down through Perthshire and sometimes calling in on my childhood home.

My memories are full of midge moments. I washed my hair in the pure water of a burn in an idyllic glen only to find myself covered in the "wee beasties" as I stood up to dry my hair. We stuck our arms out of the car windows to test our midge repellent cream, only to bring them back in covered with dozens of midges stuck to the cream. The legendary Scottish midges bear no resemblance to their Sassenach counterparts and can overwhelm the soul.

The Highlands are not comfortable, the landscapes can be bleak, hard and unforgiving. The weather can change in an instant to storms of such ferocity it is as though the protection of a tent does not exist. The Highlands teach resilience, compassion, and show us our own smallness among the vast beauty and unique nature of our planet.

After seven or eight years together our relationship began to founder, we began to want different paths. I had developed my interior design practice and was designing extensions to our cottage home. Stuart was working with an electronics company based in Devon, installing new computer systems across the West Country. At the start of our relationship we agreed we did not want children. We enjoyed our child-free years, travelling through Europe and growing our careers. Stuart wanted to expand and continue, he was often away and was enjoying stretching his wings.

I was emotionally lonely and becoming broody. I realised I wanted a family and to build a family home. Stuart had a very difficult relationship with his refugee father, who had died before we met. He was not allowed to learn to speak Polish, and as a result was unable to communicate with his father. Their relationship was one of frustration, anger and domestic violence; a father example he did not wish to repeat. We grew further apart and when the tensions resulted in Stuart having an affair, I was heartbroken. My trust and romantic views on love disintegrated. I took the view "if you can't beat them join them", gave up my hopes for an interior design practice and took the job with the fitted kitchen distributor earning a good income, driving a company car, power dressing and travelling in England and Europe.

With my resilience intact and my self-esteem recovering, Stuart and I chose to stay together. Two years later Stuart announced that he'd changed his mind and would like to try for a baby. When I was thirty-two we took a well-earned holiday and set off once more to Achnahaird, sharing the familiar landscape from a different more mature perspective. I'd developed my independence and had confidence in myself, something that had not been the case when we married so young.

We decided to climb Stac Pollaidh, something we had never tried before. Not the highest mountain, Stac Pollaidh is a relatively easy climb. The mountain-top is a series of tooth like protrusions from narrow steep slopes that contrast with the round sculpted mountain base. We took our two dogs,

Ben the collie and Sunshine, an early version of a several things- oodle, with us. Mature and well-behaved dogs, they set off with us enthusiastically along the lower slopes. We climbed steadily for an hour or two and paused to take in the view. Below the series of lochs and lochans opened out in magnificent splendour and we could see for miles. Above was becoming a rather forbidding prospect with much steeper, scree slopes. I suffer from vertigo and we tried to see whether the path went round the mountain.

We probably took the wrong path at this point for we headed straight up the mountain at a steep angle, the dogs gamely keeping up with us and even running ahead, Sunshine pretending to be a mountain goat. When I paused in my climb and looked behind me I was shocked to see how high we had climbed, the landscape now opening out in a way I could never have imagined. I clung as best I could to the scree with hands and feet, remembering my father's admonition to always keep my feet sideways when climbing a scree slope otherwise the inevitable slide back cannot be stopped, and decided the only way was up. We got to the top intact and the view was incredible. Looking over the top of almost all the mountains except Suilven the 360 degree panorama that was unveiled was stunning, unforgettable. Equally stunning was to find the narrow unstable path that we had reached at the top had a steep fall, both in front of and behind us. We gingerly made our way along the top and, with relief, found an easier path to descend.

Our relationship would never be the same again as in those early years but we felt we had reached new heights. On our return home I learned I was pregnant. We were both delighted, ready to embrace change.

Part Three Deconstruction and Transformation 1984 – 1997

The Mendips, water colour by Morag Smyth

St Michael's Hill

I was walking up the steep hill wondering which bright town planner had designed Bristol's maternity hospital to be sited on one of Bristol's steepest hills. I wondered how many heavily pregnant women have made this walk, counterbalancing carrying weight equivalent to a sack of potatoes in front while bending at an uncomfortable angle over the sack to protect it, and somehow climb the exhausting last few metres to the hospital entrance as part of their prenatal experience. This, accompanied by growing anxiety about parking tickets running out while the long wait for the overdue appointment occurs, must surely have pushed many women's blood pressure up to alarming levels by the time they are seen. I can't blame this alone for the diagnosis of pre-eclampsia and my admission to hospital for bed rest, but I believe it was a factor.

Another factor was continuing the building work at The Cottage while pregnant. Stuart and I had moved into the new bedroom we'd built and I was stripping paint from windows in what had been our old bedroom and preparing the room for the baby when the midwife arrived. She sat me down and made me a cuppa while she waited for my blood pressure to subside and then tested me again.

"Mmm," she said calmly, "it is a little high". She asked me some questions about Stuart and his work. He and a colleague from his former work place had begun a new business in Bristol and were cresting the wave of new computerised point of sale systems.

"He'll be home this evening," I said. The midwife sceptically eyed the decorating tools and asked about me. My design practice had not died the death that I'd expected when I went to work for HMW. A few clients still contacted me over the years and what had begun with my designing a kitchen or sitting room for them had, over time, become my designing two storey extensions to their homes. I did not mention to the midwife that the month before I had been on the scaffolding of one of these extensions, explaining to the builder how to lead flash the complicated join of roof pitches. Nevertheless, this wise woman referred me for this appointment at the hospital - I was a few days after my due date. It was clear the midwife felt that enforced inaction was what the baby and I needed.

Another factor was my age. I was thirty-two and in 1984 a first pregnancy at this age was considered unusual. Instead of being referred to the local cottage hospital, I'd been referred to Bristol. Here research identified a small increase in the number of what they called 'elderly Primigravidas' (first time mothers) and a specific prenatal course was designed for us. I'd been attending weekly for the previous six weeks.

"As an older mother you may find it is difficult not to cope," we were told. "After all you have been coping with life, career and complicated things for some time and you may not be prepared for how vulnerable having a baby can make you feel." We shuffled uncomfortably as the tutor midwife explained how tired we would be from sleepless nights. She explained how a young mother – who usually has the support of her mother and other family members, together with the resilience of youth and lower expectations - will often find this stage easier to manage.

She also identified that we might be lonely and isolated. "You have your careers and friends and colleagues," she said, "but you may find that they are busy and you - alone at home with your baby - will be sharing this important period of your life in common with other much younger mothers and may feel alone. This is particularly true for those of you who live in the countryside," she concluded, looking directly at me.

My journey by car to and from Bristol went past Chew Valley Lake and over Dundry Hill. Taking in the spectacular views across Bristol to the River Avon and the Suspension Bridge, and - if you knew where to look - St Michael's Hill. I reflected on what I was learning. I bought books and was doing yoga for pregnancy but, until this course, I'd not fully appreciated how different my experience was from that of my friends whose children were now in their teens.

From the prenatal ward on the top floor of the hospital I could look across to Dundry Hill with the sun setting behind it and felt sad and homesick. It was nearly midsummer and the weather was exceptionally warm – hot, and the nights were light and bright with moon.

Prenatal wards are not fun to be in. Women are there because they are recovering from having miscarriages or natal emergencies or, like me, waiting and being observed because there may be a problem. The heat wave and the moon were bringing many women to labour or to Braxton Hicks contractions or to more major concerns and the ward was hot, busy and noisy. There was grief, anxiety and raw emotion. It is not the calmest place in which to bring your blood pressure down and mine remained stubbornly high.

Stuart came to see me and reassured me our neighbour was looking after our cats, Minnie and Moli, and dogs, Ben and Sunshine. The Doctor told me they would induce the birth if labour didn't start soon, I just had to be patient.

"I'm just so uncomfortable," I told Stuart angrily. "I've got nowhere to sit and nowhere to rest. I'm really fed up". With the nurses' permission Stuart had taken me for a walk in what little outdoor space there was. I was restless and frustrated and I wanted to be starting my labour at home, not stuck in this distressing hospital ward.

Stuart tried to reassure me. "It won't be much longer. They are worried we live so far away from the hospital."

The following day induction began, but labour did not start in earnest for another day. The first eight hours were not too uncomfortable and I was able to walk around a little until my waters broke. The following eight hours were more dramatic and, ultimately, I was given an epidural as the midwife was concerned about stress for me and for the baby. An epidural, pain relief administered in the spine, can sometimes slow the birth down. The pain subsided and I slept. Stuart, who had been distressed witnessing the epidural being administered to me, was reassured it would be many hours yet and was sent home for a rest.

A Dad being present at the birth of his child was still a relatively new development. Part of our neonatal course had been to invite and advise fathers on what to expect and on looking after themselves in these crucial days. Stuart had left a chicken for himself on timer in the oven but when he got home our neighbour, not realising, had switched it off when she came in to look after the animals. Stuart nevertheless returned to the hospital with this tale, refreshed and ready for action. I - although I had slept desultorily - was becoming increasingly tired. By now we had had three shifts of midwives and our original midwife was back with us.

Becoming concerned about my blood pressure and other signs, the midwife called in the doctor. The young woman looked at me, "Push!" she said. "I want you to push."

"I'm trying," I replied weakly.

"Keep trying, try harder," she said and - after a cursory glance at the machines measuring me - went off to see to another woman.

I began to fade, and things became very spaced and light and white. I was vaguely aware from an out of body perspective of the midwife rushing out and calling the senior consultant in; of his standing beside me angrily calling up assistance; of a group of people round my bedside and the young doctor being advised by the angry consultant on what she was to do as the forceps were used.

"Where did he come from?" Di asked me as she looked at my big boy with his dark hair and enormous blue eyes, and we laughed together. Di, who had shared my long journey to having a child, had tears of joy and I was overwhelmingly proud, bonded and deep in love with my long-awaited son.

"So this is who all the cards I've been delivering have been for," said the postman on his rounds next day, wishing me congratulations. And there were a lot of cards and so many expressions of love.

The doctor came round and visited the young woman she had delivered the night before instead of attending to me. She was unable to look me in the eye, humiliated as she had been by the consultant. I hoped she'd learned from the experience.

There were four of us in the ward. I envied the young Caribbean woman in the bed opposite me whose mother and sisters came with great fuss and attention to braid her hair and to hold her baby. I thought it was such a loving action and I told her so as I tried to comfort her when she later had the three-day blues. The young fireman's wife had her mother and grandmother at her bedside. I realised her grandmother was younger than my mother.

My parents and Stuart's parents came to see the baby. Stuart's parents were staying with us at the cottage. I was not allowed home for a few days, I needed rest and recovery time. At last Stuart collected us and drove us home.

"They both slept for twelve hours!" Stuart's mother exclaimed. And we had, both baby and mother exhausted, slept the whole night through. I was grateful to be home in our cottage, baby in his Moses basket, cats at my feet, and dogs at my side. Sunshine immediately proved to be a perfect Nanny Dog and Ben, the collie protector. I was grateful too for the prompt action by the midwives and consultant that saved both Tom and my lives, and for the dedicated team that looked after us so well.

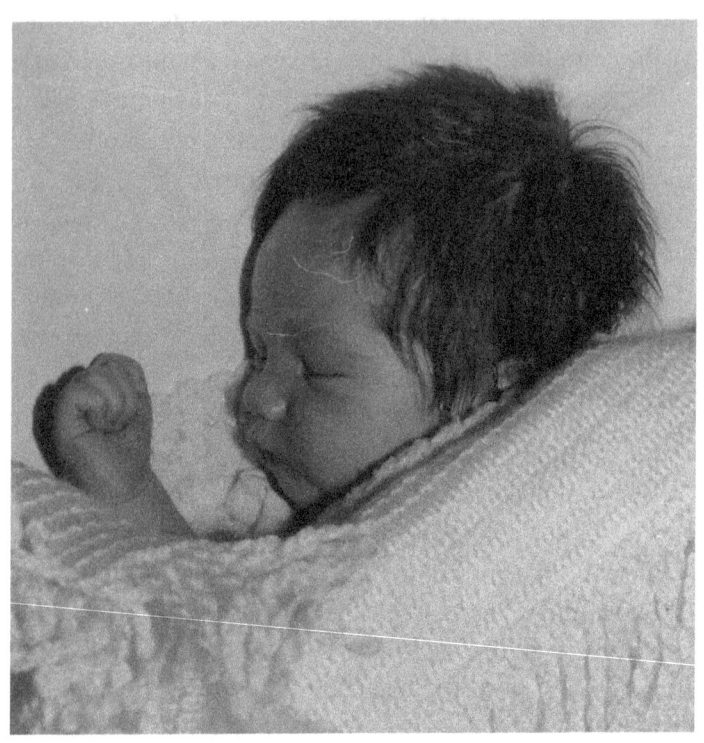

Baby Tom

Chewton Mendip

"Hi Mum. Do you think you could come and help for a week please?" I was phoning with the request just three weeks after giving birth to Tom. "I've had mastitis and I've had to stop breast feeding. The Health Visitor says I need to rest after such a difficult birth and I'm on antibiotics." Stuart had gone back to work and I was isolated and exhausted.

"Well I'm not sure how much help I will be dear, but of course I will come."

Mum came down by train and Stuart collected her at the station. "Oh he is a big baby isn't he," she said, returning him to me after I passed Tom to her to hold. When she had visited us in hospital she'd not had much contact with the baby and this was her first chance to bond with her new grandson.

"Thanks for coming Joyce," Stuart was relieved. He too was exhausted and had almost driven over the central reservation while driving down the motorway early one morning on his way to work. Neither of us were getting much sleep and the antenatal training was proving well founded.

"I've started worrying now," I told Mum.

"What do you mean dear?"

"Well I used to tell you to stop worrying all the time, but now I've had a child I have started worrying."

I was surprised how uncertain Mum was with Tom. She was lacking in confidence and clearly anxious.

Maxine, our neighbour at the farm, had come over to see how Tom and I were, and found me sitting in the shade of the porch of our cottage trying to breastfeed Tom. "You have a temperature," she told me.

"I've called the doctor but he just stood in the bedroom doorway and told me I was doing fine," I told her.

"Oh no," she said promptly, and competently called the health visitor who came at once and who called the doctor back. Mastitis was identified and I was advised to stop breastfeeding, rest and get some help.

My mother, usually so calm and confident in a crisis, was - with a baby - all of a dither. Uncertain about how to help me, she was not the practical support I had hoped for. She asked constant questions about what to cook, where to put things, what I needed, with the result that I only managed to sleep when Tom slept and continued to be exhausted.

"She's driving me mad," I told Stuart.

"Let's go out for an evening," he suggested. And with Mum agreeing to baby-sit we walked down to the pub.

"Mum always said she was better with older children than with babies," I told Stuart. Stuart's mother loved to cuddle Tom. My mother loved Tom but she held him at arm's length, clearly frightened of upsetting the baby.

Mum - Joyce - was not a tactile woman. She was brilliant, passionate, outspoken, and contact with Mum came in the form of long discussions, shared experiences and activities. After we were babies, she never held or hugged or cuddled her children, nor told them that she loved them. Mum hated all forms of sentimental outpourings of love. She was also disgusted by any excess physical needs such as diarrhoea or sickness and even by normal child toileting requirements. It was Dad to whom we went for comfort after an accident. The new disposable nappies I had for Tom were an improvement, but she still shied away from nappy changing. She'd once told me how angry Dad was when she had an accident with a nappy pin whilst changing my baby brother, and how wonderful Velcro was.

We were just finishing our first drink and enjoying our time alone together for the first time in weeks when the landlord called me to the phone, it was Mum.

"The baby won't stop crying dear. I can't cope, I need you to come home."

When Dad drove down to collect Mum we were talking about how hard it had been for her.

"I wish you could just be with him Mum," I said, referring to the baby.

"I don't know what you mean dear," said Mum, looking hurt.

"I know you don't," I replied cuddling Tom to my shoulder and, seeing my father give me a resigned smile of understanding from behind her, I gave my Mum a little pat. "Thank you for coming to help".

Stuart and I breathed a sigh of relief as they left and thereafter we coped pretty well. I loved proudly walking up the lane with Tom in his big second hand Silver Cross pram, with the two dogs beside and in front of us and the two cats following along behind.

One of the advantages of waiting to have a child meant that I made the most of every moment. I loved singing to and playing with Tom. I made him toys, a shape sorter for bricks through a lid into a dried milk can and a mobile from different materials and textures that reflected and captured light. I loved reading to him and talking with him. And when we were both tired, I would settle in front of the television and watch soaps while he drifted off to sleep in my arms.

Recently my sister and I visited the Foundling Museum in London on Mother's Day. We saw hundreds of tokens cut in patterned halves paired with mementos, hope of being reclaimed. There were paintings of mothers handing over babies to the wealthy few. We read survivors' accounts of the absence of love, regimented marches, cruel PE teachers. A dormitory was thought better than starvation on the street. In one room an artist shared with us a recording of children in care today, laughing as they recount the comfort of contact, the power of a cuddle.

Afterwards, emotionally exhausted, Sheila and I sat on a bench in Brunswick Square and remembered our grandmother. I have her sampler dated 1896 - it is an embroidered alphabet with her name and the name of the institution she was sent to as a child. The institution had a work-house history and, although it was a school by the time she went there, it was undoubtedly similar to the Foundling Museum in its history and culture. Sheila and I went on for a meal and raised a glass to our grandmother, our mother, and to ourselves.

Our grandmother's experience of disruption after her father died had profoundly affected her mothering of our mother, and in turn our mother's mothering of us. My grandfather travelled for work and as a child my mother took charge of the household from an early age when he was away. Grandma was a withdrawn woman who'd been unwell since her daughters were children. My mother thought it may have been agoraphobia, as Grandma rarely went out of the house. When I developed a thyroid condition, I recognised some of her symptoms and wondered if this was part of the cause. It may have been a mixture of the psychological impact of her childhood experiences and something physical that went undiagnosed. Whatever the cause, her symptoms became worse after the birth of her second daughter and my mother recounted managing the house from an early age for her mother, grandmother and younger sister.

The lack of physical contact with our mother was painful for my sister and me, but Mum's love for us was shown in other ways. Food was one of her main expressions of love. Coming home to a cheese and egg surprise or her brownie, and receiving nurturing meals every day was a matter of course for us children. We never thought twice about the work that went into ensuring we were fed. Nor did we appreciate that not every home was filled with discussion, conversation and commentary as she tried to give her love to us in intellectual ways.

Blackford, where my maternal line came from, is famed for its Highland Spring water. In Chewton Mendip, where I was attempting to rebuild an imaginary idyll, most of the water is underground. The copious pure water runs through the porous limestone and gets filtered through the Mendips. The River Chew that feeds Chew Valley Lake starts here, and the underground water appears in springs in the Bishops Palace in Wells and in Bath. I wheeled Tom round the moat of the Bishops Palace and we fed the ducks and swans.

Morag and Tom

"Don't worry, you are doing everything right" Mrs Green, a farmer and mother of five boys, told me. "Each of my sons was different. The first three slept through the night and it was only when I had my fourth, who never slept through the night at all, that I realised it was more about the child than what the mother did."

This was very reassuring. We were in the village hall for the rural baby clinic. The midwife weighed and checked Tom. "He's developing really well," she said. There was just the health visitor, nurse and a few mothers and babies at the clinic, all from scattered homes in the area. We were offered cups of weak tea.

"What a lovely smile," said one of the young mothers to me.

"And what a head of hair," said another.

We shared our experiences, connected with each other over the heads of our babies, and soon we became good friends - our days of rural isolation were over.

Greenfields

When I was a child I had a recurring dream about a madman who set fire to the world, and whose laughing face appeared in my dream in front of a burning globe. I woke terrified each time.

When my son Tom was a baby, Sheila was a peace campaigner and activist. With her husband and son, they joined the anti-nuclear protest at Molesworth (in John Major's constituency). A peace chapel was erected and in 1984 a MolesworthGreen Gathering grew into a peace village called Rainbow Fields village of about a hundred people living in vans and tents, including my sister, her husband and their son.

On the 5th February 1985 I was watching the news on television and was horrified to see 1000 troops with helicopters and assault weapons being deployed to evict this small, unarmed and harmless camp of peace protesters. Michael Heseltine, Defence Secretary, was dressed in a flak jacket and appeared with the troops. It was clear it was a carefully coordinated media campaign. With his maniacal laughing face Heseltine brought me back to my childhood nightmare.

It was a few anxious days before we knew they were safe. We were all worried and our mother was distraught and angry, bubbling over with the anger of anxiety.

"It's about the child," she said to me on the phone. "It's too dangerous for him".

I naively could not understand why peace campaigning should be dangerous. I thought it was a ridiculous and over egged response on the part of the government. To use armed soldiers against men, women and children peacefully protesting seemed a waste of resources, and counterproductive if the government wanted to defend the proliferation of nuclear war.

But it was dangerous. I began to suspect my phone might be tapped. There were strange sounds and delays on the line. The Thatcher Government had many undercover detectives working in the protest movement. Free speech and protest was becoming increasingly discouraged and was seen as a threat. In June the Rainbow Fields Village joined up with other travellers in a peace convoy heading for the Stonehenge Free Festival. A high court injunction had been issued aimed at preventing this year's festival, following concerns from the previous year.

"Look Stuart", I called my husband over to the television. A brief news report saying the peace convoy had been stopped before reaching Stonehenge showed a few photos of hippies, but there was little other information. Over the next months and years more about the violent and illegal way the convoy had been stopped became known. Over a hundred vehicles, buses and vans that were homes to men, women and children had been corralled by police road blocks on a side road before entering a beanfield.

Over a thousand police and agency police officers armed with truncheons and riot gear entered the field at 7pm and launched a violent assault on unarmed men, women - including pregnant women and those holding babies - and children. Years later it became public knowledge that the police used the tactics that had been learnt during the miners' strike earlier that same year.

Vans and buses and personal belongings were smashed up and trashed, terrified children were separated from their families and taken into care, and all the adults, about five hundred, were arrested in the largest mass civilian arrest in English history on the spurious grounds of obstructing the highway.

I was relieved when Sheila and her son came to see me at The Cottage a few days later. They were still in shock and traumatised by their experience.

"I wanted to ask you. Will you be Ali's guardian if anything like this should ever happen again?" she asked.

"Of course, I will. It would be a privilege," I replied and we hugged each other and our sons.

Initially both Police and the Government denied the violence. The shocking truth slowly emerged and eventually, two years later, the courts recognised that twenty-one travellers who fought for justice had been subjected to false imprisonment, wrongful arrest and damage to property. The Beanfield came into peace activism legend, the event is recalled in several popular songs and remains an example of inexcusable totalitarian action.

CND, the Campaign for Nuclear Disarmament, peace and green movements were close to the heart of the original Glastonbury Festival values. Following the Green gathering at Molesworth the previous year, a Green Field was established on the Glastonbury Festival site as a place for those with alternative views. A few weeks after the festival I visited Sheila and my nephew there. The clear up of the festival was nearly complete. The field sloped away looking out over the peaceful Mendip valley, with just the smoke of a few bonfires in the distance and some remaining tee-pees, vans and tents in situ with children playing contentedly nearby.

"You were always the brave one," I told Sheila, remembering how she had loved to play gypsies when we were young, building tents and envisaging camps just like this one, loving the idea of the freedom of the road. While fully supporting the values of the peace movement, I never had the courage to be a peace activist and to put myself on the front line, in the way my sister has done. I support the values of the peace movement, and am writing this at a time when Trump and others who threaten potential nuclear Armageddon are gaining power, I am grateful to the movement of which my sister was a part and to all those who influenced the Cruise Missiles ultimately leaving the UK at that time.

In his book The Spy and the Traitor, published in 2018, Ben Macintyre shows how deep the machinations were during the Cold War in the UK, the US and Russia. He says historians disagree on how close the world had come to war in 1983, the authorised history of MI5 describes the impact of a nuclear exercise, Able Archer, in 1983 as the most dangerous moment since the Cuban Missile Crisis of 1962. In 2016 an article in the Independent newspaper confirmed that MI5 were monitoring Peace Activists at RAF bases in the 1980s, and the photo which heads the article shows the Minister of Defence, Michael Heseltine, in his combat fatigues beside the barbed wire of the Molesworth Base in February 1985.

Litton

When Tom cut his forehead on the sharp corner of the porch wall, I'd never seen so much blood. Terrified, I ran with him in my arms to my neighbour Maxine at the farm. She calmed me, held the sides of the cut together, and arranged for a lift to our local cottage hospital eight miles away. There they taped the cut together and Tom and I soon recovered.

Tom was an active toddler. I read that with a Gemini child you can think you have given birth to twins due to the child's capacity to be in two places at the same time. And this was certainly the case with Tom, he often moved from one place to another at great speed. I soon got used to my heart frequently being in my mouth as well as visits to hospital. I bought a first aid manual and began to keep a 'hero' bag of little treats to be given after tumbles or upsets.

We new mums started a mums and toddlers group at a hall in the nearby village of Litton. It was great fun, very energised and dynamic. The children produced an amazing amount of noise as they ran round and played with each other with a selection of toys and trikes. We held fund raising jumble sales and cake sales and the demand for the group grew rapidly.

It was great to share these special early years with other mums, the highs and lows of the emotional and exhausting challenges, and to learn from each other's experience. This was long before the advent of 'yummy mummies' or competitive super mums. We were from all walks of life and - mostly happy in each other's company - we were able to enjoy and talk about the days that were not going so well, as well as the days that were.

Four or five of us had children within months of each other and we soon became close friends, our children also developing lasting friendships. The afternoons spent nattering over a cuppa while our children played in the garden or the woods, the times when life's challenges meant one or other of us needed to call on our friends for support, the social times of parties and the rhythm of a rural life with its harvest festivals, spring services and summer fairs were immensely pleasurable for Tom and me. I had the deep solace of a strong and loving bond with my son, the sense of being accepted, welcomed and rooted in a community, in short the sense of belonging that had until now often eluded me.

My relationship with Stuart had changed. He loved Tom and was a wonderful father, but he saw and treated me differently as a mother. Sometimes he found it difficult when The Cottage was often filled with children and mums and he wanted to work, make phone calls or have some quiet time. Sometimes the fathers shared time together too, but that was infrequent and Stuart found it very difficult to share his emotions.

So it was to my friends I turned when Tom was two and my parents called me on my thirty-fifth birthday to tell me that my father had cancer. They were wonderful - kind, supportive and caring, patient with my tears and taking Tom to play with their children when I needed time to grieve.

I drove up to Derbyshire regularly. Tom was a good traveller and I sang to him in his car seat as I drove up the motorway. My parents had recently sold Ladygrove House and moved into a converted barn in the same village, Two Dales. My sister and Alan sometimes met us there and we supported each other as we tried to support our parents through the months of gruelling operations, treatments and the ultimate "nothing more we can do" diagnosis.

My once strong father was wasting away before our eyes. Tom hated visiting him in the hospital in Chesterfield, with its long impersonal corridors and the altogether different atmosphere from our local cottage hospital. One day I arrived at Dad's bedside to find him missing.

"Don't worry" said the nurse, "he's just gone for a wash".

When another half hour passed with no sign of him I asked the nurses to check. They found he had fallen and been unable to get up or to reach the help cord. My father was like a felled tree. His sense of humour was intact and the equanimity with which he met his impending death was remarkable. He sipped his water with a weak shot of whisky, in preference to morphine.

"Ah, well," he said, "I've had my three score years and ten".

My mother was frantic. She tried every alternative cancer diet and remedy, desperate to get him to eat, to rebuild some strength, to not die. Dad had only been retired for a few years and

Mum had been looking forward to travelling with him, and to sharing a full life together.

Sheila and I walked in the woods, our sons running ahead of us using sticks as guns and leaping and calling, letting off the steam that built up in our parents' home.

"It's so difficult, we can't keep telling the boys to be quiet," I grumbled.

"Mum needs us," Sheila replied, both of us acknowledging how hard Mum found it. The life energy of her grandsons sustained her as her husband's life energy slipped away.

Stuart came up to see us. "I miss you," he said. He'd recently started up his own business and he brought with him some administrative paper work for my help. I found it hard to concentrate on his needs and he found it hard to compete with our son and my parents' needs for my attention.

When Tom and I came home to The Cottage we were very relieved and so happy to see our friends and animals again. Dad was having some respite time at home, and Mum was happier to have him in her care, if only for a short time. There was a deep grief, a kind of weight in the pit of my stomach, but there was nothing more to be done for the time being. Nothing really prepares you for the loss of a parent. As the autumn nights grew longer and colder and darker I could feel my life closing in, and I sat close to the fire watching the flames and waiting.

When the phone call came in January it was not the expected one about my father. Stuart's mother rang in tears from the hospital. Stuart's step father had an unexpected and sudden heart attack. Tom was asleep in his bed. We gently put him in the car and he slept all the way, waking only the following morning to find he was at his Nana's home. On our way there I had the words from a song "You don't miss your water 'til your well runs dry" running repeatedly in my head. Leon died before we got to Chesterfield.

Now I began to fully understand how much this kind gentle man had given to our family. Stuart's mother had a number of complex difficulties and Leon had been her rock. Recently he helped her to move into this modern sheltered bungalow where she would be able to manage alone. Maybe he had some intimation or early warning signals about his health that he had not shared with us. We shall never know, but for us all it was a complete shock.

The funeral, in the Catholic Polish church, was intense and sad. Tom was distressed and I took him out into the churchyard, thinking about the loss to Tom of all his grandfathers, Stuart's father having died long before Tom was born.

"Where is the motorway to heaven?" Tom asked me. And with tears in my eyes I had to reply I did not know.

A few weeks later Dad was admitted to hospital. His heart was giving up the struggle. He was peaceful and calm, occasionally removing the mask giving him oxygen, it irritated him because it reminded him of war.

My brother Alan took my mother for a cup of tea. She'd been holding Dad's hand, unwilling to let him go. Thus it was that I was alone at his bedside when he died.

"God bless you, we all love you," I said and held his hand as he breathed out, never to breathe in again.

Dad's death blew a hole in all our lives. He was our lynch pin and his death changed us all. Mum in particular was sometimes overwhelmed with grief.

A few months later I was lying on the bathroom floor crying. "Come on, you should be over this by now," Stuart stood in the doorway frowning at me. But I wasn't, and it would be some years before I was fully able to process the grief. Meanwhile, I got on as best I could with our busy lives.

Grief comes over us all in unexpected ways and waves. One

day I was driving Tom to his new nursery school. Suddenly the tears started to flow and I had to stop in a layby to cry. Tom unbuckled his car seat strap and climbed into the front seat and gave me a hug. Never have such small arms carried more comfort.

On the first year anniversary of Dad's death I needed to find somewhere to be with the spiritual moment alone. Tom's nursery school was near Downside Abbey and I hoped to light a candle there, but it was closed. I drove round the country lanes and serendipitously found a closed and deserted church. Standing in the overgrown graveyard thinking about my father the wind suddenly whipped up and dark clouds whirled around me, like an archetypal biblical storm. And just as suddenly the clouds cleared, the sun came out and the birds sang.

Szczecin

Why I thought going to Poland might cheer us all up, I'm not quite sure. I wanted Stuart to have the opportunity to meet his elderly aunt and his cousins. I wanted Tom to have an experience of his Polish roots, Jewish on my side, Catholic on Stuart's. Poland had been the source of severance and loss. My Jewish great grandparents had come to the UK as refugees from Warsaw in the 19th century. Perhaps with the loss of Tom's grandfathers I hoped for some healing to our family history.

Eighteen days after the start of the Second World War, with Germany's invasion of Poland, the Soviet Union, in an agreement with Germany, invaded Poland from the east. All of Poland was then under German or Soviet rule. The repression and dislocation of Polish people began. Four waves of deportation sent hundreds of thousands of people to Siberia.

Stuart's father was incarcerated in a Russian prisoner of war camp. Two years later when the Germans began to invade the Soviet part of Poland, Russia changed loyalties and Stuart's father, with many other Polish prisoners of war, was transferred to camps in the UK, where he continued his service with Polish regiments based in the UK. We had the bronze Monte Cassino commemorative cross, awarded to all the Polish soldiers who fought this fiercest of battles. The Polish cemetery at Monte Cassino holds the graves of over a 1000 Poles.

At the end of the war Poland, given over to Russia and Soviet communist rule, continued to suffer great deprivation for another forty years. Stuart's Aunt Helena and others in Poland with family connections in the west were punished. Helena lost her job and Stuart's mother sent out little parcels for her. Polish servicemen were killed or imprisoned if they returned to Poland. In the UK Stuart's father was treated as an 'alien' and had to report weekly to the Post Office with his passport.

Solidarnosc, a broad social movement using civil resistance to advance workers' rights and social change, was the first trade union in a Warsaw Pact country that was not controlled by a communist party. This development made the UK newspapers. Stuart and I read the coverage with interest. Formed in 1980 Solidarity rapidly came to represent more than a third of the working age population of Poland. The movement resulted in political repression and martial law was imposed in 1981, resulting in a strike by the dockyard workers of Szczecin. By 1983 the government had been forced by pressure from the USA and Pope John Paul II to negotiate with Solidarity. The hard line was softening, border restrictions were beginning to improve and, seizing the opportunity, we planned our visit to Stuart's family. The Pope visited Szczecin in June 1987, four months before our visit.

We took the car ferry to Hamburg and drove across West Germany to the inner border crossing with East Germany.

This was our first shock. The Cold War between the UK and the USSR was active, and crossing to the East at Lubeck was a frightening experience. We left West Germany with its ostentatious wealth - gold jewellery, large cars - and entered a no go zone between two borders. Crossing the distance of two fields separated by rows of watchtowers and barbed and razor wire, took us to a different reality.

The Border Guards thoroughly checked our passports, luggage, permissions, visas, and grumpily waved us through. Stuart's cousin was meeting us at the border between East Germany and Poland and we had no plans to linger in East Germany, but the few hours we spent driving through were significant. In East Germany poverty was evident in the thin sallow faces of the people who stared at us, and in the dilapidated buildings and towns people viewed us with great suspicion.

Our route took us close to Rostock, East Germany's largest seaport and a city that had gained massive support for the Nazi Party prior to the Second World War. They had a council composed entirely of Nazis in 1938 and, during the notorious Kristallnacht, they oversaw

Rostock's synagogue being destroyed and many Jews being beaten, killed or imprisoned. The RAF heavily bombed Rostock during the Second World War. We should not have been surprised that our car bearing its GB plates was viewed with such antipathy, but we were taken aback by the strength of passive aggression we encountered.

We soon realised we were being followed both by car and by helicopter. Stuart's hands gripped the steering wheel. We kept going and prayed we would not break down. The whole journey began to resemble a James Bond movie. Luckily Tom had fallen asleep in his car seat and we said little to each other as we approached the border with Poland. Here the East German Guards took all our passports and documents, corralled us into a separate holding area and left us there for three hours.

"Don't look at them," Stuart admonished me when I turned to stare angrily at the guards. "Just wait it out – it's definitely best not to confront them."

Tom woke up, I gave him a drink and put his favourite Roald Dahl story on the tape deck.

"They can see we've got a three-year old," I said crossly.

"Let's just hope they are still waiting for us," Stuart replied, referring to his cousins.

And there they were, waiting patiently for us. Alek and his wife Krista had taken the bus to the border crossing and, with no facilities at all, had had to wait out in the open all that time. The Polish guards greeted us with evident joy, commenting on our name, welcoming us in Polish, stroking Tom's cheek and rapidly waving us through. The contrast with the dreary totalitarian and threatening experience in East Germany could not have been more marked. Five years after our visit the worst violent mob attacks against migrants in post war Germany took place in Rostock, home still to militant right-wing extremism.

Gryfino, a town on the River Oder in the Szczecin Volvdeship, was not far from the East German border and soon we were at our destination. Polish hospitality is traditionally abundant and generous. Stuart's family put all their ration vouchers together to give us a warm welcome and a rich meal. Aunt Helena was crying as she greeted Stuart and held his face in her hands. She spoke only Polish and our Polish was very basic but many of the things she was saying needed no translation. She was speaking of a generation of loss.

In England it was as if we were the only family who had experience of disruption. In Poland it was every family. The entire population had been dispossessed, dislocated and separated. We toasted each other with small glasses of strong vodka and many cries of "na zdrowie" and went to bed in a happy glow. For Stuart, growing up in poverty in Northern England, he was the one who had been deprived. For his family in Poland he was the lucky one, the one who had grown up with freedom, food, education and autonomy. Everyone we met commented on our wellbeing, our clothes, our car, our skin and everyone we met had endured deprivation and loss.

Helena and family lived in a three-room apartment in a purpose-built utility block exactly like the neighbouring blocks. Each room served dual function as bedroom and living room and were furnished with sofa-beds. Below us we looked down on a solitary remaining original cottage with steep roofs, dwarfed among the blocks of flats, reminding us how this town must have been before the war.

In many ways life in Poland in the eighties was similar to post war Britain in the fifties, with rations, queues for bread, limited supplies and restricted freedom of movement. There were still tanks on the streets and the Poles seemed to hate the Russian domination. They watched the American series 'Dallas' on old television sets in black and white and longed for the goods they saw readily available in the west. I saw a young couple proudly carrying their new twin tub washing machine home on the bus. Everywhere we went people stopped to make a fuss of Tom and I was acutely aware of his evident glowing energy compared with the undernourished and slightly cowed children I saw in Gryfino.

Krista was somewhat sharp with her son Marek, who was nearly two, and did not hesitate to slap him. She seemed to think that I was very soft with Tom. Tom and Marek played happily together. Her parents lived inland in rural Poland and we were invited to meet them, giving Krista a rare opportunity to visit her family. It was a long drive through the fertile countryside and miles of forest. The village was a straggle of houses on the road, some with storks' nests on tall chimneys.

Krista's father was a schoolmaster and the family lived in a flat above the school. We were shown round the classrooms, with rows of desks, blackboards and a cane in the corner. The toilets were outside and were long drop toilets - a wooden bench had seat holes accommodating several bottoms along its length. The waste products dropped some distance into a not too smelly trench.

Upstairs we were treated to a welcoming feast and more glasses of vodka. Krista's father and brother could speak some English and we were talking for hours. Tom, who had been fascinated by the school rooms, asked if he could go down and have a look around. Stuart and I asked Krista's father about the derelict hamlet of thatched cottages we'd found on a walk around the village. It had been a peaceful and idyllic location and we wondered why it was deserted.

Hamlet in Poland

"Ach that was a village for Jews," he replied with a dismissive shrug. I realised how near we had travelled to the site of the concentration camps built by the Nazis for the extermination of Jews, homosexuals, and gypsies. Before the Second World War there were nine million Jews in Europe and afterwards, three.

Some time later Tom came back and tugged on my arm in alarm. "Mummy, Mummy the school is on fire!"

Krista's father rushed off downstairs and soon a commotion ensued with much shouting and activity and running up and downstairs with water and cloths. The huge boiler had been left on the hob of the stove downstairs and, now red hot, had boiled dry. Fortunately, it was steam, not smoke, that filled the room. By raising the alarm Tom had prevented what could have been a catastrophic fire. Krista's father was furious with his son, who had left the boiler on. Tom became the hero of the hour and was hugged and kissed and volubly thanked by all.

Stuart and I wanted to visit the town of Szczecin, a major seaport near the Baltic coast. Alek was not sure about our leaving - by signing the permission for our visas he was held personally responsible for our visit. Our presence filled their flat and despite their being so hospitable we felt the family could do with a rest. Reassuring Alek we drove to the city, relieved to have some time for ourselves. The whole visit was exhausting and emotional on many levels for us all.

We stayed in a hotel with fifties Brutalist design and thin partition walls. Szczecin was mentioned in Winston Churchill's famous Iron Curtain speech in 1946, describing the post war division of Europe into two separate areas, "from Szczecin in the Baltic to Trieste in the Adriatic an Iron Curtain has descended". The city was the third largest city in Germany. Prior to world war two it had only 2,000 Polish and 2,000 Jewish inhabitants. Bombing during the war destroyed more than half of the city and in the agreements with the Soviet Union it became a major Polish city after the war.

In 1987 much of the city was still being rebuilt and there was a strong sense of a new and displaced population in recovery and resettlement, as well as a sense of desertion and loss. The river Oder flowed into a huge bay that entered the Baltic Sea. The water was brownish, we managed a paddle but a passer-by drew our attention to the signs in Polish warning of effluent outflow and we quickly washed Tom and ourselves off and walked to the town centre.

We had a meal in a restaurant that advertised accepting Barclaycard. When I came to pay with the card the waiters had no idea how to use it. The manager was called and eventually a machine to record the card transaction was found and I signed the docket, and six months later the transaction went through on my account for £2.

I saw an elderly woman walking rapidly away down a side road and took a sharp intake of breath. Her build and looks were so familiar she could have been my mother or my aunt. And I realised this was the only Jewish person I had seen throughout our visit to Poland.

Our last day with the family in Gryfino was sad. We knew this was probably the last time Stuart would see his aunt. Aunt Helena pressed a gold ring into my hand and hugged me. I knew I would never have the strength she had demonstrated - to survive great loss and deprivation and to remain strong and intact, with a warm and loving heart.

Two years later, in 1989, the chain reaction of revolutionary change had spread from Poland and Hungary to East Germany. I cried as I watched on television the Berlin Wall being torn down by the hands of euphoric people. The division was over, Poland's borders were opened, and Germany's reunification took place in 1990, three years after our visit.

The Road to the Isles 4

West coast Highland Scotland

Our visits to Scotland always helped me to keep life in perspective. When Tom was two years old Stuart and I took him to Achiltibuie on the North West coast of Scotland for a camping holiday. We drove up and stopped in a campsite at Aviemore on the way. Tom, normally a happy child, cried all night and we could not console him. We tried everything, lighting the tent with lamps and torches, reading stories to him and then sitting in the car, but the dark remoteness of the Scottish Highlands was filling him with a primitive terror.

When we got to the campsite in Achnahaird Tom's response

was completely different. He loved it. Responding to the free-range vast space where the mountains meet the sea and the sky, he played in the sand, made himself a bed of stones to lie on and delighted in full body contact with the ground and sea. He ran into the sea and pulled up long lines of kelp brought in by the storms and draped himself in them, laughing with glee. Together we laughed and jumped over the waves. The water was bitterly cold but it didn't seem to affect Tom at all. I had chittering bites at the ready for him and wrapped him in a towel and rubbed him warm.

I developed a temperature and started to feel really ill. I went to see a GP in the nearest town, Ullapool, twenty-five miles from the campsite. She sounded my chest and pronounced bronchitis, prescribing a hefty dose of antibiotics.

"What were you thinking of, camping up here with a baby?" she asked, clearly appalled at my foolhardiness and lack of respect for our remote location. "You need to look after yourself as well as the baby."

Undaunted Stuart took Tom off in the backpack for a hike in the hills while I lay in the tent and waited for my temperature to come down. I reflected on how far away from help we were should anything else happen and, when they came back, Stuart and I discussed it and decided to move to a slightly less remote site further south, near Gairloch.

Stuart and Tom near Gairloch

Gairloch is a more gentle area, protected by the Gulf Stream it stays relatively warm all year, and the Inverewe gardens pride themselves on the rare plant species they are able to grow 'where the Gulf Stream meets the Highlands'. The landscape is more rolling and sheltered than the rugged north and there is a sense of respite from the wilderness. We camped in a well-equipped and sheltered site at Badachro, and treated ourselves to a meal at the Badachro Inn. I started to feel much better and realised I was relieved to be closer to luxuries such as hot water, flush toilets and showers.

A young couple from Germany were staying on the campsite. They had a young son with them of similar age to Tom and the two boys got on immediately, with the instant rapport children find irrespective of language or culture. The family had a huge luxurious camper van and soon we were invited to join them for a barbecue. We sat in the sun and drank cool beer from their fridge while our sons played and built castles in the sand.

Further along the road the soft sand dunes of Red Sands were perfect to roll and tumble in. Tom was born with a sense of humour and he had a glint of mischief in his eye as ran up to where I was lying on a towel to pour freezing cold water over me fresh from the rolling waves. The healing light and sounds and magic of the highlands soon brought me back to full health and I realised how exhausted I had been. Caring for my parents and my son had taken its toll and this holiday was a welcome respite and gave me the strength to cope with the demands to come.

We returned to Achiltibuie when Tom was five. Mum rented a cottage for us all for a family holiday. Sheila and Alan joined us and the two cousins climbed, explored and built dens while the adults talked and read and enjoyed the comfort of living in a house. Although in a strange way I missed the direct contact with ground and granite and wildness, I enjoyed the space and protection of home living.

Tom was only four when he started school and this holiday was the half term before the end of his first year. I was frightened when he started school, bringing up as it did the memories of my own first school days in Dollar, but I needn't have worried. The first class at Tom's school was designed to be a bridge between nursery and primary and I was fascinated by the change in education from my own primary days. There was so much research about children's development and, as a result, approaches to child nurture and education had vastly improved. Watching Tom and Alan play and build universes in the dens they constructed and the sand towns they created was fascinating. In my teaching I was helping young students to develop their spatial skills and I began to realise spatial ability was immensely variable and rarely taught.

Watching my mother with her grandsons was illuminating. She watched them with great love in her eyes, and I knew having them with her helped her to cope with the loss of their grandfather. Her way of giving love was to make sure we all had food and our needs met.

She never held, cuddled or touched her grandsons, unlike the family in Poland who had held Tom's face lovingly in their hands, she seemed to drink the love in through looking. She would speak in her loud clear diction words of warning - "Boys…" – that would stop them in their tracks just before a fall or spill. And they loved their grandmother, accepting her as she was.

While the boys played, I rested and sketched. Once again, I was in Achiltibuie while taking strong antibiotics. I had recently been for two gynaecological treatments, both unpleasant and painful, and at two different hospitals in Bristol. It felt rather like being in pieces and I needed to restore my whole being. I had not discussed my health issues with my sister or mother and I did not discuss the details of the reasons for my medication. My family shied away from medical or physical matters and preferred to discuss literature, politics or art.

We had books to identify the wild flowers and bird life unique to the area. With binoculars we hopefully watched the sea for whales. We walked and talked and enjoyed spending this rare time together. I drew in my sketch book and wrote poems and gradually the healing power of the Highlands worked for me again.

We took a boat trip to the Summer Isles. From Achnahaird

watching the sunset behind the Summer Isles is a time-stopping experience. Professor Brian Winley discovered in 2009 that rocks on the Coigach peninsula are three billion years old, some of the oldest rocks in the world. I always had this sense of ancient uniqueness in this landscape. Plate tectonic theory was only accepted in geological science when I was seventeen, I learnt nothing about it at school, but I always realised that this area must have been subject to extraordinary forces. We now know that this area of land has moved around the globe, due to plate tectonics, from the South Pole to Novia Scotia, ultimately breaking off and banging into the UK six million years ago. Just twenty two thousand years ago the area was an arctic fjord environment, valley glaciers converged here and became one of the major tributaries for the ice stream that was the drainage route for the British Ice Sheet.

On the boat we talked about volcanic forces as we motored what appeared to be perilously close to the steep granite cliffs and watched the seal colony from a respectful distance. Gannets spear-dived into the sea and gusts of sea birds flew round the boat, hoping for fish remains from the boat's other use as a fishing vessel. Volcanic emotions in the family after Dad's death and Sheila's recent separation from her husband were beginning to calm. The fleeting quality of life is apparent where time is measured in the span of billions of years, a time before any life was present on the planet. And all about us now, life teemed with intensity and vibrancy as the sea slapped the side of our boat and our little family bounced around at the mercy of the skipper and the tides.

Wallisdown

Unravelling is a gradual process. Events start to fray and tear at the fabric of structures, finding weaknesses and pulling at loose ends. Grief layered on grief for me and, invisibly at first, the bonds between Stuart and me began to undo. I longed for another child - all around me my friends were having their second and third babies. At last I felt I was pregnant. The familiar feelings in my body confirmed this. Three weeks late for a period felt too soon for a test, and I kept my knowledge wrapped inside me. As a result, when I lost the baby or embryo there was no one to share the loss with.

I was gardening, digging up ground elder, a weed with an extensive and pervasive root system. I dug up great forkfuls of the writhing white roots and was carrying them to our bonfire when I felt a sharp pain in my womb. I raced to the toilet in distress. Blood and my tears flowed. I'd imagined a little girl. I had begun to think of names. And now there was nothing.

There was no suggestion of going to see a doctor. After all the pregnancy had not been confirmed. Stuart shrugged it off and I had no idea how to process the loss. The long-term physical effect became clear over time - untreated infection, secondary infertility. The long-term effect on our relationship was like placing the final domino in a long line, ready to fall at the slightest push.

We were struggling financially as well as emotionally. Lawson's boom and bust economy was beginning to fall apart, and interest rates were going up to 9%. Stuart's business was not faring well and I had a very small income from my freelance design work.

"You'll have to go back to work," he told me.

I knew this meant the end of my hopes for increasing our family. "Well," I replied, "if I'm going back to work it will be to do something I want to do."

More grief was to follow when our dear dog Sunshine died. She had been like Nana, the dog who acted as nanny in Peter Pan, to Tom and she was irreplaceable. Ben pined without her, as we all did. For Tom's fifth birthday we visited Bristol dogs' home and adopted Sparky, a gorgeous collie mix puppy who Ben immediately started training in good behaviour.

Our friends visited and I told them I was job hunting. "What do you want to do?" Martin asked me. I'd become very interested in child development and learning, and was reading about education practice. "I'd quite like to teach" I told him. Martin worked in an art college in Dorset. "They are often looking for part-time lecturers," he said. And a few weeks later I received an invitation from the Head of the School of Spatial Design to deliver a guest lecture.

Dusting off my portfolio and cleaning my drawing board, returning it from its use as a nappy changing table back to its original purpose felt good. I was nervous driving down to Poole but as I drove into the art college campus in Wallisdown I felt alive, excited. And when I arrived in the purpose built studio with its copious daylight, pitched ceilings and red laminated timber beams, I felt at home.

The students were generous and attentive, enthusiastically looking at my designs and asking many questions. The day sped by and after my lecture I spent time with them discussing their own designs at their drawing boards. I was shown round the extensive workshops, the photography and film studios, the library full of art books and the pre computer state of the art resources. The studios were equipped with the very first tiny Mac computers. I loved it all, and driving home was filled with a sense of joy and of longing.

I was delighted when I was asked to come back to work as a part time lecturer for the National Diploma in Spatial Design. Stuart was less keen. It was a long way to travel for a day's work, two hours driving each way each day. Tom had started school and the local village school was in walking distance. Stuart would have to take Tom to school and collect him afterwards.

"It's only one day a week and the pay is great," I said. "Let's try it".

Martin used to say being in the studio was like walking on the surface of a cow pat, it looked smooth and dry on the surface but you soon realised you were sliding all over the place and could hardly hold a task in mind for a minute before being interrupted and over taken by a dozen queries or events. It was true, I would arrive with the day's projects and plans clear in my mind, by lunch-time I considered myself lucky to have completed one task. There were about forty students on the national diploma in two-year groups and all of them were active, engaged and lively.

On my way home I mapped the studio in my mind, picturing where each student sat and memorising their names. The course was a combination of project work, workshop practice and materials and drawing studies. Spatial design was a relatively new course and was mocked by the industrial design students, "Ooo designing rockets are we?" they would laugh. "Spatial", a term used to describe working with three and four dimension concepts such as interior architecture and exhibition design, has become a common term used regularly in architecture. At that time we were forerunners in the field.

"Where is Bournemouth?" Tom asked and I promised to take him one day. They were long days and I was rarely home before Tom's bedtime. Gradually the hours I was working increased. Mark, the Head of School, asked me to do two days a week the following term.

"We need the money," I told Stuart. I was thoroughly enjoying the teaching, getting great pleasure from watching the students' development and participating in the wide range of projects. Stuart agreed.

I spent many of the teaching days at student's drawing boards, working with them on projects. I was teaching on the National Diploma in Spatial Design. The new course structure was in sections designed to give the students basic design skills, materials and construction knowledge and experience of a range of design practice. The workshop was large, modern and well equipped, and the studios were generous and shared with the students studying the Higher National Diploma. The College was, and is, internationally renowned for its successful Film and Photography Studios. This relatively new course sat alongside courses in Fashion, Graphic Design and Industrial Design in a purpose-built new building, completed a few years earlier.

The full-time staff on the course included David Ridout

who, like myself, had been trained by the team headed by Norman Potter who taught me in Chesterfield and had then moved to Bristol. Two of the part time staff were also from the Bristol school. Mark, the Head of School, specialised in interior design, his work brought colour and energy to the studio, while David developed systems design with detail and black and white geometry. Mike Rowbotham, one of the tutors who taught both David and myself, laughed when he heard David and I were working together.

"I can see it now," he told me. "David's work will be precise and organised and rigorous and yours will be creative and colourful and innovative". And he was exactly right.

All students bring energy and commitment to their work, but there is something extra lively and invigorating in art colleges. They are sexy dynamic inspiring working environments and not for the faint hearted. Emotions and energies run high and there are dramas playing out while students learn as much about themselves as about the discipline they are studying. And so do the staff. I became more and more drawn in to the course. When I worked two consecutive days I sometimes stayed with friends, but often I travelled on two separate days of the week.

It was a two-hour drive across Somerset, Wiltshire and Dorset and included spectacular views. My route took me up zigzag hill past Shaftesbury and on my way home I stopped to admire the sunset. Purple orange and red clouds streaked across the sky below me and the Dorset and Wiltshire countryside spread out in cushioned fields. It was a recovery of my freedom, and in a similar way to the way I had recovered myself when I worked for HMW, I felt I was able to get perspective on my life and my priorities.

At the end of my first year of teaching my mother decided to move to Wells.

"I've had long enough of living on my own and I want to be near you all, and near enough to walk to the shops," she said. I made a short-list of houses in Bath and Wells and we went house-hunting together.

"Too hilly" was her summary for Bath.

"Too big a garden" in response to a house in Wells with a walled garden.

I was surprised, having seen the many acres she had gardened, she was wise and at seventy was thinking of her future.

In the end she found a small cottage with a courtyard and roof garden that was manageable for her on her own and near enough to us to be connected to family without being too close. The night before she moved from Derbyshire, we had the end of school year celebration for the children at Tom's primary school. The children had all grown so much in that year and were a delightful secure and close group. We were proud parents and happy the first year at school had gone well. The relief and infectious happiness led to us drinking too much Pimms and when Mum and the removal truck arrived the next day I was a little the worse for wear.

"Are you all right dear?" asked Mum.

"Just about" I said as I ran for the toilet.

"I hope it's not the strain of me moving in," she said.

"No of course not" I replied, but I guess in some ways I drank too much because all the parts of my life were coming together and at the same time falling apart.

Bournemouth

"It feels like a ten-ton truck coming," I said to Alec. We were walking along the coast path above Bournemouth beach in our lunch hour. The sea was flat and calm and perfectly reflected the grey sky. The tension between Stuart and I was reaching a crisis point and I could not get Stuart to take any responsibility in the failure of our relationship. He seemed to feel persistent denial would make it, or me and my needs go away. Alec patted my back in sympathy. We'd become close in this second year of my teaching at the art college. Alec was trained in Bristol by the same team that I studied with in Chesterfield and we had a mutual understanding of design principles. Our values were similar too. Alec had a young daughter and, recently separated from his wife, he was very understanding and empathic to the conflict I was feeling.

"I think I'm getting close to Alec," I told Stuart, who was furious.

"It would be better if you hadn't told me," he said.

I guess in telling him I hoped Stuart would somehow become emotionally articulate and able to prevent the crash that was coming.

Later a friend said the same thing, "It would be better if you hadn't told anybody."

But I could not live with the duplicity that may have enabled me to retain the status quo. I wanted to make changes and to be free. My feelings for Alec were intensified by his recognition of who I was and his seeing me as a woman rather than a label 'wife' or 'mother'.

"I never thought I would see you looking this happy again," Stuart told me, and in this he voiced his recognition that we had not been truly happy together since our first break and the accompanying loss of trust.

And I was happy - ecstatic, joyful, alive.

A 'friend' took one look at me. "You're having an affair," she said and went straight off to console Stuart.

Being loved, rediscovering yourself and in a close relationship with another is that crazy thing, the madness of love. The intensity of love, being awake with every fibre of your being is wonderful and overwhelming. The sorrow of separation from Stuart was eased by this love, but the end of our marriage was still deeply painful after our many years together and our shared love for our son.

Women 'police' women and in Chewton Mendip I was the subject of intense disapproval. "I don't approve of what you are doing at all," said one mother. Most of the mums felt very sorry for Stuart, saw him as the victim and could not understand how I could be separating from him and leaving my son to go to work. It seems extraordinary now that working mothers are the norm, but this was the prevailing culture of the time. They did not realise how unhappy I had been and they certainly did not approve of my having a career, or a lover, far less did they understand me being the main wage earner. A few very good friends rallied round. One gave Tom breakfast and took him to school in the morning with her daughter, and one collected him from school and shared tea with him and her sons until I got home in the evening.

It was of course most painful for Tom. It was shattering that his loving innocence and secure home should be subject to such upheaval. I felt terribly responsible and even though I'd read 'I'm OK, You're OK' with its clarity of explanation for transactional analysis, and 'Women who love too much' with its tree shaking exposure of power dynamics, and 'A Good Enough Parent' with its reassuring approach, I still took more than my share of responsibility for the decision to part. Somehow, I had always known I would have to manage being a parent on my own. My new relationship protected me from that reality for a while and I indulged in fantasies of a new happy family with Alec and his daughter. But it was not to be. Rebound relationships are often a bright brief flare. At the end of a spring holiday Alec made it clear he did not want what I wanted and the relationship ended.

Now I was truly heartbroken. All the loss in my life flooded in on me. I went through detachment trauma, and talked endlessly and obsessively about it to my patient friends until Di said, "I can't help you anymore. You need to see a counsellor."

The counselling appointments were in an attic room in Bristol that was a safe calm space. Paper and pastel crayons were on the table beside me. Carol, my counsellor, gently guided me through the process of unpacking the compacted layers of grief in my soul. Aunt Katie used to sing "Cry me a river' and the lyrics stayed with me, now I found myself crying that river – I could not believe there were so many tears. Carol helped me to see how isolated and coerced I had been and the counselling process enabled me to rediscover trust in myself.

I used to pass Emborough Pond on my way to work and would sometimes stop and gaze for a while at its calm flat surface. The reflection of the sunset and the beech trees that surrounded the water soaked up my grief. Tom, aged six, tried to mow the lawn and make tea and effectively tried to become my carer. But I managed to recover enough to show him we would be fine and that I could cope. I decided not to go back to teaching in Bournemouth after the end of that academic year. It was a painful decision but I knew Tom and I needed the time to recover and explore our future together. Mark tried to persuade me to stay, but I was resolute.

I still wanted to pursue my teaching career and had become very interested in spatial ability.

I saw an unusual opportunity advertised for an interdisciplinary Master's degree in Art, Education and Psychology and applied. My application had to go before the Board because my art qualifications were from a time before Art Colleges had degree status and a first degree was a must for Master's study. Thankfully, the case I made and my references swung it and I was offered a place on the course at the University of Wales in Cardiff. My mother, her non-judgemental support unwavering throughout, generously offered to pay the fees.

A friend invited me to see Shirley Valentine, the play, at the theatre in Bristol. It was great to revisit the joy of a middle-aged woman rediscovering her freedom. I was happy as I got off the bus to walk home. The village had no street lights and I was soon away from the main road on dark unlit lanes. I heard footsteps behind me and realised I was being followed. I sped up and so did the sound of the footsteps. I decided to go through a field that cut through at a steep angle and would avoid a particularly dark bend in the lane. As I entered the field two horses came towards me in curiosity. I greeted them like old friends. "Oh hello there you are," I said loudly and with that I heard the footsteps behind me running away.

Mum and I went to see Single Spies, the two-play production by Alan Bennet exploring the life of Guy Burgess and Anthony Blunt. When the two men kissed on stage Mum flinched, she had never seen a gay kiss before and although she knew the spies were gay, seeing a live kiss was still a shock to her. Afterwards we talked about our gay friends and how difficult it had been for Mum's gay friends in the sixties. Mark, my friend and colleague at Bournemouth, was gay and I had been shocked at the sometimes overt and often unconscious homophobia he experienced daily. Men would say "I'm not sexist", unaware that they were doing something ridiculously sexist such as bum pinching or overtly scanning a woman's body. My male colleagues would describe how they had had to prove they were not gay when they were studying art, yet at the same time they mocked Mark's skill with colour and his flamboyant energy.

A couple of years later I was telling Tom that Mark was lonely after he had visited us one day.

"He should get himself a girlfriend," Tom said.

"He's gay," I replied.

"Well, he should get himself a boyfriend then," Tom said without a moment of hesitation. I was quietly pleased in the change in attitude over three generations, but it would be many years before Mark would be free from prejudice.

Di and I and our boys watched the Freddie Mercury tribute concert for Aids awareness on TV. We danced in her living room to Mercury's exuberant performance in film of 'I want to break free' and we felt and lived the change.

"I don't want to do this," I told John, a design client who had become a friend, and who made me a business proposition. Already a successful businessman, he felt together we could design and develop a company supplying balconies. I was unsure how much demand there would be, but he was willing to invest in research and development. We visited blacksmiths and I developed some designs loosely based on a Macintosh theme. We had our first trial surveys in London and commissioned the first build. I knew this was not the right direction for me. There was chemistry between us, complicating things, and I shied away from developing the relationship or the company. I shied away from other potential relationships too. I realised, after marrying so young, I had not had the opportunity to be with myself and with who I was before sharing myself with others. This was my time.

With sadness I said goodbye at the end of term to the students, friends and colleagues in Bournemouth and returned home alone to spend the summer playing with my son, trusting that I would find a way through for us both.

Cardiff

I was standing in the queue in the student's union building in Cardiff, my photo and documents in hand, hardly able to believe I was registering for a Master's degree. As soon as I had my library card I explored the stacks of books in the Education Library – thousands of them. Whole areas devoted to child development and shelves of books on feminism and exclusion. I was not alone, many people had been researching and writing about these issues, and the results were fascinating. And thus started an expensive reading addiction.

I would take a stack of books home and pile them up beside my bed.

"It doesn't do to go too deeply into everything," Mum said, viewing some of the titles with concern.

"We can't follow you where you are going," said Di. But she did, and several years later she took her own Master's degree at Cardiff after taking an Open University degree.

If I hadn't read them I couldn't bear to take the books back, and racked up substantial library fines. So much so that over three years of study it was cheaper to buy the books new. I ended up purchasing some of them from the library, as the cost of purchase was less than the fines.

"Will you see it through?" asked Tom's teacher in disbelief when she learned about the course, making me more determined to do so. She had come to see me to apologise after Stuart had unexpectedly collected Tom from school and taken him to Derbyshire for the weekend without informing me.

One day I was walking Ben and Sparky in the fields and Ben, who was aged fifteen and showing signs of rheumatism and arthritis, just sat down and could not walk on. I called the vet and he came and put Ben down at home. The moment Ben died Sparky let out a huge howl, and when Tom came home from a day out with Stuart he did the same.

Stuart and I had shared custody rights, but Stuart saw Tom intermittently and when it suited him. Following the divorce agreement he paid maintenance for a short while, but he stopped after I took on a sole mortgage and paid him his share of the equity in The Cottage. Soon after that he started a new relationship and moved on.

I loved the drive through Bristol to Cardiff, a route that took me over the first Severn Bridge which had been opened by the Queen in 1966. I find suspension bridges stunning, the way they appear to float in the air. Bristol is, of course, known for the suspension bridge designed by Brunel, which hangs over the River Avon. The first Severn Bridge crossing, from Bristol to Wales, is much longer and has spectacular views. Now I felt queen of the world, as I drove over the Severn, playing my tape compilations at full volume.

There was a weekly evening lecture in Psychology during the first year. Two fellow students lived in Bristol and we soon car shared, I picked them up in Bristol. Claire was studying the course full-time, a huge undertaking. Carenza and I had opted to take the part time route to fit in with our work commitments. We shared ideas and experiences and the strains of completing our first course assignments. One of my first essays was titled 'Not the Nuclear Family'. I wrote it on my little Amstrad with its floppy disc storage and tiny flickering green text. I forgot to save the first draft and had to rewrite the entire thing, but it was probably better second time around, and I got a B, which felt fantastic - B for my first assignment at University – wow! I knew I could never have undertaken this course without a computer, the ability to cut and paste and redraft was essential to my woven method of writing. Reading type written dissertations in the library archives, I was in awe of the work involved. I tended to make sketches in abstract form of my ideas and then weave in words until an essay structure began to appear.

I was still in psychotherapy and it was fascinating to compare psychology theory and academic research with a therapeutic approach to the lived experience. For me, I needed both approaches - head and heart. Some of the dry experiments in human psychology appeared to miss some of the essential aspects of being human, others often involving case studies, were fundamentally illuminating.

During the first term Carenza asked me if I would take over her part time teaching role in the Chew Valley. She had a group who were part way through a course in watercolour painting. "It's too far for me to travel," she said. And since it was near me, I took it on. The group was delightful. They had a mixture of abilities; one woman had always wanted to study art but had dropped any creative study before she was twelve, one man had retired and wanted to develop his skills. For the first session I set up a complicated still life, straw hat, suitcase, dry flowers on the table. The group gently and kindly showed me this was too much. We discussed their needs and settled on a weekly technique exercise, and looking at the work of other artists, followed by sketch painting.

I was researching spatial ability as part of my study in Psychology and initially could not find any texts on this in Cardiff library. The nearest thing I found was about the spatial ability of migrant birds following their 'head compass'. I asked Tom's school if I could do a little study with the children, and they were very helpful and invited me in as a volunteer. I had the sense that all children knew they were creative and could draw, but at an early stage in their education most children lost that confidence to the extent that they stopped drawing or modelling their ideas altogether. I took a small group of children on field drawing sessions. I still have the delightful drawings they made of the village.

In the second term Mark rang and asked me to come back to Bournemouth to do some teaching. I agreed to one day a week. I did miss the studio, the students and, of course, the money. But I couldn't have committed to doing this without the fantastically generous support of my friends, something I could never repay. "Don't worry," Pat said, "you will be able to help others in the future." Their faith in me was amazing and their support helped Tom to recover his sense of security. It does take a village to raise a child.

Alec and the other part time lecturer from Bristol had left the school. Mark had appointed two new part time tutors, an architect who was London based and a Dorset artist. It was great to meet them. "We've already heard all about you," they said and welcomed me back to the lively and productive studio. Most of the students I taught the previous year had finished their courses but there was a new, even larger year group keen for attention. We worked through lunch-time and on into the evening. Tom was asleep in his sleeping bag when I collected him from Di's home and I drove home and gently lifted him into his own bed without waking him.

My hours at Bournemouth gradually increased to two days a week and, with my travelling to Cardiff one evening a week as well as being a single mother, my week was full. Mum realised how tired I was and generously offered to treat me to a holiday for my fortieth birthday. Two of my friends offered to share Tom's care for the week and, for the first time in seven years, I had a whole week to myself. I booked an apartment in Menorca and flew out with just a few books and my straw hat for company.

Each morning I walked down to the secluded cove and swam, then returned to my terrace for brunch and to read. I was reading the trilogy "Attachment, Separation and Loss" by John Bowlby. His seminal work showed the importance of the child's bond with the mother and the effects if such bonding is disrupted or insecure. He describes a child developing secure attachment, where the child is free to come, go and to explore and return securely; and contrasts this with insecure attachment, where the child clings to an attachment person or thing and cannot let go, and insecure detachment, where the child cannot attach and rejects overtures of connection. I found it intensely interesting and absorbed myself in his ideas. It let me reflect on my own and my family's experience of all three forms of secure and insecure attachment. Without Bowlby's work mothers would still be separated from their child when the child is born, this was common practice until the nineteen seventies. The history of separation in my family was felt through the generations. Perhaps everyone who absorbs themselves in research is essentially finding out something about their own lives, like the Greek Delphic maxim "know thyself", I found I was understanding more about myself as my studies progressed.

On the flight home I spoke with some fellow passengers. They asked if I'd had a good holiday and said they had seen me every day on the beach. Clearly I'd been a woman of mystery for them, and unusual in my single status. I'd been oblivious, involved as I was in my own inner journey. Tom and I were very happy to see each other and he reattached to me comfortably and securely. I'm grateful for the support for me that made his secure attachment possible.

In the second year of my Master's course the art education lectures were structured around self-motivated research and that enabled me to develop my thoughts around spatial ability. Tom's school continued to be supportive, as was Mark on the spatial design course. As a result I was able to compare the development of adult and children's spatial ability in the art college and the primary school through a series of projects. I was fascinated by the different skills and began to find that students with dyslexia tended to have better spatial skills. A colleague brought me a checklist for dyslexia and I read down the list with an increasingly loud bell in my ear:

- often late for appointments, or attends at the right time on the wrong day,
- often misses digits in telephone numbers,
- has difficulty finding and remembering numbers and names,
- has difficulty with organisation and short term memory,
- has difficulty planning and writing essays,

- has areas of strength as well as weaknesses.

Wait a minute, I thought. This is describing me. And I added dyslexia to my research. Our knowledge of how the brain works was in its infancy. With the advent of Magnetic Resonance Imaging technology a great deal of research around the brain's hemispherical functions was just getting under way. I read 'Left Brain/Right Brain' by Springer and Deutsch and had already been influenced by Betty Edward's book 'Drawing on the Right side of the Brain'. I realised much of what I was teaching was right brain dominant and required right brain dominant thinking skills. This was at a time when many people dismissed the research and believed dyslexia did not exist. Dorset County Council refused to support students with dyslexia. I discussed my concerns with the principal.

"I've found there may be a relationship between spatial ability and people with dyslexia," I told him. "We do seem to have quite a high proportion of students with dyslexia on the spatial course. They need support for their dissertations."

"Then don't take them in Mo," was his memorable reply.

What do you mean don't take them in, I thought. These are our best students. Something needed to be done.

"They're going to advertise for a full time Course Director in Spatial Design," Martin told me. "Why don't you apply?"

I thought about it and discussed it with my dear friend and neighbour Jan. Jan had been steadfast in her support for me, and as a fellow design teacher (in textiles) and a graduate of the Royal School of Art she had a full understanding of the decision before me. She suggested writing a list of pros and cons.

The cons list was pretty long. Getting this job would mean

moving, and the upheaval for Tom would be huge. I would lose my support network and, although I had a few friends in Bournemouth, I would still be pretty isolated. I would have to conform to the institutional framework with its huge administration demands. I would get drawn into the politics of teaching, something I was really trying to avoid. I still had a year of study on my Master's course and could not possibly travel from Bournemouth. My mother would miss us as she aged.

"Well," said Derek, the course leader in Cardiff, "the final year is all about your research and dissertation. We could meet occasionally, it doesn't need to be weekly, and you could send me your drafts as they are done."

The pros list was simple; secure income, consolidate my work in one place, new start for me and Tom. I applied.

I was one of four short listed applicants. The others had already qualified with Master's degrees and had impressive portfolios. As is usual in Higher Education interviews, we were introduced to the studio and course design then taken for an individual interview with a panel, which included the Principal and Mark, the Head of School.

The Principal opened my portfolio at my watercolour drawings and poems, then turned to my architectural drawings. "Which do you prefer?" he asked.

"I enjoy doing both," I answered, "I like the emotional aspect of the painting and the rigour of the drawings".

I'd been asked to bring a presentation for how I would develop the course. I did this in a visual way by drawing a DNA structure with the core components of the course as the ladder and the abilities being developed as the ribbons that connected the rungs. It made it easier for me to explain my thinking around developing spatial ability and describe how I would approach this. I answered all their questions and was just about to go, when Mark asked me about my Master's course.

"I knew I'd forgotten something," I said and pulled out a smaller portfolio with my research and assignments. I still had one more year of the Master's course to go and I had a title for my draft dissertation, 'Ourselves in Place'. The ability to map, orientate and know where we are was central to my lived experience and to my thinking about spatial skills. I used the bridge that I travelled over to Cardiff as my metaphor for making connections between the hemispheres of the brain in order to develop spatial ability. But it seemed too much to show at the end of the interview and I left unsure whether I had done justice to my work.

The next day, to my amazement, they offered me the job. And, after a hectic few weeks of teaching and completing the second year of my course in Cardiff, I was at Chew Valley Lake with the watercolour group. We had decided to have my last teaching day with them as an outside painting day. I really enjoyed working with this group, they had such interesting journeys through life and were very kind to me. "We knew we wouldn't be able to keep you for long, you're too good," they told me. And with this boost to my ego I could say farewell to the sparkling lake and the river valley that had sustained Tom and me for so long.

West Moors

The car was packed with the last of our belongings as we set off for our new life in Dorset. Sparky and Tom were on the back seat of the Vauxhall and Minnie, the cat, was in her basket. Halfway there the cat got out of the basket, jumped onto the parcel shelf and peed all over the dog, making her feelings clear.

"Mum!" Tom shouted and Sparky looked at me in disgust.

"Not far now," I told them and stopped in a layby and cleaned up.

I'd rented out our cottage in Chewton Mendip and rented a bungalow in West Moors, a village on the fringe of the Bournemouth and Poole conurbation. It was near forest and built on sandy heathland, giving us places for dog walking and sand lizards in the garden. The bungalow's previous tenants had left it in a basic and grubby condition, but my friends helped me to clean up and Tom and I soon settled in.

Tom was starting his new school and said, "It's all right for you Mum, you already have friends here, I haven't."

"You'll soon make new friends," I said, and gave him a hug, regretting having to put him through yet more upheaval. The school was larger than his village school in Somerset, but smaller than the Middle School that he would be going to the following year. "We'll both be OK" I reassured him.

The first few weeks were hard, with adjustment to new challenges, routines and places. Tom had a child-minder after school, I sensed the same judgement from her about my single parent status as from some of the mothers in Somerset, and her perfectly ordered home left little room for free play. Tom ate little with her and often had a second tea with me when I came home. One evening when we were feeling a bit low, we decided to go to the local shops to rent a film. The video shop was also the pet shop and we ended up coming home with a hamster. Tom called him Freddy and his excited squeaks filled the house.

I trusted that the right people would come to me and, soon enough, my colleague Jane was staying with me overnight when she was teaching. Jane, an architect from London, loved building Lego cities with Tom. We would all eat pizza and the bungalow began to fill with laughter and discussion and life. One day Tom was taken ill at school, I was in the middle of student reviews when the school rang. The students volunteered to come home with me. They played with Tom in the sitting room and each student had their work review with me in turn in the kitchen. Sometimes I would pick Tom up from the child-minder and take him to the studio so that I could continue working while Tom explored the studio, or sat at a drawing board drawing, or slid around the vast space on draughting stool casters.

My friend Di rang me. "Mo - my house has burnt down!" she cried. Her eldest son had been about to cook chips when there was a power cut. He went to the pub for his lunch and while he was there the power came back on, with the hob switched on ready to heat the oil the entire kitchen went up in flames. Luckily the rest of the house was smoke damage and the house had been empty apart from two kittens and a poodle, all found alive and sheltering at the back of the house. I offered to look after the kittens until Di's home was repaired. Tom and I went to collect the kittens and brought them home to meet Minnie and Sparky. They were adorable and – just like the Siamese cats in the Disney film The Lady and the Tramp - they were prone to domestic disaster. Sliding down the curtain linings with their claws, leaving long lines of rips in the material, pulling off the table cloth along with everything on it, condiments, cutlery, plates and all. They delighted in chasing the hamster who took to escapology when they succeeded in tipping over his cage and he hid under the floorboards. Sparky and Minnie would look at us with accusing eyes, appalled by their behaviour. We never quite knew what to expect when we came home.

My Vauxhall car had been playing up for some time. It had been backwards and forward to the garage. Sometimes it just stopped unexpectedly and would not restart, other times it coughed and lurched through its timing like a car with bronchitis. The garage I'd taken it to locally had not sorted it out and tried to charge me several hundred pounds. Tom and I loaded the car for our Christmas visit to Somerset and half way there it stopped on one of the most remote parts of the journey. The car was full of cats, a dog and presents. The kittens were being returned to Di in her repaired home, Minnie and Sparky were coming with us to my mother's house for Christmas. Tom and I walked down the dark unlit road in cold wind and rain until we found a lane with a few houses scattered along it.

We knocked at the door of the first one. The occupant

took a long time to answer. There was no outside light and, somewhat like a horror movie, the door creaked open and a man peered round the edge suspiciously. I asked if we could use his phone but he gruffly directed us to the next house along the lane and closed his door. The people in the next house welcomed us in, allowed me to use the phone and the car was collected. It was towed to a garage in Somerset where they at last identified that sugar had been deliberately put into the petrol tank. This act of sabotage, another vicious attack on my independence, happened before I left Chewton Mendip and caused problems throughout my first term in Bournemouth.

Back in West Moors the local garage attempted to intimidate me into paying for work they had not done. The garage owner knew I was a single woman and he turned up in my home and became threatening in my kitchen. I stood my ground - having paid for the time they spent looking into it I was not willing to pay any more. The man shouted abuse and eventually left. Although shaking afterwards I was proud of myself for not being brought down by the bullying and prejudice of others.

I was becoming stronger too at dealing with the resistance to change in my teaching. The Higher National Diploma had a previously sound but limited curriculum and in my interview I'd been clear about the changes I intended to bring in. Firstly, based on my developing understanding of spatial ability, the focus would be on working with the plasticity of structures and materials, by having projects that played with scale and form to enable understanding to grow. I was also focusing on social and environmental context. For example, an established and popular project, designing a beach hut in the style of an artist, was completed at the end of the first term. A line of colourful and beautiful beach hut models adorned the studio. On their return in the second term the students were given a project brief called 'transformation' which informed them that due to an ecological disaster two thirds of their beach hut had been destroyed and they were to build a shelter with the remains of their beach hut and found materials.

Some students (and colleagues) were appalled by the loss and found coping with the transformation very difficult. The project was designed to help the students grapple with scale and deconstruction, and to engage both the linear and spatial sides of their brain. Many of the students rose enthusiastically to the challenge and some even built full size shelters in the college grounds. We had fantastic workshops and equipment, crucial in facilitating the development of spatial understanding. Working with structure was essential, and we explored bridge engineering designs and geodesic dome structures as well as building models for designs and for full-scale exhibitions.

Spatial Design Studio, BPCAD

As part of the EU initiative there was an exchange programme between the art college in Ghent, Belgium and Bournemouth. Mark and I were invited to visit the students from Bournemouth studying there for the year and to meet the staff. Ghent is a beautiful city and the art college was similar to an art college of the sixties in the UK. There seemed little need for Health and Safety in Ghent. Our workshop in Bournemouth was professionally managed with strict safety rules, and was maybe a little sterile. In Ghent students were using drills in random locations with trailing cables and building installations with a freedom and energy that was reminiscent of the sculpture studios of my youth. Our students were having a brilliant time in Ghent. So good that some of them formed permanent links and even settled in the city, and all the students made significant development in their careers.

The Head of the School in Ghent commented on my gender.

"You have a female Principal," Mark replied. "Do you have any problem with women lecturers?"

"Oh no," he laughed, "we sit back and just let them do all the work."

This attitude was unfortunately still prevalent. The BTEC examiner for the HND course came to visit us. He looked me up and down and took in my no make-up or feminine flounces appearance and, in front of me, said to Mark, "ah yes one of the lesbian lecturers." Despite his prejudice our students' work gained his approval and I was made an external moderator for related courses. One day when I was late getting home from visiting one of these in Devon I found Jane and Andy, one of the mature students on the course, sitting on the grass waiting for me outside the bungalow. We had supper and talked about a forthcoming live project. Live projects were an integral part of the course and were vital for giving the students experience in real clients, deadlines and budgets. This one was for the Mayor of Poole's celebration banquet. The students had designed banners and temporary sail-like structures to lift the space of the hall and we were planning the installation. I had been invited to attend the banquet and, as Jane would be in London, Andy offered to join me.

A little nervous to ensure the installation worked well and

did not collapse on anyone's meal, we entered the hall and were introduced to the Mayor and his wife. In her late sixties, she had thick pancake make-up and powder that gave her face an unusual sheen, scattered grains fell onto her shoulders. They were, however, very welcoming. I was grateful for Andy's support, and we had a good evening. The Mayor wrote an effusive letter of thanks and congratulations to the students.

Andy was in his final year of the course. His wife and young family lived in Dorset and in term time he was living in Bournemouth with friends. "I feel sorry for your family," I told him. We were all, students and staff, completely immersed in the intensity of finishing final major projects and there were long queues for student tutorials outside my office. At the end of the academic year we mounted an exhibition of the students' work in Bournemouth and two weeks later took the exhibition to the Mall Galleries in London. In addition to their major projects, the students designed and constructed the exhibition, and the studios and workshops were very busy and energised.

During one particularly intense student crit session I clashed with Andy about the nature of his design. He had some outstanding elements to the design but I felt he had missed an essential aspect that would greatly improve the whole. We had a fierce intellectual debate, with other students and staff joining in. This was not unusual in crit sessions, but afterwards I sat by the shore reflecting on how much this particular conflict had shaken me and realised I was becoming too close to him personally.

We found out later that some of the students sensed the chemistry between us long before we had acknowledged it ourselves. I knew there were difficulties in Andy's relationship, and I'd no intention of breaking up a family or of using my position and compromising my professional career. We met and talked with Mark, the Head of School, who was fantastically supportive.

"I don't think there is a problem," he said. "Especially as Andy is a mature student and finishing the course. I'll check and talk it over with the Deputy Principal."

Recently Andy and I visited an exhibition called 'In Relation: Nine couples who Transformed Modern British Art' at the RWA in Bristol. Seven of the nine couples met at art college, some when they were both students, some when they were in student and lecturer relationships. This combination of shared interest, depth of process and electrical connection is not unusual.

Mark and the Deputy Principal came back with the advice for me to take no part in assessing Andy's final work and we focused on finishing the academic year.

I was looking for somewhere to live for the next year, the tenancy was up on the bungalow and I did not wish to renew it. I looked at a National Trust property, available for rent with the proviso of being a steward for the historic house and occasionally showing people round. Andy came with me to help me to survey the building, a mediaeval stone court house in an extraordinary location by the river. I loved it but knew it would be very expensive to run.

A couple of days later Andy came up to me at college. "Come and see what I've found," he said, and excitedly showed me agent's details for a farm cottage in North Dorset. "It's a long way out," I replied, but I agreed to come and look at it. The location was wonderful and, while I was worried about Tom and myself being lonely, it was too good to miss and I signed the lease. The property was not available until August and another mature student, Linda, very kindly loaned me her house while she was away so that Tom and I had somewhere to live until the end of term.

We were in the car driving to my friend Anne's house – she'd generously offered to look after Minnie while we were between houses. Andy had Minnie in her basket on his knee and Tom and Sparky were in the back seat. Minnie, who hated being in her basket, promptly peed and Andy had to sit with a warm puddle coming through the towel in the basket onto his knee.

"It's a test," I said. "Love me, love my son, love my animals," and we laughed all the way there.

Glasgow School

I was sitting on my sofa having my morning cuppa when the television news showed graphic film of the 2018 fire that destroyed the Glasgow School of Art overnight. The iconic building, designed by Charles Rennie Macintosh and completed in 1910, was completely gutted, and so was I. When I posted my heartbreak on Facebook friends could not believe that another fire had devastated the school.

In 2014 a fire swept through, destroying the famous library - the restoration from this fire was almost complete when this new fire hit the building. All over the world people mourn the loss of the school. I am not alone in having an almost physical love for the building and the design. Many years ago I was alone in the library preparing a talk for the Design History Society. The vivid memories of the feel of the wood, the tactile quality of the desks, the sensual nature of the articulation of the space and the uplifting quality of the light stays with me.

My Grandfather studied art in Glasgow, pursuing a course in textile design; I still have his sketch books. My Aunt Stella also studied art, she was a talented artist and I kept some of her drawings. My father's family were friends with the artists and musicians of the time and one of their friends, the highly regarded Glasgow School artist John Laurie, painted portraits of my cousins when they were young. Before the Second World War my parents met and fell in love in that rich culture of shared art and music, internationalism and gender free opportunity.

Born into this connection with Scottish Art practice, when I was twenty I wrote a thesis on Charles Rennie Macintosh for my first Diploma in Environmental design. As an interior designer I loved Macintosh's approach to rhythm and change, never having static repeat, always adding alteration to pattern. As an artist I particularly admired the organic space within his drawings that translated fully to his buildings. There was something very intimate in the way that, as you explored the building, new details opened up and continued to surprise even when you knew what to expect.

The Glasgow School of Art had a unique curriculum devised by its Director, Francis Newbery. The course was divided into four stages and students moved through those stages at their own pace, some taking seven or eight years to achieve the award of the Diploma. A version of this system was still in place in the 1970s in Glasgow. Lorna Edmiston, a colleague and artist who taught life drawing in Bournemouth and was a graduate of the Glasgow School, described to me how disconcerting it could be. Unlike most art and architecture education full of critical reviews, here you were encouraged to develop your work without active critique and feedback. Instead, you exhibited your work each year and were subsequently told whether or not you could progress. One of our full-time lecturers, Donald Melvin, was also a Glasgow School of Art graduate and we all had spirited discussions about the different methodologies and the value of one of the last remaining independent art schools in the

UK.

When I was eight, I ran an art competition for my family. My grandparents were still living in Glasgow. I carefully typed up the rules and entry details and posted these to them. My grandfather replied with his entry asking, if he was lucky enough to win could he receive the third prize. I'd set the prize amounts in reverse order. My family dutifully entered, I still remember their drawings, and my grandfather was duly awarded first place and the third prize award of sixpence. I don't know why, at the age of eight, I had the precocity to assume I knew which would be the best drawing or how to make such a judgement. Setting rules and criteria for art was already in my consciousness. Teaching at Bournemouth involved a series of discussions and criticism sessions throughout a project development and a range of assessment criteria and outcomes. We tried to make the critical discussion balanced and positive, but presenting their designs and drawings to the group was nerve wracking for the students, and for many of them having to present and defend their ideas in depth for the first time was an intense and emotional experience.

Teaching staff at Bournemouth were occasionally encouraged to share their own work with the students, but were discouraged from working on their own projects during teaching terms. Every teacher at the Glasgow School of Art had their own studio and was expected to work on their own practice as well as to teach. I walked through the corridor, known as the hen run, at the top of the building that ran alongside these studios. The whole floor was suffused with light and with the imbued palimpsest of generations of art practice. Here the light and space still invited you to just be, come in, write, paint.

Recently, while exploring my family tree, I discovered another reason my sense of connection to the Glasgow School of Art was so strong. Following clues left by the Scottish tradition of naming daughters through the mother's line I found that Dorothy Carleton Smyth had been my paternal Grandfather's cousin. Dorothy was a student at the School in 1914 and became a successful artist. Returning to teach at the School she was appointed principal of Commercial Art Teaching. She continued her work as a professional artist and her designs, in the Glasgow style inspired by Celtic art and the curved lines of organic forms, are visible in her exquisite drawings. The resonance with my own path in art and design astonished me, and when I saw her photos I could see her resemblance to members of my family.

Dorothy's father, who was an organist in Glasgow for twenty years, turned out to be the man who influenced and taught my grandfather. He subsequently also became an organist for twenty years, and Dorothy's sister Rose was a composer. I realised this music influence reached down through my family, my father, sister and brother, and now I had found one source of the art influence on us too. When you grow up in a creative environment you take this as a given, a natural part of human life. Only later do you realise what a privilege it is.

Dorothy was a contemporary of Macintosh and the artists known as the Glasgow Four. She lived with her two sisters in Glasgow, Olive also taught at the Glasgow School. In 1933 Dorothy Carleton Smyth was appointed as the Glasgow School of Art's first woman Director at the age of fifty-three. Tragically Dorothy died unexpectedly that same year and was never able to take up her appointment as Director. A recent exhibition at the National Gallery, Scotland - Modern Scottish Women, Painters and Sculptors 1885-1965 - described how Francis Newbery did much in terms of gender equality at a time when women's art was generally being dismissed and excluded from art references. Francis described Dorothy as 'a living force contained within a human body ... she is the light and life of anything we may do here'.

Work is now being done to address the exclusion of women artists and poets from art and literature history and much still needs to be done. Artists from the Glasgow School are forerunners in the field of contemporary art today, and their courses in sculpture and environmental art now focus on the language of spatial and material practice in much the same way we were approaching the development of the spatial design course in Bournemouth in the 1990s. Ciara Phillips, a graduate from the Glasgow School of Art, for example, was one of four artists shortlisted for the 2014 Turner Prize.

Unlike the extreme under-representation of women when I was a student, the female representation of students on the HND in Spatial Design in Bournemouth had improved and was almost fifty percent by the mid 1990s. Female students still found it harder than their male counterparts to gain entry to architecture courses and many were put off from applying. However, we were getting our first successes in placing women on good architecture and design degrees and were helped in changing perceptions by having the architect, Jane Tankard, as one of our part time lecturers.

Jane's passion for architecture and exploring the lived experience of space was infectious. She had a great rapport with the students and really engaged with their struggles to articulate their designs. There was always a queue for her attention on the days she was in and the energy in the studio went up a level. We became great friends and she stayed with me when she was visiting Bournemouth.

Jane also taught at London Universities and brought contemporary architecture theory and practice to the course - a perfect fit with the developments in spatial theory I'd been making. We sparked off each other and at the end of the teaching day would continue the conversation at home. One of the most important things for us both was to ensure that students had the opportunity to model their ideas, to make maquettes and sketch models and play with scale and form. Organic form in architecture was very much in its infancy, to go against the 'linear grain' was resisted by some male colleagues.

"What do you think this is – an art college?" laughed one of them when he encountered my students making large-scale models from found materials.

Developments in ecology practice and material technology were making curved, sensual and human scale designs more possible. Zaha Hadid, a forerunner in this field, has been described as 'liberating architectural geometry', but it was to be many years before her work gained acceptance. Her major projects were not built until the twenty-first century and in 2015, the year before she died, she became the first and only woman to be awarded the Royal Gold Medal from the Royal Institute of British Architects. Acceptance of this practice in contemporary architecture was some decades away, but the potential was before us all.

I had many encounters with resistance to the changes I was making in the course structure. One day Jane told me she had a dream where I was walking around the studio topless "like an Amazon woman" she said.

My mother also felt I was brave and vulnerable and she too had a dream about me walking naked and unprotected. "Just be careful dear," she said. Both these strong women consciously and unconsciously aware of the level of attack I might face.

The connections between the Glasgow School and Dorset go back to the beginning of Art and Design education in the late nineteenth century in the UK. Francis Newbery's early education was in Bridport and the foundation art and design education he received in Dorset fundamentally informed his work in Glasgow. We were therefore delighted when we were invited to present our students' work at the Glasgow School of Art.

The students' work had been selected as a winner in a national project competition, 'Retail Futures', held by the Design History Society. The project was exploring the changes on the horizon in retail methodology. The huge growth in online shopping was not yet apparent but the changes in store design and ranges were becoming clear, with unified store identity coming into vogue. Our students had developed colourful, textural and circulation flow designs and we were to exhibit these at a conference with the same theme, and I was to give a talk explaining our studio practice. I invited Chris, one of the students, to come with me and we flew to Glasgow with a large portfolio containing the work.

"Oh my God Chris where's the portfolio?" I said when we reached the hotel. At the same moment I realised I'd idiotically left it cruising round the luggage carousel. I rang Glasgow airport and with characteristic Scottish generosity they found and sent the portfolio to me in a taxi. Chris and I were then able to go to the Glasgow School and mount the exhibition the day before the conference began. And so it was that I was alone in the Art School library preparing the talk in a space that was the antithesis of rigid, unified design. The struggle to go against the trend of linear homogeneous design had begun.

Tarrant Launceston

The Tarrant River is a tributary from the River Stour, and the sheltered river valley is home to a string of picture postcard villages with thatched cottages and rose filled gardens. Tarrant Launceston has a thatched pub, a shallow ford over the river where ducks and coots weave through the reeds, and a timeless feel of bucolic charm. The farm cottage was semi-detached, brick walled, steep roofed and purpose built for workers on the neighbouring farm. It had a large garden which backed onto fields, rambling outbuildings and a swing.

We soon found there were two boys in the village the same age as Tom and my fear for our isolation was unfounded. The space around us, with its open Dorset skies were complete balm after our hectic first year in Bournemouth, and while Tom cycled and played with his new friends I joyfully unpacked our things for this new home. From the kitchen window I could see swans gathering at the river and in the back garden a peregrine falcon perched on the swing. From the bedroom window I could lie in bed and gaze at the field of golden corn swaying in the breeze, moving like waves on the sea.

I did, however, have work to do. I was also completing my dissertation and my MA supervisor, Derek, said "just finish it" in his feedback to my last piece of work. The deadline was looming and I knew I had to get the work done before the next academic year began. On the tiny green Mac screen, I wrote the last few chapters, and pulled together my research with children and students. Ultimately, I was making proposals for reconnecting and synthesising the way we develop creativity and spatial ability and understand ourselves in place.

Tom was starting his new middle school in West Moors and our morning journey through the rolling Dorset landscape was exquisite, mist rising in the valleys and the sun glinting on rolling hills. We enjoyed talking and singing along with tape compilations on our hour-long journey, "I can see clearly now the rain has gone" was a favourite. Tom quickly settled in, joining his friends from first school, and he thrived on the more advanced curriculum.

I designed a project called music and space, which aimed to enable students to explore structural design in a fluid way. I wanted the students to access the creative side of their brain and allow connections to grow. The project asked them to design a space based on the structure of music. I made a tape compilation of various non-verbal tracks, from world music and classical, to jazz and club music. The students were free to design in a new way and built wonderful exploratory models that could become buildings or exhibition spaces. It was a successful project and one that I ran for several years, with Jane and Andy contributing to the development of the tape selection in later years.

I was beginning to understand the separation between right and left brain thinking was sometimes necessary. The linear sequential left brain is needed in structural thinking. The difficulty with this way of thinking is that it can be a bit of a dictator and does not consciously allow right brain processes, often seeking to eliminate them. The right brain being the holistic one (rta is Sanskrit for whole) includes and accommodates the left. Because the left brain controls the right hand, and vice versa, dominance of the right hand has been common particularly in western cultures, giving weight to the old saying "the right hand does not know what the left hand is doing". Research in neuroscience was beginning to confirm these differences and magnetic resonance imaging was beginning to show us, 'seeing is believing'.

Most recent research shows us there is a great deal more plasticity in the brain than was recognised at this time, and that there are more potential connections in the brain than there are galaxies in the known universe. If we were to have all these connections all the time we would be overwhelmed. With information overload people's mental health can suffer and the brain gives us the ability to close off and forget. This division, commonly known as long term and short term memory, is different for people with dyslexia, who often have poor short term memory and exceptional long term memory.

The music and space project was aiming to help students to access their long term memory and right brains in a safe contained way by using design methodology to explore without verbal reasoning. Breaking down boundaries can be liberating. In my own life I erected layers of shell to my heart to enable me to recover from life's losses. Andy's love began to melt this shell away and with his warm and humour filled presence I began to let my guard down and enable love to enter.

Andy had been away with his family over the summer, determined to resolve his issues. On his return he and his wife had decided to separate. Andy's wife and children, David and Marie Claire, came over and we talked it through.

"I know," said David, aged 3, "we could all live together," and we laughed at the loving simplicity of his solution. The separation also meant a separation from Andy's parents and from the farm they shared that was on the verge of being repossessed. Andy and his family were caught by the collapse of the British housing market and the resulting mass emergence of negative equity, a new and previously unforeseen phenomenon that manifested on a mass scale in 1991.

Life was complicated and painful for us all. Andy's wife had also started a new relationship and was moving with the children to Bournemouth. Andy was returning to college to do a post-graduate media course and part time teaching on the spatial design course. A few weeks after term began he became ill with bronchitis following the stress of the break-up and the fight to save the farm from repossession. He moved in with me, initially on a temporary basis.

"How long will he be staying?" asked Tom. I replied that I did not know.

Andy and I became good friends before we became lovers and this gave depth and strength to our new relationship. Strength we would need to cope with the many challenges ahead. The pain of separation was balanced with joy and we were basking in new love, new hope, shared passion. Andy gave me a book on the relationship between Georgia O'Keefe and Alfred Stieglitz, 'Two Lives'. His intention was to share the conversation between artists who are also lovers. Ultimately the relationship between Georgia and Alfred broke down because Alfred was too dominating and Georgia lived alone in New Mexico to produce her best work. Andy and I drew our perfect scenario with separate creative spaces for our work and shared space between as the way we wanted to live our lives.

The autumn term had begun and the dissertation deadline was approaching. I gathered together the books I needed to refer to in my bibliography. Jane and Andy helped me and we set out the books in large piles with me writing down the references while they called out dates and details. We worked into the early hours of the morning. I took the floppy disc with my thesis to college to print it out. Sometimes I have a highly charged electrical field around me. I could never keep a pre battery watch on my wrist going, and occasionally stopped clocks when I was meditating. When I entered the school administration office I was highly stressed about getting the printing done.

"Oh," said Gill, the secretary. "The computer has frozen, I don't know why. Go down to the main admin office, they will help." And she took out the floppy disc and handed it back to me. In the main admin office they were happy to take the disc, but the energy around the disc - or me, or something, froze the entire college computer system.

Now I was really running out of time. The dissertation had to be printed, bound and presented by midday the following day in Cardiff. Andy drove me to Cardiff first thing in the morning. The dissertation was printed and bound by the library services and I handed it in with half an hour to spare.

"Remind me not to do that again," I told Andy as we drove home exhausted.

Andy moved in while I was in Glasgow. Tom was staying with my sister in London and Andy worked non-stop to clear the family farm and move his things in. I rang him from Glasgow after I'd given my talk. "You won't believe it," he said, "the electricity has gone off and I can't have a bath or a meal."

Soon Andy settled in, our difficulties with electricity calmed and Tom accepted his being with us. Marie Claire and David were coping with many changes and Andy was missing the children terribly, but they came to stay with us regularly and Tom, who'd always wanted a brother or sister, gradually got used to being part of an extended family. Marie Claire immediately took on the task of organising me. Like her father, who had quietly organised a place for my keys and sorted my piles of papers, Marie Claire began putting my scattered books and decorative boxes in order.

The children too needed space to process the changes and took turns to spend hours on the swing looking out over the Dorset fields. They were active den makers and built dens from fabric, stools, branches and cushions and created new spaces for themselves.

Andy, having accrued massive negative equity from the farm, which had been sold at the last minute, chose to do some of the after school care for Tom in return for his keep. He collected Tom from school and Tom was much happier than staying with the child-minder. Sometimes, when we were both working, Karen, a friend and student who also became a member of our extended family, collected Tom and took him home. Their various old bangers - Minis, Morris Minors - often resulted in adventurous journeys for Tom. Tom and Karen once had to hitch home after her Mini had broken down. Mothers with shiny four-wheel drive cars and smart coats more usually collected pupils from his middle school. The series of art students with long hair and battered cars embarrassed Tom and interested his friends - who thought they were really cool.

At weekends our favourite walk took us to the fields, bluebell woods and open downs above our home. Tom, Marie Claire and David were climbing the hill, Sparky running on ahead of them. Tom was bashing the tall cow parsley with a long stick, Marie Claire was anxious not to get her new boots muddy.

"Do dinosaurs still live here?" David asked. We explained that they had lived here a very long time ago.

Sparky disappeared in the long corn of the field and the children ran after him, laughing and calling to each other, just the tops of their heads occasionally visible above the crop.

From the top of the hill we could just see the roof of our home with smoke curling out of the cottage chimney. Andy and I linked arms, called to Sparky and the children and headed for home.

Family at Tarrant Launceston

Bonnington Square

Bonnington Square, in South London, became squatted during the late 1970s and 80s when all the houses in it were vacant and awaiting demolition. Many of the squatters, including my sister, by then a homeless single parent, formed cooperatives, established a community and successfully negotiated to save the buildings. The Square, along with neighbouring Vauxhall Grove and Langley Lane, became renowned for the community gardens and café. The calm, cool and peaceful vibe as you enter the area is all the more remarkable because it is directly off one of the busiest traffic interchanges in London at Vauxhall. I walked past the banana tree, now over twenty feet high, and the olive tree growing from a bin and flowers from the street planting that fills the Square and rang Sheila's doorbell.

When Tom and I first visited, Sheila and her son were living in a squat with a toilet room that was gradually separating from the structure of the house, so that you could see daylight as you sat there. We'd taken a group of students on a trip to see the Turner Prize Exhibition at Tate Britain, walking distance from Bonnington Square. Tom found Damien Hirst's exhibits, which included a cow mounted in a formalin tank, bisected, with its embryo calf intact, disturbing. The installation reduced one of the mature students to tears. Married to a dairy farmer she explained how distressing the treatment of cows, with forced calving for milk production, can be. "I fully understand what he is saying here," she told me. Hirst's career was just taking off and he did not win the prize, but the impact of his installation was seminal.

This time, Andy and I were in London with Tom to present an exhibition of the students' work at the Mall Galleries. Tom loved playing with the pigeons in Trafalgar Square and we had fun combining sight-seeing with work. Sheila, now living in a different squat in the Square, gave us a warm welcome.

Tom in Trafalgar Square

'Would it be OK if I suggested your home in the Square as one of the projects for the students?" I asked Sheila. The Royal Society of Arts ran a student competition every year. The next one was for designs for multi generation living, with the aim of getting away from the ghettoization of age groups. The diverse community in Bonnington Square was ideal for the brief. Sheila and her housemates generously agreed and the following term a group of students descended on Bonnington Square.

The day was adventurous: one student, Alison, had a panic attack on the underground. Three students became so enamoured of the Square they over stayed and they travelled home separately. The community garden was designed to enable residents to stay connected to nature, and the students later described how they wanted to stay there. The experience brought home to all the students how different the Bournemouth culture was from that of London. The Square with its diverse community, families, including refugees, members of the LGBT community and people of all ages from all over the world, was vastly different from the predominately white and mainly aged community then in Bournemouth. One of our students won the competition and the discussions we had around diversity as a result of our visit undoubtedly contributed to the success of his design.

For Tom's twenty first birthday Sheila hosted us all for a family gathering. We went to the Tate Modern and walked up to the London Eye where we had booked tickets for the ride. By the time we got there we were soaked by a sudden cloudburst and our clothes were steaming as we took in the view across the city. We walked back to Bonnington Square along the South Bank of the River Thames with the views of the Houses of Parliament and the Waterloo sunset to accompany us.

More memorable still for us all was the evening in the

Bonnington café that had started off as a squatters' kitchen and developed into a collective café where different groups provided meals from different cultures. There we enjoyed a delicious vegetarian meal, then went upstairs to the Community Centre where we were treated to a wonderful night of music from a Venezuelan band.

Sheila and Ali outside the Newspaper House an art installation in Bonnington Square.

I was invited to give a talk on 'Ourselves in Place' at a Matrix conference at Central St Martins College of Art and Design, known as CSM. This was somewhat daunting but very exciting for me. The conference was held just a few years after St Martins School of Art merged with Central, and the international influence of the College was immense. The impressive list of alumni, from fashion designers John Galliano and Alexander McQueen to musicians P.J. Harvey, Jarvis Cocker and Paloma Faith, and the range of artists and designers working across the sector today, speaks for itself.

On this occasion Sheila was away working and I rang CSM to ask if there was child-care provision for the conference. Stuart Evans, who took the query, immediately said "Ah well, of course we should have. Let me look into it and I'll get back to you". And in this way, I was introduced to the remarkable Jane Graves.

Jane was a Cultural Studies Lecturer at CSM and when she heard child-care was needed, she volunteered to look after Tom while I was at the conference. Tom and I entered the CSM building in Southampton Row, Camden and were directed up the huge central staircase with its immediate feeling of space and light. We found Jane in her office, a room brimming with energy, colour and life. Postcards from grateful students and quotes of the day adorned her door and the desk was piled high with student essays and papers.

Jane welcomed us in her deep plummy, Oxford educated voice and invited us to sit down, clearing her chairs of more papers. We were made at ease, and Jane and I hit it off immediately. My paper went down well at the conference, but it was Jane who was most interested in what I had to say. She helped many dyslexic students pass the written component of their degrees, and had encountered the same resistance to identification and support for dyslexic students as I had. Jane also recognised that it was often the most talented design students who had the most difficulty with written work. We carried on talking long after the conference had finished and agreed that we needed more debate in academia on these issues.

"They're frightened," said Jane. "Most of them are covering up their own dyslexia and art colleges have such a fight for academic recognition they are too scared to face it in case it tarnishes their reputation."

I was heartened to meet another woman in Higher Education for Art and Design who was thinking the same way as I. Most of the time I encountered resistance or derision from men and to meet Jane, a highly educated and brilliant woman who with the force of her warm and strong personality had carved a way into the heart of the system, was deeply satisfying. She was to become my mentor and supporter and to be powerfully instrumental in getting funding with Ian Padgett for a research project on creativity and dyslexia at CSM.

I was to learn that I was not alone in exploring the differences and difficulties between verbal and visual spatial thinking. Sue Parkinson from the Arts Dyslexia Trust organised an exhibition opened by Lord Gowrie, then Chairman of the Arts Council, of dyslexic artists' work at the Mall Galleries in 1994. And two years later I was invited to present my paper 'Music and Space, Differently Able' at a conference organised by CSM at the culmination of their project.

By now we'd realised Andy was dyslexic and we both found the conference very moving and pertinent to our experiences and work. Bruce Gernard, a sculpture tutor, and John Gunter, Head of Theatre Design, talked of their experience of dyslexia and their different ways of working. Afterwards Sue Parkinson came up to speak with me and was very encouraging about my work.

Jane Graves died in 2007 after a long COPD illness. Andy and I went to her packed memorial service. Jane worked as a psychotherapist in Silver Town after she retired from CSM and was active in the community until her death. Her friends and family talked of the many contributions she had made to others and we celebrated her life.

Afterwards we sat with Sheila in her lovely new flat in Bonnington Square and talked about all those creative and exciting years. "Jane was just one of those people it was a privilege to know," I said as we raised a glass to her. We also proposed a toast to CSM. The Art School, now part of the University of Arts London, has been moved in its entirety to new buildings near St Pancras at Kings Cross, and the old building with its imbued history of art is now a hotel.

Shortly before she died Jane said to me, "Mo, I think things are getting worse for people with dyslexia, not better, despite all our work". She would be proved right but at the time of the conference I returned to Dorset with validation for my approach and with renewed vigour to fight for support for the students and staff. My approach remained controversial but the outcomes spoke for themselves and many students were beginning to value the course.

Recently Sheila and I sat outside in the sun at the Italian deli (once a corner shop) that now sits at the centre of the piazza. We were mulling over the changes in the area. Terry Farrell's design for the fortified MI6 building on Vauxhall Cross is omnipresent when you walk over Vauxhall Bridge. A new American Embassy building and the huge development at Nine Elms is nearby. What was once a run down and forgotten part of London is now a desirable area, sought after by property developers. Social housing is limited, especially in London, and squatting is now illegal in the UK. As opportunities to develop true communities, like this one, become increasingly scarce, the achievement of the people in Bonnington Square is all the more remarkable and cherished.

Dartington

Sometimes in life synthesis and synchronicity occur at such a deep level it is felt in the bones. When I stood on the stage of the mediaeval Dartington Hall to present my paper at a conference, it was one of those moments where everything overlaps and time pauses. "No less than the trees and the stars you have a right to be here and whether or not it is clear to you no doubt the universe is unfolding as it should". Jane Graves had a copy of Desiderata on her office door, and I kept one in my bedroom. I had a sense of the universe unfolding, but how this would influence my life was certainly not clear.

Gradually my work on dyslexia was becoming as demanding as my work managing the spatial design course. Students from other parts of the college and staff approached me with their stories of exclusion in education. Each one was devastating and painful.

"I was put in the divi class," said one talented member of staff who was sent to a school for children with learning difficulties. Others were humiliated, publicly mocked and abused by teachers.

Dyslexic students also shared their experience of exclusion in life. One had been to prison, she had low self-esteem and fallen into bad company, there is a high proportion of people with dyslexia in prison. Another had lost all contact with her dyslexic family abroad because none of them could cope with the very real and practical difficulties of letter writing, finding addresses and getting to a post box. The advent of email and mobile phone technology today is a wonderful thing.

I could not understand why dyslexia was not being addressed in education. Research had shown that from multiple ways of learning, our current academic system only validated two. I went to a conference on Education in London. Andy was with me and we were both shocked by the presentations. One described how technology was going to completely transform education in the 21st century. Another described the persistence of resistance to change and why attempts to bring in change were met with hostility.

Denial of dyslexia was changing and gradually gentle winds of change began to breeze through the system. Our students designed and built sensory rooms and music walls for schools in live projects, and some of them went on to pursue careers in education. Every dyslexic student who recovered their self-respect and understood and utilised their strengths flourished. Many of the students were going on to degree courses in architecture. The award-winning architect Sir Richard Rogers had recently come out as dyslexic. He powerfully described his difficulties in education, making him believe he was "stupid because he could not read or memorise his schoolwork".

Some things have fundamentally changed for people with dyslexia and new technology has been massively empowering. However, a 2012 report by the British Dyslexia Association identifies a continuing resistance to change in education 40 years on. They estimate 7 million people in the UK are dyslexic, most of whom are adults and half of those adults may not realise they are dyslexic. They show the persistence of issues, such as the cost of getting a diagnostic assessment, lack of access for young people to funding for adjustments and poor support in education, to poor treatment and disciplinary procedures in the workplace. They identify that while "dyslexia" is now common currency "there continues to be widespread ignorance on what the condition actually is... The basis for this lies within our education system".

In 1995 dyslexia was certainly not seen as common currency. The existence of the condition was mainly denied, hidden and unsupported at all levels of education. So much so that data identified very low numbers of people with dyslexia in Higher Education. There were a mixture of reasons, primarily exclusion of would be students due to non-existent support in education, resulting in entry exam failure. There was also a total absence of identification of dyslexic students in the system. What was becoming apparent in these days of early data collection was a significantly higher proportion of students being identified with dyslexia in art colleges.

The 1995 Disability Discrimination Act required all Higher Education Institutions to provide access for people with disabilities to their services by 1996. To help Universities prepare for this 'Dyslexia in Higher Education', the 2nd international conference, was held in Dartington Hall, Devon. Dartington, home of the free education influence of my childhood, and the Schumacher College, founded by the Dartington Hall Trust, describe in their handbook: 'This College is part of a long and distinguished heritage of radical experimentation. Dorothy and Leonard Elmhirst, inspired by the work of the Indian poet, educationalist, social reformer and Nobel Prize winner, Rabindranath Tagore, founded the Trust in 1925. They bought and rehabilitated the 1,300 acre Dartington estate to develop and demonstrate models for rural regeneration through diverse economic, educational and artistic activity.' They quote Dorothy Elmhirst's aims for Dartington for "a place where education could be continuously carried on and where the Arts could become an integral part of the life of the whole place".

The conference supper was a noisy lively affair. Academics from all over the country came to this landmark event, and the papers they published afterwards were influential and are still available online today. I sat next to Leila Edwards, a Dean of Students from the University of Bath and we had an animated discussion about how to address the resistance to change in academia. She was a powerhouse woman who had no truck with resistance, seeing it as something to bulldoze down. I was impressed by her strength.

I visited Jack Whitehead, an academic in Education at the University of Bath. He too was open to change. I showed him my dissertation and his warm and positive response was heartening.

"Look at the bibliography," he said enthusiastically and commented on the poetry in my writing. He described to me how feminists were challenging the lack of the subject, me or I, in academic papers and how he felt I'd been compromised by having to write this dissertation in the third person, 'one'. We explored the potential for my undertaking an interdisciplinary PhD, but the inter-discipline avenues in Higher Education were hard to navigate.

The light bulb moment came when I realised that while I'd been writing the dissertation, I'd always also been writing poems alongside, but the poems were always kept separate and were the way I managed the emotions of the work. Andy read my poems and encouraged me to meet with David Caddy in Blandford Forum. David was editor of the poetry journal 'Tears in the Fence' and was also running a monthly poetry group called East Street Poets. David was generous in his review of my poems and Andy and I joined the group. At first my poetry voice was barely more than a whisper, but the poets were kind and encouraging and I gradually grew more able to share my work.

In Bournemouth the resistance to change was led by the new Head of both the Industrial and Spatial Design Schools, Peter Dawson. He sought a more ordered and contained environment and did not have any truck with 'arts becoming an integral part of the whole place'. It became apparent that he was considering merging spatial design with industrial design to have a three dimensional design degree course. He had worked for the Design Council and wanted clean modernism.

"Mo," he said, "if there is a problem with the design, of a cup say, you change the handle".

Where for me, if there was a problem with the design, cosmetic change was not the answer. What was needed was more a flattening of the clay and taking it back to the potter's wheel for a better outcome.

Andy left the spatial studio and Mark, the former Head of Spatial Design was side-lined and ultimately left the College. Andy was working on a public art commission for Swanage Pier. In the studio political controversy was growing. New contracts were being implemented and staff either had to sign or be penalised by remaining on the old contracts. "I need to talk to Jack about this," I told Andy and he drove me to Bath.

Jack is a remarkable academic whose work is on values and action learning in education. He had the courage to challenge his own institution about their practice and to publish his lived experience, with names. His research now focuses on "understanding and spreading the influence of Living Theory Research as a social movement… with values that carry hope for the flourishing of humanity".

"Ah," said Jack, looking at the contract, "probably the best thing you can do is sign the contract and document the whole process".

I was silent all the way home. I knew signing the contract would seem like a betrayal to my colleagues who were determined not to sign. But I recognised that my standing against it would make no difference to the outcome. Maybe by staying within the system I could have an effect. It was not a happy decision, and it meant I would no longer have school holidays off with Tom. The colleagues who did not sign were disappointed that I had, and my relationship with them was damaged.

Jack invited Andy and me to the first international Action Learning conference at the University of Bath. Humanity and lived experience was common in the poetry world but rarely discussed in Higher Education. The event was a breath of fresh air. Jack introduced us to some colleagues and encouraged me to develop my PhD proposal. Art politics at Bournemouth were appearing increasingly retrograde.

The following year I spotted an advertisement in the Guardian for a Learning Support Manager based at the University of Bath with the brief to develop access for dyslexia across the region. "That's interesting," I said to Andy. "I bet that came out of the conference at Dartington."

We were in the middle of the very busy live project part of the course and I did not have much time to pay attention. New technology was developing and computer design programmes were in their infancy. The college was entirely Macintosh based and Mac was undoubtedly the best platform for visual work. The workshops were being reduced to accommodate more computer spaces and drawing software was rapidly developing. I decided I needed to up my PC skills and I bought a Hewlett Packard computer, with Windows 95 software and the first rudimentary access to what would become the World Wide Web. Andy, still something of a Luddite, and Tom, bonded to his Playstation, were surprised by my purchase. The personal computer cost more than a laptop does today and had much less capacity than a modern mobile phone, but it was exciting and soon we all began to use it.

Tom had been unwell. He had one of the first MMR vaccines at the age of 12, and was then stung by a hornet. He had not recovered as he should, and was still low in energy and wellbeing. The GP referred us to a Paediatrician who reassured us and told us this was probably just delayed recovery from a virus, and quite normal for a boy of Tom's age. Outside in the car park Tom and I both cried, we felt it was more than that.

I too was having health issues. I was referred to the gynaecologist who advised me I had an ovarian cyst. This can be quite serious if cancerous, and is often described as a silent killer. A bit shocked, I went in for a minor operation. Andy and Tom came to visit me, and both gave me a hug. I was still blurry from the anaesthetic, ultimately, I was lucky and it was not cancer, but the experience changed my life in a different way.

While I was at home recovering from the operation, I saw the job advertisement for the Learning Support Manager at Bath being re-advertised with the by-line "previous applicants need not reapply". I regretted not applying for the post the first time round. I loved my work, but things were changing and I knew I could not work with Peter, our values and approach to design were too different. "Your intelligence has been recognised," he told me in an avuncular patronising way. I'd put a lot of work into developing the 3Dimensional Design Degree and we were well on the way to gaining validation. The post for Course Leader was being advertised. It was clear the choice would probably come down to me, or the course leader for industrial design. I decided not to apply.

Instead I applied for the post at Bath and was shortlisted for interview. "Well," I said to Andy as I prepared and rehearsed my presentation. "They either want me as I am or not."

"And if they don't then you don't want to be there," Andy replied.

The panel, which included Leila Edwards, asked me to explain my approach to the job. I produced some string and made a cat's cradle in front of them while I described how I would build a supportive structure and environment for students with disabilities at the University of Bath. I was offered the job.

It was hard to leave Dorset. We knew we would miss it terribly and would hate being further away from Marie Claire and David. It did seem meant to be. Even our tenancy of the cottage was ending as the house was needed again for farm workers. Tom's time in his middle school was ending and he decided he wanted a disco for his 13th birthday to say goodbye to all his class. Karen and I stayed in the kitchen of the village hall. We were in awe of the advanced development of the 13 year old girls at the party. Karen and I were both free range children, make up and heels were not in our lexicon at that age. The boys, however, were active and awkward, and the DJ was great - they all danced and we had a brilliant time.

We decided to give the students a party too. One of the students was able to get access for us to a field on Arne Point in Poole Harbour. The location was stunning and at the end of term we set up a mini festival with music, food, bar and dance tents. The students brought their own tents and we all danced into dawn, celebrating everything the spatial design students had achieved.

"I wish I'd had a course director like you," one of the industrial design students shouted over the music. I laughed. Our spatial design course may have ended in style but all over the country new spatial initiatives were beginning in art and architecture education, and spatial ability, a term so reviled when I began, would become common parlance within a few years.

Part Four Change, Backlash, Continuum 1997 – 2018

smoking room, University of Bath 1997

Woodbury Close

I sold my cottage in Somerset and we went house hunting in Bath and Wells. Bath was too expensive and somehow felt daunting. The ancient city of Wells is the smallest city in England with the longest intact mediaeval street in Europe. My mother chose to live there - it was practical, with beautiful countryside, the high street and the market square all in easy walking distance. By moving to the city we would be close enough to support her as she approached her eighties, and Tom would be able to walk to school, see his friends and be more independent in his teens.

We'd lived in rural environments for over twenty years and still needed space to walk Sparky, our collie, and a distant view in which to allow our thoughts to roam. It was a big ask and house hunting was a dispiriting experience, but eventually we settled on a very ordinary semi-detached dormer bungalow at the end of a cul de sac. After paying the deposit I could just afford the mortgage, and it had potential, it needed work but we agreed we could do this 'low road' bit by bit. The small estate had been built in the nineteen seventies to generously proportioned sixties plans on what had been the Bishop's fishponds fields. We were above the flood plain and a large bay window overlooked national trust woodland bordering

St Andrews Stream, and with mature trees in neighbouring gardens we were in walking distance of the town centre yet had a remarkable country feel. We moved into the house with the bare essentials, having put our things into storage.

"I hate it," I told Andy in tears. The dowdy carpet and beige everywhere had all the feeling of an old peoples' home and the feeling of enclosure, after living in the limitless space of Dorset downs and skies, was overwhelming.

In a few weeks we stripped it back to the purity of the sixties design, taking out walls and letting the daylight flow through the house, as we knew it would. We sanded the floorboards and polished them to a golden glow. With organic paint we brought white clarity and depth and colour to the walls, and with mirrors we made the most of the reflected light.

My mother helped us financially, enabling Andy to rent a studio space in a disused industrial drawing office with excellent space and light. When the two removal trucks arrived to bring our contents out of store, one came to the house and one to the studio. The driver of the first one was amazed. "You wouldn't believe this was the same house," he exclaimed. "You should put that in a magazine".

We soon settled in and began to feel at home. Early one morning Tom called me, "Mum! I think Princess Diana's died". And we watched together in disbelief as the television news unfolded. Deeply sad, we watched as the crowds expressed their grief and the piles of flowers grew. Diana had affected us all, reflecting as she did the cultural change we were all part of. Somehow her death seemed to provide a collective call, something had to change.

It was hard for us to come away from the art college environment and my dream was that arts and academia would be integrated at the University, one day. Andy and I made a conscious decision that one of us (me) would work inside the academic system and one of us (Andy) would work outside. This would enable us to continue our creative practice while I took, what was essentially, an administrative role in Higher Education. We called our creative partnership 'Monday Studio' an anagram of our names, and Andy set to converting the studio into the Black Square Gallery while I started at the University of Bath.

Built in 1966 in modernist style, very different to the city of Bath famous for its Georgian architecture, the University sits above the city on the edge of the Cotswolds. It was a fifty minute drive from the Mendips to the Cotswolds. This gave me time to process my thoughts and prepare for the day on the way there, and to reflect and recover on the way home. At rush hour the roads were clogged and the drive time increased by at least fifteen minutes. Luckily the University had a flexible hour policy and I was able to go in for 10am and finish at 6pm, often driving home through exquisite sunsets with views across the Glastonbury levels and the Tor.

On my first day the Dean of Students gave me a cursory tour of the University. "Here's your room," she said, leading me to a small office on the ground floor with a lobby opening to a public thoroughfare. I was given the task of finding my own desk, chair, filing cabinet, phone etcetera, but soon had the space in order. Half of my role was to facilitate access for students with dyslexia to Higher Education and the idea was immediately met with hostility from some academics.

"Oh you won't find people with dyslexia at the University," I was told by one ill-informed individual.

"What makes you think you can be a Learning Support

Manager?" asked a large imposing man as he arrived at my door.

"Well," I replied, "I have a Master's Degree from the University of Wales, College of Cardiff." He harrumphed and introduced himself as a Professor of Social Policy, and I got the impression he felt he should have had a role in my appointment.

It rapidly became clear that my appointment was a political challenge. Academics vigorously protected their Departments and resisted what they saw as intrusion and interference in the admissions process, especially since my role was in an Administration capacity. It was a lateral move for me to take a step from academia in art to administration in University, unusual in a hierarchical environment. I saw it as the best way to work towards achieving inclusion for students with disabilities and dyslexia.

I was asked to show a prospective student who had tetraplegia round the University. He was a lovely young man who was hoping to study Science. His injury had been caused by a rugby accident and the University of Bath was famous for its rugby connections. I started by taking him to the Library. This was my first mistake, the Library had a revolving door that was inaccessible and an opening side door that was too narrow for his large electric wheelchair. "I'm so sorry," I said and, continuing my tour of the campus with him, soon learnt how many physical barriers to access there were.

The psychological barriers were equally impenetrable. The Head of the Science Department sent me an abrupt email, in reply to my request to introduce the student, and copied it to the Registrar and the Dean of Students. "How dare you suggest a disabled student could access my Department?" he asked, and continued with a diatribe about health and safety in a laboratory environment, accusing me of giving the student false hope.

The Dean of Students was furious on my behalf and the Registrar, discussing the email with me, just said "That says more about him than it does about you, Mo." The exchange revealed the depth of resistance to inclusion in academia and I knew I had my work cut out. "I'll just have to get a flak jacket," I said in reply.

Academia at that time was exclusive and excluding. This was seen as a good thing. Intense competition ensured that only the best of the best got in, until now only a tiny proportion of the population had been able to go to University. The idea, that as a result many highly able and intelligent people were being actively excluded, was challenging for the system. Initially the exclusion of women was the issue, now growing research and understanding was showing that people from all diverse backgrounds were systematically excluded. The University of Bath was proud of being one of the top Universities in the country, and feared lowering its reputation by becoming more inclusive.

I was working with a joint three-year project with the University of Bristol and the University of the West of England. My colleagues in these Universities experienced similar resistance and together we explored ways of overcoming the barriers to inclusion and shared the challenges we encountered. It helped me a great deal to have the regional and national overview, and there were regular meetings and conferences with people working in the same field.

Nevertheless, I was often isolated in my home University. Still a smoker, I would sit with a coffee and a roll up, looking out over the lake and thinking. Students, well aware of the resistance therefore fearful of declaring their difficulties openly, often felt more able to approach me here than in my office and the café was known as 'my second office' by the students. Soon the number of students coming forward rapidly increased, and the issues they were encountering became apparent. I called the project the three I's of Dyslexia: Identification, Intervention and Institution issues.

Tom completed his first term at his new school and had begun the second term. It's never easy to enter a new school at a different time to everyone else, and Tom had a series of colds and viral infections. We went to the doctor, who told us it was quite normal at a new school. Tom's energy was low and I was worried, but he seemed to be settling in well.

In February Andy had an exhibition with our friend Karin Mathews at the MOMA, Museum of Modern Art in Wales. It was a long drive to North Wales and we left on Friday with a car full of Andy's paintings and the three of us squeezed in. Karin and Rodney made us welcome in their beautiful home on the hills above Criccieth. Tom was fascinated by Rodney's drums, which filled one room. They were both artists and we all loved being there, with the roaring log fire warming us after the wintry journey and the house full of children and dogs and exhibition preparation.

There was a good turnout for the exhibition and a busy private view. I realised Tom had been in the toilet for a long time and shared with Karin my concerns about Tom. Next day, on the long journey home, he was feeling very unwell. "I must have a water melon," he cried, and luckily we were able to find one at the service station. He feasted on it hungrily, and I wondered if it could be carsickness. We got home late and he went to bed, still feeling very unwell.

"Do you want me to call the doctor?" I asked him. "I don't know," he replied. Of course I should have done, but it was very late and we were all tired and fraught.

Andy reassured me. "You go to your meeting in the morning - I'll look after him and take him to the doctor if he's no better."

In the morning I went to my meeting in Bristol. Andy gave Tom toast and honey and ran him a bath. When Andy realised Tom had gone very quiet he called to him through the door, breaking it open when there was no reply. Tom was unconscious in the bath and Andy pulled him out, rang the doctor and put Tom in his car, taking him straight to the surgery where they looked after him until the ambulance arrived.

We had no mobile phones and, unaware of all this, I came home to an empty house and a brief message from Andy to come to Taunton hospital. I drove there in a daze and found Tom in intensive care with Andy pacing the floor.

Tom's sugar levels were through the roof and he was critically ill. He was diagnosed with Type 1 Diabetes, a complete shock. As we learned about diabetes we realised many of the signs had been there, very thirsty, tired, lethargic, weight gain, mood changes, prone to infection. All had been missed by all the doctors we had seen, and all were typical issues for a teenager.

The hospital were very clear, we needed to learn how to support Tom with the new insulin regime delivered by injection, and Tom needed time to recover. I rang the Dean of Students who was very dismissive. "Oh I have a friend whose son is diabetic, it's no problem," and she wrote me a letter saying I couldn't have time off unless it was for a bereavement.

Distressed, I rang the Human Resources Manager who was very helpful and advised me to visit the doctor, who in turn signed me off for six weeks. This gave me time to support Tom. I stayed with him in hospital and luckily, with insulin, he began to recover. When you nearly lose a child the shock is overwhelming. I felt spaced out, gravity free like an astronaut. All the details we were learning, how to check blood sugar levels, how to give injections, were in slow motion and had clarity like at the time of an accident or trauma.

Tom's sense of humour saw us through. He did find it difficult but he was glad to know what was wrong, that it was not his fault and that the insulin was what he needed. He was also able to face the facts. When we came home he asked if he could watch the film Trainspotting. We watched it together, both of us acknowledging the difference between injections for good and those for drug dependency.

I thought of giving up my job to care for Tom and discussed it with the doctor. "That's probably the worst thing that could happen," he said, "best to keep things on an even keel." Andy offered to care for Tom and I would be the sole wage earner. Tom seemed happy with the arrangement, at thirteen he did not want his Mum hanging round him. I put my grief on hold and went back to work, with a new layer of anxiety underpinning my day.

On my return to work the Dean was less than impressed and entirely unsympathetic. Our relationship was damaged. A few years later a friend of hers had exactly the same experience with his daughter and the Dean came in to tell me. "It's terrible, his daughter nearly died," she cried. "Oh," I said, "that's exactly what happened to Tom". And she looked at me in sudden realisation and, without a word, left the room.

I write this a few days after World Diabetes Day. A fourteen-page pull out in the Times newspaper has been published with information about the different types of diabetes, new treatment and new research. Type 1 Diabetes is when the auto immune system of the body has sensed insulin as an intruder, attacked the pancreas and prevented the body from making insulin by killing the insulin producing cells. It often emerges at puberty. Some research has recently revealed that babies born to mothers who have undiagnosed diabetes in pregnancy and pre-eclampsia are likely to develop Type 1 Diabetes. Possibly this is what happened for Tom. Until his collapse we knew nothing about it at all.

Within a year of taking insulin, Tom had recovered his strength and was tall and slim, he'd grown about 6 inches. The change was so rapid that everyone including the doctor commented on it, and friends sometimes didn't recognise him in the street. I used to tell him his puppy fat was like chewing gum, and that one day he would stretch out, making him tall. I just didn't expect it to happen so fast, he's over six feet tall today.

Claverton Down

The three years of the Dyslexia project flew by. Funded by the Higher Education Council for England and developed from new Labour initiatives in policy and funding for inclusion, all Universities were being required to reflect and improve on their practice. Half of my time was devoted to the project, developing inclusion for students with dyslexia at the Universities of Bristol, West of England and Bath, and half to actively developing learning support provision at the University of Bath. Both halves of my role rapidly grew in demand and, as numbers of students being identified with support needs increased, I was able to make the case for more staff. It was great to have support and colleagues and I was no longer isolated. We became something of a small hub with constant activity coming and going, and we were very busy.

Kathy, to my immense relief, quickly took charge of the paperwork. Digital records were in their infancy and our files and piles of paper were engulfing the small office. A queue of students was forming outside our door and it quickly became clear this was just the tip of the iceberg. Philippa joined us as Student Adviser and students had more structured support. For every member of staff who expressed their bias against inclusion, another member of staff would appear at my door, telling me about their daughter who was blind, or about their son who had Asperger's Syndrome.

Much of the prejudice was simply lack of understanding. One student who was registered blind and had requested copies of lecture notes from the lecturers, came to enlist my support when the notes were not forthcoming. Many conditions that cause blindness are not immediately evident and I arranged a meeting with the course leader. We explained to her that the student had peripheral vision but was blind. The course leader, sitting opposite the student at my table, asked her somewhat defensively whether the student could read the title of the book she was holding up. The student replied "What book?" The course leader's understanding immediately changed and the notes were made available. The student told me when she was at school her sight condition, initially believed to be 'hysterical blindness', was eventually identified. The school realised they had made a mistake in treating her as though the condition was not real, but when they presented her with an award to acknowledge her achievement against the odds, they gave her a book which of course she could not read.

Understanding is slow to grow, often lacking in imagination and large in fear. One lovely student with a condition that affected her mobility as well as her sight was bullied by her housemates. At night they deliberately put things on the floor in front of her door so she would stumble over them, and they excluded her from group meals in the kitchen. We arranged to move her to a flat with welcoming and empathic students, and worked with the Students Union on developing student awareness.

Technology to support inclusion was developing. Email was

in its infancy and staff used a system called Pine. Much of the new assistive software becoming available was compatible only with Windows 95. When I suggested to the Library that we could have some rooms installed with computers with assistive software for disabled students I was met with great support. Unfortunately the Computer Services Department was initially less supportive. The University computer system was a secure Java network and having Windows 95 was seen as a significant security risk, prone as it was to hacking. Inclusion won out and three rooms were put in place. Introducing students to the embryonic voice recognition technology, and magnification and mind mapping systems often reduced them to tears as the potential for them to succeed opened up.

As students began to realise their full potential, staff reservations began to ebb away. One lecturer told me when a dyslexic student first arrived, and he saw the difficulties they were having with written work and exams, he would never have believed that the same student with support provision could possibly achieve a first class honours degree. "It's made such a difference," he told me. Other academics were still suspicious of support, thinking support meant it was not the students' own work they were marking. Some thought seeing students achieve meant they had no real problem. "Well if he can get a first in Maths Mo why did he need support?" asked one member of staff in Registry.

It was difficult for an academic environment to recognise that limiting measures of intelligence to the ability to read and write was in itself a failure. Soon those limitations would be completely overturned by the advances in technology. Professor Stephen Hawking published 'A Brief History of

Time' ten years previously, in 1988, and when in 2000 a blind student achieved a distinction in his Master's Degree in Computing Science at the University, he was cheered on by staff and students alike. It was never going to be easy for those first students to fight their way through the system, but they educated us all and opened a route for others to follow.

More difficult for an academic system was to recognise that students with specific learning difficulties such as dyslexia and dyspraxia could be highly intelligent. Dr Mary Haslum, a Reader in Psychology at the University of the West of England, had been developing research into screening for students with specific learning difficulties. Using new screening assessment software for dyslexia, we designed a research project that gave us data across all three Universities. Among other things the data revealed that students with dyslexia often had high IQs and higher visual spatial skills.

I enjoyed meeting with Mary, her acute intelligence would cut through to the essentials we needed to discuss, and her warm and generous nature made me feel welcome and gave me support. UWE is spread across several sites in Bristol and her office was initially based on the St Mathias campus in Fishponds. Later she moved to the new Frenchay campus. When St Mathias departments were moved to Frenchay, UWE claimed 'the historic emphasis on community spirit and the importance of an institution devoted to teaching and learning will remain'. I experienced the way those values were imbued in Mary herself.

Being inside a University is a bit like being inside a giant brain, and the single site campus in Bath exaggerated the feeling for me. The plan of the campus with its large rectangular pedestrianised centre, the modernism of the campus buildings, and its development in science and engineering gave it something of a brave new world feeling. John Le Carre, the former spy turned novelist, wrote about the University of Bath in his novel 'Our Game' in 1995. His character Larry is a double agent and poses as a left-wing political lecturer at the University 'tiresomely bleating on about the failings of the West and espousing various good causes'.

The refectory for academics was then kept separate to café facilities for students and administration staff, and was known as the Claverton Rooms. A classic sixties design, aspiring to be like London's Festival Hall, the rooms included a separate room where smoking was permitted. I occasionally smoked my roll ups in there, and felt like an interloper in a man's club. The scent of cigars hung heavy in the air, sometimes when I went in a few men were playing cards in a smoky club-like atmosphere. Sometimes there was just me at one table, and at a separate table the American Vice Chancellor David Vanderlinde with two Professors, hunkered over in serious discussion. It was easy to imagine the spy world Le Carreinhabited here.

Alan Turing, the mathematician whose work developed the code breaking Enigma machine and who is widely regarded as the father of computer science, is believed to have had Asperger's Syndrome. This autistic spectrum disorder affects social interaction and nonverbal communication. The first student with AS who arrived at my door was a delightful young man called Simon. Simon was given excellent coping strategies by his family, and he was thriving in his first year in maths. He taught me how important it was for him that I be in my office at exactly the right time to meet him. The difficulty he found in managing the flexibility of life was immediately clear. We shared humour about my learning to be there for him, and his managing the times I was late, and his absolute recall of all the buses that were not on time.

This facility with numbers and long strings of connections was fascinating. One of the first problems Simon encountered was when he was asked to leave a lecture by a Professor whose lecture he kept interrupting to correct errors. I met with the lecturer, who told me other students had been upset on Simon's behalf and the whole thing had caused quite a stir. The Professor turned out to be dyslexic. His chalk equations were drawn on the board as he talked. "I like it that he has the courage to speak out Mo, and sometimes I do make errors. The trouble is, his interruptions make me lose my flow of thought and the students start laughing more at the corrections Simon suggests than paying attention to the principles I am teaching." We came to an agreement that Simon would wait until the end of a lecture to discuss the errors with the Professor. Simon thrived in a Department where some Professors had Dyslexia and some were AS, and when he completed his degree he was head hunted by a major technology company.

Peter, a mature student whose AS we identified, had a very difficult life before the identification, including expulsion from schools, arrests for violence, and alcohol dependency. "I use alcohol to try and switch my brain off," he told me. He came to see me because he was struggling with the curriculum and deadlines. "I thought you came to University to read a subject," he said and showed me the research he'd undertaken before he even started at University. The identification helped his entire family, his brothers and father were also AS. "My mother wants to thank you," he said. "She always used to say I was dictatorial, a bit of a Hitler, and I've found out Asperger, who identified the syndrome, was a Nazi who even sent children for euthanasia." The condition is now more commonly known as ASD. The lack of guile and of tact and the honesty associated with the condition is wonderful, but can cause serious social friction. Peter reminds me of the film about the pianist David Helfgott, 'Shine'. I was realising there were as many students with AS who had not been identified as there were with dyslexia.

The association with some conditions and exceptional ability is now well known, the autistic savant, the dyslexic genius. I knew I would find staff at the University who had these conditions and it helped me enormously when they came to talk to me. The dyslexic architect, for example, who knew he was dyslexic but who would never tell his colleagues because of the mindless prejudice against dyslexia he was used to hearing from them. The dyslexic Professor of Engineering whose office was swamped in paper work, his day-to-day life was scatty and his engineering designs transformed systems.

When our work began to make inroads at higher levels in the University, these same prejudices were aired in Council meetings and to my great good fortune Professor William Gosling was at these meetings. He listened to all the prejudices being aired, the puerile jokes being made, and when they had all finished he announced to the entire council that he himself was dyslexic. "You could have heard a pin drop Mo," he said. I was grateful to him and to all the academics willing to support us, they turned the tide of prejudice and at the end of the project we felt the entire situation had changed at the University. There were still hurdles to be overcome but much of the initial antipathy had changed.

The funding had enabled us to have more staff and, with our growing student advice and administration support team, we had outgrown our office. We moved to a new office suite and continued to develop our services. We wanted to celebrate the success of the project and disseminate our findings, and decided to hold a conference 'Cascade: Creativity Across Science, Art, Dyslexia, Education' in the summer of 2001.

John Struthers, Director of Creative Arts at the University, supported our aim to integrate and include art in the proceedings. We planned performance events, including a play by Ketaki Kushari Dyson, an art exhibition in the Library, including work by academics at the University, and music and installation events to underpin the presentation of papers in the lecture theatre. The papers included findings from the Project, outside contributions and a closing address from Dr Jack Whitehead.

Professor Margaret Herrington, in her foreword to the book that emerged from the Cascade conference, identifies the conversational space in which dyslexic and non-dyslexic listen and speak. "It is a conversation in which the unexpected jostles with the familiar, 'messiness' with clarity, and dazzling glimmers of insight with solid positions. This kind of open space is rare in a field dominated by disciplinary boundaries and conventions". Sadly, this is still the case as I write in 2018.

St Andrews Stream

I was having a coffee with a colleague when someone told us a plane had attacked New York. The normally busy cafeteria went quiet and, as word spread through the University, many of us went to watch the news on the television in what used to be the smoking room of the Claverton Rooms. We watched in disbelief as first one and then another plane flew into the twin towers and the horrifying spectacle that would become known as 9/11 unfolded on the screen.

My mother was living in a Nursing Home in Henton, a village near Wells. I was visiting her every evening and after work I went to her Home, very worried about how this news might affect her. Televisions were on in every room of the Home, replaying over and over the horrific events. The doors to each room were open and as I rushed to Mum's room the sounds of devastation, accompanied by the strange smells of disinfectant with the faint whiff of urine, laid another level onto the impact for me.

We had made Mum's room as comfortable as we could and, surrounded by her familiar things and photos, she was lying in bed watching the television quite unconcerned. "Isn't it awful Mum," I said, giving her a peck on the cheek.

"Well dear," she replied philosophically, "it's not as bad as the blitz in Glasgow during the war."

She had been a social worker in deprived areas of Glasgow during the war. Sixty years previously one of the most intense Luftwaffe bombing raids of World War 2 had been the Clydebank blitz, which affected Clydebank the most but also hit areas of Glasgow, including Govan, where Mum was working. I remembered her telling me how she'd been caught in the blitz and stayed overnight in a shelter. It was days before her worried parents knew she had survived. Mum remembered the bombed out buildings, the flames and the smoke and for her 9/11 seemed small in comparison, contained as it was by a television screen.

My mother's honesty and fortitude were as strong as ever despite her frailty, and it put my concerns into perspective. Mum, now in her eighties, was in the Home because she'd had a major stroke. For some time she'd not been too well and I had been with her to her GP and consultant appointments. Scans showed she'd had mini strokes (known as TIAs). She was a bit shaky but still sharp and with it, and determinedly independent.

It had been healing for me to have these years of closeness with Mum since we moved back to Wells. When I had been so distressed about Tom's diagnosis of diabetes she had said, "I don't know what to do dear, shall I give you a hug?" Such a rare and difficult thing for her to do and the most memorable for me to receive. She'd been a listening ear and constant support through the challenges at work too. "I just wish things could be easier for you dear," she said.

Tom and Andy had kept a closer eye on Mum while I was at work. Andy took her shopping and Tom called in on her after school, but we could see she was becoming frail, so when the phone call came from her neighbours to say she'd not taken in her milk bottle that morning, we knew at once something was wrong. We found her on the floor in her bedroom; she had collapsed with a major stroke and was rushed to hospital. At first the hospital didn't seem to be doing much and she was left in an admissions ward for twenty-four hours. I felt as though they were waiting to see if she would survive and when I complained she was moved to a private room and given first class support. My brother and sister and families came to see Mum and we celebrated Tom's seventeenth birthday by her bedside.

My brother told us she had made a 'living will'. By the time I eventually found it Mum had recovered enough to return to a cottage hospital in Wells. The will made her wishes clear - she did not wish to be resuscitated should she have a life-threatening condition. Always able to look facts in the face, my mother had a horror of becoming incapacitated and reliant on others. Day by day in the cottage hospital she slowly recovered, but not sufficiently to resume her independent life. Sheila visited regularly and my brother Alan came and looked after Mum for a week, giving me a break. Andy and I went on holiday to Malta and while I was away Alan researched nursing homes in the area. It was a decision we were reluctant to take, but it was becoming clear it would be necessary.

The cottage hospital was near our home and Andy and I wheeled Mum round in her wheelchair for a visit. We couldn't get her into the house and were making adjustments to create an accessible door. We were able to enjoy a sunny hour or two in the garden and sat by the pond Andy recently built. Mum asked to throw a stone into it, and with the splash it made we shared a realisation she would not be able to come home to her own home or to ours.

"A Nursing Home is Mum's worst nightmare," I told my GP. He replied that we'd chosen the best one in the area. "You can't nurse her twenty-four hours a day," he told me, "and she needs nursing care."

Mum had been a magistrate, the name for this work used to be Justice of the Peace and Mum was always a seeker after truth, peace and justice. She did voluntary work for the Red Cross and maintained her social conscience to the end. The staff in the Nursing Home liked her, and we were never sure if the sweet compliance she showed them was resignation to her situation or an understanding and knowledge of how to survive her situation. Sometimes she understood exactly what was going on and sometimes she thought she was in an Edinburgh Guest House. We were able to take her out for lunch in a pub and to a café after a visit to an optician. She knew she was near her old home and asked me if we could go home now.

Her deterioration continued and she began to stay in her room for meals. I went to see her every evening and we shared a small glass of sherry and talked like old times. When I had suggested to my mother that she may have dyspraxia she said, "It feels like a relief, dear. I could never catch a ball or ride a bike, I always thought I must be a bit spastic" (the dreadful old term for cerebral palsy). She watched a documentary and it was healing to be able to forgive herself and understand some of the difficulties she'd had throughout her life. I think she would have been a writer had she had the support available today, and I wondered if her ability to adapt to the damage caused by the stroke was partly due to her versatile neural pathways; some of the earliest brain research was with stroke victims.

She was not the easiest mother, not given to hugs or loving endearments and preferring honesty to empathy. She was fiercely intelligent, generous, emancipated and courageous. She had survived the anti-Semitism of her childhood, and embraced diversity and freedom from prejudice.

Without words or physical actions for love such as hugs, the love between us was unstated and yet powerfully strong. My mother becoming incapacitated was deeply sad, heart wrenching and frustrating yet had moments of sheer wonder. I was working on releasing the wordless bonds that bound us and stood by the stream in the garden of the Nursing Home, watching the autumn leaves slide downstream. St Andrews Stream ran through Wells from the Bishop's Palace and continued through Henton. I knew I had to let Mum go and not be pulled into the stream with her.

Her limited speech still allowed her some extraordinary communication. One of our favourites was a phrase she wrote while in the home, "Ach na morbid, Welcome strangeness". This curious and very clear injunction to avoid sentimentality and embrace change was somehow heartening.

When the next stroke came she lost the ability to speak or swallow. The Doctor respected her wishes, "I've read your living will," she told Mum. "Is this what you still want?" Mum nodded vigorously. "That's good enough for me," she said and the decision was taken to allow Mum to die peacefully without further hospital intervention. Over her last few days we were all able to be with her, and in her final hours the nurses were midwives to her death, sitting with me and calmly talking as she took her final breaths.

As I write, a candle is burning for what would have been

Mum's hundredth birthday. I feel her strength and spirit is still with me. Although she did not believe in an afterlife she once told me "It would help if I had faith" and we would light candles together for Dad and family in Wells Cathedral. She died on All Souls Day. A few weeks later I was watching an old Christmas movie when in an emotional scene the words "I Love You" were spoken and in precise unison the fairy lights on the Christmas tree - which were not flashing ones - came on and off three times. That was good enough for me.

Don Valley

My brother Alan started the now famous 2fly studio in Sheffield in the same year our mother died. As a very young child he believed he could fly - when he was a toddler he was waiting at the stair gate at the top of our three-storey house in Dorridge and, aged six, I tucked him under my arm and carried him downstairs. Our Mum was furious with me - of course I could have dropped him and her anger was from fear - but Alan always remembered the sensation of flying.

Alan loves music and like our father has a natural ear for rhythm and tone. We grew up with the jazz sound track of our Dad and Aunt and Uncle's music, our Dad's trumpet was always around and the piano at Ladygrove was in constant use. Our Dad, my brother Alan and my son Tom all constantly drum with their fingers to a silent rhythm when they are thinking and music is where they process their thoughts. Alan pursued an Arts degree but his career has mainly been in the music industry. From his early days as a sound engineer on the Pulp 'Separations' album in 1982 his interest in music production never wavered.

Alan was in a number of moderately successful bands. In the late 80's in 'The Man Upstairs' he played mellow café jazz and was in a Melody Maker centre fold. He joined Don Valley and the Rotherhides, their name was based on an area of Sheffield, between 1986 and 1992. They were an indie country and western band and were fantastic live performers. When they came to stay with us at The Cottage in Chewton Mendip I saw them performing in the Hole in the Wall nightclub in Bath. I remember the entire room erupting to their performances of 'Thatcher's Dead' and 'I'm so far in the red I'm blue'. I loved their energy and was proud of my brother, but at that time we saw little of each other and dipped in and out of each other's lives.

That changed when our mother moved to Wells and when my niece Tasmin was born in 1996 we started to see each other more regularly. Our extended families have all formed strong bonds over the years and we share many memories. There is only a year between Tasmin's brother Tom and my son Tom. Anne Marie, Tom and Tasmin's mother, and I soon became close friends. When Alan joined the band Seafruit he visited us in Dorset and brought a tape of their forthcoming album - I spent hours listening to it. I felt sure the album was going to make it big, the songs were powerful and the lyrics - from the prophetic "You can't keep living on Rocket Fuel' to the moving 'Looking for Sparks' – were great. Their single 'Hello World' made it to number 59 in the charts in 1999, and they featured in the Radio One Road show that year.

Alan and Anne Marie took Tom with them on part of the Radio One Roadshow tour and we all went to see the band, performing in their iconic white lab coats, at Weston Super Mare. Tasmin danced on the beach to the music while the two Toms played it as cool as young teenagers can. But the big time was not to be, even though the album is selling for £20 on Amazon as I write. Reviewers give it five stars and called it "absolutely fantastic the more I hear it the more I like it" and "if you like your music to refresh and stir the soul... Seafruit really are pearls in a shell" and "one of the best albums I have ever bought". I remember a Guardian reviewer at the time describing the music as at once familiar and totally new, and I thought of how I hear the many influences Alan had experienced and the fusion he brings to the music he writes, irresistible rhythm, like our Aunt from the Rhythm Sisters.

Alan and Anne Marie also made an income from developing the wood sculptures he had begun to make at Art College into a small business, the Flying Duckters. Anne Marie's drawing skills and the sense of humour and fun in the work was successful, and they gained contracts with among others John Lewis Stores. But music was never far from Alan's heart and when the opportunity came to open 2fly studios he took it. In an article for Counterfeit magazine he recalls rehearsing with Seafruit in the Stag Works and that Joe Moskow wrote 2fly on the doorframe after Stu Doughty had called Alan "too fly". Alan describes how the studio was already set up, just needing a wall built between the live room and the studio. This was built at an angle to accommodate a sofa and accidentally produced "a very nice sound".

From this 'very nice sound' a Sheffield music dynasty was to emerge. Developments in technology were rapidly changing. Alan always used technology in his work and as the changes in music production evolved, so did he and the music he produced. Alan has said that most people then thought of Sheffield as the closure of the steel industry and the Hillsborough Disaster, and Sheffield had suffered terribly in the financial crises. Like with so many places in the North of England the South remained unaware. It was to be the music that would bring the cultural scene of Sheffield back to life.

Musicians tend to know each other and, in a city like Sheffield where pubs have live music stages and the energy is quite vibrant, young bands had the chance to develop their skills with small gigs and many rehearsal and studio spaces. One of these was the 2fly Studio. Some of the bands Alan worked with such as Milburn and Tate were becoming well known, and when Reverend and the Makers and the Arctic Monkeys first started recording at 2fly the shared friendly rivalry and collaboration meant there was an extra edge to the way the music developed.

Alan advised the Arctic Monkeys singer, Alex Turner, not to use the American accent he was attempting, but to stick with his Sheffield vowels. Alex was singing about the abuse of young women and of Rotherham years before the news of the grooming gang and the failures of the system to protect girls there was finally exposed. The songs were powerful, and they recorded a demo of 18 songs at the 2fly Studio that were burned onto CDs, given away for free at gigs and through file sharing. Alan brought us one and, sitting on our sofa early in the New Year 2005, he said "You're going to hear a lot more about this band. They are very good".

The Arctic Monkeys 2fly's demo is widely credited as the first ever example of free digital music being circulated on line. I listened to it on my drive to work in the morning, knowing this was something extraordinary. It seemed to combine the rhythm of Sheffield steel hammers with a 'get up and dance through the crap' energy that was irresistible.

Their live performances were popular and soon they were

playing to large audiences at Leeds and Reading Festivals. By June they were signed to Domino records and their first single release 'I Bet You Look Good on the Dancefloor' went straight to number 1 in October 2005. The album 'Whatever People Say I Am, That's What I'm Not' became the fastest selling debut album in the UK chart history and is in the 100 Best Debut Albums of All Time. Alan has credits for the production on track 9, 'Mardy Bum', and additional recording on track 11, 'When the Sun Goes Down'.

It was exciting to be so close to such a stratospheric rise for Alan, but he was very cool - his long experience of the toughness of the music business stood him in good stead in managing expectations and he took no credit for their success, rightly saying it is all their own work. But for his family, we felt he underplayed the role he played in influencing and bringing the album to the world stage, and were frustrated for him that he was not better rewarded financially.

Mum always used to say she had made a mistake in giving her children a social conscience but not making us more money conscious. "He'll make it one day," I told her when she voiced her concerns for her son. "I hope I live to see it," she replied. Unfortunately she didn't but I know she was always proud of him, and I found the words to 'Thatcher's Dead' written out in her hand after she died. Lyrics were always important to her, a lover of Frank Sinatra, she once wrote a short article on song writing long before her son was born.

Years later I danced to a special performance, from former members of Seafruit and Don Valley and the Rotherhides, of the song 'Thatcher's Dead' at Anne Marie's birthday party. A few people in the packed room found the lyrics distasteful but for most people in Sheffield, a city that suffered so much at the hands of her policies, they were one hundred per cent apt and the room was still jumping when the performance ended. Standing next to Jon McClure, a tall man and leader of the Reverend and the Makers - known for his outspoken political views, I raised a glass to the end of that era unaware that the policies, and much worse, would return.

Jon McClure was determined to ensure Reverend and the Makers retained their unique identity. They released their nine-track demo in 2006, also recorded at 2fly Studios, and their first single release was 'Heavyweight Champion of the World' in 2007. Alan has credits with Jon McClure and Ed Cosens, acknowledging the work Alan did towards the demo of the song. My favourite track on the album is 'Machine' which Jon co-wrote with Alex Turner of the Arctic Monkeys. I played it over and over on my way to and from work when things were difficult, with its line "Don't forget you can get off the conveyor, when you want you can get off the conveyor" echoing in my head and reminding me that one day I could leave the machine of academia.

Alan moved to a larger studio in neighbouring Harland Works. These disused industrial buildings were reminiscent of New York loft living and a steep narrow stair led to Alan's new and busy studio premises. The South had woken up to the power and energy of the North, and the BBC Imagine programme decided to explore the Northern Music scene. Starting in Manchester, they ended the programme in Sheffield. I stared in astonishment and huge pride at the television as I saw Alan Yentob sitting in my brother's studio. His last line before the closing credits was "Right now, here - in Sheffield – this is the coolest place to be."

Blue Mountains

As I walked through the beautiful historic campus of the University of Queensland, surrounded on three sides by the Brisbane River, I saw a Professor heading towards one of the School buildings. He was an Indigenous Australian person who was wearing a suit and walking in his bare feet, the soles of the feet being the intuitive way to know the world. So much of our left brain dominant culture has given western culture supremacy and failed indigenous populations, and this includes the exclusion of different ways of learning and being in our academic systems. Here in Australia I was learning the depth of change needed to facilitate diversity.

I'd been invited to give a talk at a conference on support for students with disabilities. I flew to Sydney with Tom and his friend Declan who, at eighteen, were having their own road trip and sharing some of the travel with me. I'd always wanted to see Sydney and the long journey was an endurance test, but worth it. "No worries mate," came the greeting from a cheerful coffee vendor at the airport, and this set the tone for the Aussie way of life. "It's like Brits in the sun," said Tom.

Aunt Stella, her husband and young son migrated to Australia when I was four. My grandparents never quite got over the loss. Letters from Australia were devoured hungrily and re-read many times. Once when we were living in Dorridge a friend of the family paid for a very expensive phone call to our family in Australia. We gathered round the Bakelite phone, admonished to speak slowly and clearly. There was an extended pause as I waited for a reply, which made me think of words on wires under the sea, and the spoken "Hello Morag" that came in return was bubbly, coming from a long, long way away.

Exotic parcels from Australia arrived at Christmas, a tortoiseshell hairband, a string of sparkly crystals, small framed prints of paintings of the outback. I kept and treasured my Aunt's drawings and imagined one day meeting the cousins I met in photographs, two boys and a girl. As time went on communication deteriorated.

Grandpa was very deaf and Grandma was frail. When Grandpa suggested they visit the family in Australia he was told Grandma could come, but he could not. It was impossible for Grandma to travel independently and so the visit was never made.

My mother decided to visit Australia in her seventieth year. She rang Aunt Stella to tell her, hoping to be able to visit the family. "I don't want to know," Stella told her and brusquely put the phone down. Mum was very upset and we talked about it. A friend of mine knew someone who lived in the same part of the Blue Mountains and we arranged for Mum to stay with her. Mum enjoyed her visit to Australia and New Zealand. She went to look at Aunt Stella's house from the outside but did not knock on the door.

The rift between the sisters started long before Stella migrated to Australia. Mum took over running the household when their mother was ill and Stella, always closer to her mother than her father, resented that. Mum, being several years older than Stella, went to Glasgow University before the Second World War, and Stella, a talented artist, was proud of the career she developed after the war in fashion design in London. The rivalry is evident in letters between them and Mum herself resented Stella being Grandma's favourite. Mum was the sole carer for her parents for many years and, as often happens, the carer takes the blame from those they care for and from absent family.

They were beautiful girls and it always seemed sad to me that the rift had widened so far. It wasn't until my sister visited the family in Australia after Mum died that we understood what may have underpinned the situation. Stella never told her children that their Grandfather was Jewish. Anti-Semitism was rife during the Second World War and continued in many parts of Australia after the war, alongside racism towards the indigenous Australian people, still known as Aborigines. I think Stella wanted to put the past behind her, protect her children, and move on with her life.

Visiting Sydney gave me an opportunity to connect with my cousin Carole, Stella's daughter. She made us welcome and we met her two sons, and shared an Aussie barbecue. We talked about the family, and Carole recalled being out for a walk as a child with her mother and her younger brother in the pram. A neighbour made a comment suggesting the baby looked Jewish. Carole remembered her mother's fierce denial, a denial that carried such energy it was held in Carole's memory for nearly fifty years.

Sydney is now such a vibrant wonderful city that it was hard to imagine, as Carole told us, how isolated and cut off from a cultural life Stella felt when she moved to the Blue

Mountains from Glasgow. Now modern art galleries that feature contemporary art, fine architecture, the Opera House and the Bridge, are stunning. The hotel we were staying in had huge and magnificent Indigenous Australian peoples' paintings in the foyer. Smoking in public places had been banned some years before and the cleanliness of the city, compared with London, was remarkable. The city shimmered with colour and culture - I walked for miles soaking it in.

My Aunt did visit the UK after her parents' death and we met her in London. Mum and Stella's cousin Gaby arranged afternoon tea at the Ritz for us all. All the women except me had dramatic dark good looks, in contrast to my fair hair and blue eyes. Stella had always been particularly beautiful and my sister shared her arched eyebrows and poise. I brought with me an embroidered sampler that Stella made as a young woman, and that I treasured. She was pleased to receive it, but said somewhat ungraciously, "It's good to get something back." She was not interested in me and I was disappointed.

It seemed too short a time before we had to take the flight to Brisbane for my forthcoming talk at Queensland University. On arrival we decided to visit North Stradbroke Island. This paradise island in Moreton Bay is the second largest sand island in the world. We went by bus and ferry and had a magical day swimming in the calm waters and lying on the soft sand, listening to parrots calling and keeping an eye out for dolphins. The day flew by and we suddenly realised we would have to make a run for it to catch the last ferry back to the mainland - as we set off we heard a phone ringing. When we located and answered the phone, the very relieved owner explained she'd left her bag on the island and we arranged to meet her from the ferry. She was so grateful for its return she insisted on taking Tom and Declan to the Gold Coast the next day as a reward, and they enjoyed a coast that was in total contrast to the Island while I went to work at the University.

I was impressed by how far ahead the Australian Universities were in facilitating access and in pioneering the social model of disability – one that shows how an environment disables a person. For example, insisting on delivering information in text to someone who cannot read, or assessing their understanding of a subject in a way that prevents their ability to do justice to their knowledge. I was giving a talk on our leading work at the University of Bath in making alternative arrangements for exams. It was well received and there was an animated discussion around academic resistance to changes such as use of a computer or additional time, reasonable adjustments that are now common place but that were then unheard of. I learnt more from the conference than I gave and knew I would be able to return to the UK with renewed confidence in persuading the academe of the value of becoming an accessible University.

After the conference finished we went to Maleny in Queensland to visit Gaby's daughter Nicola. Nicola's home was in the rolling green hills of the sunshine coast hinterland. This area was once rain forest, before 19th and 20th century logging activity cleared it, and the sense of being on the edge of sub-tropical rain forest was strong. Nicola was planting trees on her smallholding, wallabies browsed in her garden, a kookaburra called from the eucalyptus tree and cane toads chirped at night.

Nicola's father was an Oscar nominated film production designer and her film library fascinated Declan and Tom. The way Nicola used strong colour and shape in her home recalled for me the home of her parents. Beautiful objects from her travels round the world were in each room, a large Chinese ceramic bowl in my bedroom, ethnic sculpted tools in the living room, and stone figures in the garden reminded me of the props from film sets, the mermaid figurehead and prow of a pirate ship that once stood in her parents' garden, in Hertfordshire. The open plan kitchen and living room recalled her parents' living spaces whose design influenced Steven Spielberg's own home after he visited there. After her father's death Nicola gave me the plan chest he'd used for drawing up his storyboards for blockbuster films. "I've just been very lucky," he would say and told me "You have to be able to draw Morag," advice that would prove invaluable in my design career.

Gaby also cut free from her Jewish heritage, both her parents were Jewish. It was not the big secret it was for Stella, Gaby's children knew some of their Uncles, including my Grandfather, but family was just something she never talked about. I was very fond of Gaby, she was close to our mother and more of an Aunt to us; when Sheila and I stayed with her as children she showed us round London, taking us to the Science Museum or China Town.

Nicola left us in charge of her smallholding for a few days - we fed the chickens and watered the newly planted trees. The views from the hills were panoramic and the sagebrush blue of heat washed over the landscape. While I never got to see the Blue Mountains where my Aunt lived, here in Queensland the enormity of space gave me a new perspective. There was an untouched unpopulated element that reminded me of Britain in the nineteen fifties, yet the twenty first century multi-cultural Australian milieu seemed to frame my experience.

Secure attachment enables us to connect and to come and go with ease, whereas insecure or broken attachment can make us entirely cut contact. My family history, my Great Grandfather's rejection of his son when he married out of the Jewish faith, naming him as dead, and Stella and Gaby's subsequent cutting away from that history was understandable. My Grandfather forged the way by marrying out of the faith and I was grateful my mother had found a way to celebrate the diversity in our family, and to keep an archive of photos and letters that in due course our disconnected cousins would come to share and value.

Joyce and Isaac

Growing up in the anti-Semitism that existed before the Second World War was difficult for the young women. Joyce's

father's mother asked to meet Stella and Joyce after her husband died. My mother always remembered it and the recognition, almost reconciliation between them. Uncle Joe, one of my Grandfather's brothers, died in the First World War. Two other brothers left my Grandfather small parts of their estates when they died. This journey had strangely reconnected me with my roots and given me a boost in confidence for my work. Andy met us at the bus station in Bath and, exhausted after our long journey, we gratefully sank into his car for the last leg home.

Poacher's Pocket

I painted my first oil painting when I was seventeen from a photo I took by accident on a beach in Gotland, Sweden. It featured the startling white sand, vivid colours of a beach towel, and the bleached out blue of an over exposed sky that could only be Sweden in summer. The image captured the spontaneity of a moment and this theme tended to permeate my art from then on. I was proud when Mum hung the painting on the wall in our sitting room, but the work didn't get strong feedback from the all male tutors at Art College.

Owning my life as an artist has been a long journey. I lacked confidence and tended to conceal my art while building my designs. I always needed to work out my thoughts, physically in drawing and installation, and visually in photography. Often there were not words for concepts I was struggling with and the process of drawing and making helped me to clarify my thoughts and translate this to words. I did not have the wonderful craft skills of many of my friends and the spatial concepts I worked with were often derided. The year after we moved to Wells Tracey Emin's installation for the Turner Prize, 'My Bed', was widely criticised yet has become recognised as a seminal feminist work.

When we first moved to Wells, the iconic cathedral was clad

in scaffolding for repair of the stonework. Andy, with our friend and fellow artist Karen Browning and myself, proposed an installation for the Cathedral, 'Casting the Light'. Light installations were unusual and Andy was told that the masons would assist him only if he was willing to climb to the top of the tower with them. Facing his fear of heights he did so and the masons helped him to install lights throughout the scaffolding tower. The wonderful effect of a column of illumination at night attracted the attention of local media and television news, and Andy was able to secure some funding retrospectively.

We wrote a feasibility study for Wells on the inclusion of art, comparing the absence of art in the city with cities in Europe that were full of art activity. The study attracted a centre page spread in the local newspaper and Bishop George Carey, the Bishop of Bath and Wells, rang Andy to express his concerns about our proposals. We suggested opening up access to the Bishop's Palace. The Bishop lived in the Palace and viewed the Palace garden as his back garden. We called the garden the hidden jewel in Wells' crown, the huge springs that bubbled up from under the Mendips into wells in the garden had been the source of copious clean fresh drinking water for millennia and a sacred site since Pagan times. Over the years, many of the recommendations we made, including the opening up of the Bishop's Palace, and the inclusion of art were adopted without any reference to our report. It seems to me, influence often works this way – new ideas can be met with initial rejection and hostility, but sometimes ideas will slowly be absorbed, adopted and represented. Only when the idea of change is owned by those making the changes can the change be achieved.

I was an installation and conceptual artist using multi-media, a combination of film, photography, sculpture, text and image. The practice was not yet receiving recognition and I exhibited to mixed receptions. When we held an event at the Black Square Gallery, our Monday Studio, I built a den from old branches, 'found objects' and feathers and created shrine spaces in the large old workshop on the ground floor of the disused drawing office. I'd been exploring childhood spatial experience of creating safe space, dens. Friends who came to the open day told me they enjoyed exploring my den. On the other hand, my mother, who supported our exhibition, asked me what the pile of rubbish in the corner was – my den! However, my mother loved my photo, Flame, a huge angel shaped flame flickering in the heat shimmer against a fence and understood immediately it was about life and transience. I gave her the work and it was on the wall in her home until her death.

Morag's Den, Black Square Gallery

For some years, our choice of Andy working outside and me inside the academic institution was successful, and I was able to retain my creative life through our shared practice. Exhibitions became a regular event; in Glastonbury at the Somerset Rural Life Museum we exhibited work that explored regeneration and rural decline. In Shepton Mallet my installation, 'the Web', inspired by the growing numbers of students who were online 24/7 in the Library at the University, featured a pair of legs going into a computer monitor so that it appeared the rest of the body had disappeared into the Internet. It was so realistic a young boy burst into tears when he saw it.

With Andy I participated in Somerset Arts Weeks for a few years. This annual event offers the opportunity to see Somerset artists in their studios. Our friend Fiona Hingston invited us to exhibit with her in a disused dairy yard where her studio was based. In a barn I found empty stainless steel tanks once used to separate curds and whey, as well as the cutting tools and disused boards for maturing and cutting cheese. In my installation I used them as holy relics to reflect on the end of dairy production in the UK. Many dairy farms were closing down as milk production became uneconomical due to supermarkets' price cutting pressure. Recently Fiona exhibited her powerful work on the end of the dairy farm in the village where her studio is based. Her exquisitely drawn work featured the haunting absence of cows in the disused milk parlour and the fields.

One year, in a café in Wells, Andy and I exhibited our work on Identity together. This followed on from a Wessex Poetry Festival on the same theme. For the café, one of our exhibits was an imprint in white paint of our naked bodies on a navy sheet. To create this we covered each other's backs in white paint and lay on the sheet for long enough to ensure a good imprint. Much of my identity work was exploring separation, dislocation and belonging; Andy's work was exploring facing his deepest fears, working with layers of memory. The sheet print speaks to me now of relationship and connection.

Bodies, Cafe Bleu, Somerset Arts Week

When our relationship began we talked of the need to each have our own separate creative space, and drew a plan with a shared meeting space between the two. We tried to hold on to this vision in our work. When I left the Art College environment to work in the University we hoped our shared practice in Monday Studio would enable me to continue my art. Andy's partnership is a constant source of support, our deep bonds and shared values mean we can talk about, understand and encourage each other's work. But inevitably my practice declined as my work at University grew ever busier, and my art became less visible. Members of my extended family often still assume my work is Andy's, and it was only when a friend visited and asked me where my work was that I realised Andy's work dominated the walls in our home.

Ultimately the Black Square Gallery had to close because the city rates were too expensive and we were running at a loss. We remained close as partners but our practices began to diverge. Andy continued his practice at home and through an increasing and impressive portfolio of Arts Council funded and socially engaged projects. I became more immersed in the work at the University.

We both enjoyed the excellent music and hubbub of real ale and Somerset folk at the Poacher's Pocket, a Somerset pub that had a monthly open mike on Sundays. In 2002 the Poacher's Pocket agreed to be a venue for us for Somerset Arts Weeks. As a small group of artists we met and shared our work. Jeff Body and Andy were the most active, their camaraderie was inspiring and they were passionate about the work. At the Poacher's Pocket I made a votive flag fence where people could hang flags with their prayers. This was accompanied by a performance event with Andy and our friend Tom. We read poems and sang laments. I made a small poetry pamphlet, 'Stop the War'. Since 9/11 President Bush appeared determined to go to war in Iraq, and it was evident our Prime Minister Tony Blair was getting sucked in.

The performance was one of those moments where the world is stilled and rapt attention creates an art piece of its own, the atmosphere was intense. At the Poacher's Pocket, for the briefest moment, I thought maybe things could change, the course of time could be altered.

When the Stop the War marches occurred the following year it was too little, too late. I was disheartened and my creative practice began to decline. I was so busy I found no time for drawing or making work, and it was only during holidays that I could reconnect with a cultural life.

Andy believed I was using my creative skills in my work at the University, and that it was evidence of my socially engaged art practice. Certainly I was using my design skills in the structure of the support work and in the growth of accessible accommodation provision across the University. I used this creative process in my Master's dissertation and in my work at University. I often drew during meetings, doodles that ended up covering sheets of paper, but I was not being creative on a daily basis for myself, and as a result my self-care was also declining. Creative or not, I was engrossed in the work, and barely noticed my art practice slipping away. In a similar way, as technology began to dominate in the education curriculum, art began its slow decline. My art practice and the value of art in education seemed to become less visible, and less valued around the same time.

We likened the scaffolding on the Cathedral during the 'Casting the Light' installation to the Borg cube, a fictional starship in Star Trek used by the Borg collective - a cybernetic alien race. The Borg assimilated other races into its cube structure, and when my office at the University moved to the eighth floor of Wessex House I laughingly said I felt the Borg had assimilated me. There are such advantages to becoming accepted, to fitting in, and part of me longed for such acceptance, but it would not be long before my differences would pick me out once more.

I was invited to be the speaker 'for' conceptual art for a debate held at the Blue Boar in Frome. The speaker 'against' was a well-known supporter of the 'Turnip Prize', the idea being a popular Somerset derision of the Turner Prize - prizes were given to items such as a potato that mocked conceptual art. The pub was packed and, to my surprise, I was very shaky when I spoke. I was used to speaking to full lecture theatres and thought the shaking must be emotional stress because the subject was so important to me. I did not realise this was an early sign of the deterioration in my health, with less creativity and more overworking I became ill. Fortunately, I'd prepared a written talk and the audience were very attentive. During questions a woman said she valued what I said but hated not understanding the work, and as a result feeling stupid. In a similar way, my friends have regularly told me I need to write about my work, and maybe this is some of what I am attempting to do here.

After the Poachers Pocket exhibition Jeff Body told me I was a true artist, but I felt he and Andy were both stronger and more focussed, their work more accessible. Jeff's stone sheep adorn a roundabout at the entrance to Shepton (Sheep town) Mallet. They are so popular they were regularly adorned with Easter bonnets or Santa hats at the appropriate time of year until the transport authorities deemed it was too much of a distraction to motorists, especially those on their way to Glastonbury Festival.

I have a deep inner critic and my creativity can be easily blocked. These blocks seem to serve a function of deepening my creative subconscious so when my work once again irresistibly comes out, it is often stronger, more powerful. The wonderful artist Susan Hiller, who died aged 79 in 2019, said, "Artists have a function. We're part of a conversation. It's our job to represent and mirror back the values of the culture in a way that people haven't seen before". She saw the changes in gender equality and as a young woman experienced dismissal of herself as an artist, describing how people would talk to her male partner, assuming he was the artist, ignoring her. In later life she received belated global recognition for her work.

It is a great joy to me that the exclusion from the history of art of women artists is now being addressed. Every day there is news of a woman artist 'discovered' working away unrecognised all round the world. In addition, ageism in art is being challenged. Tate Britain has announced a new display dedicated to women artists working in Britain over the last 60 years. There have been huge queues for Frida Kahlo and Yayoi Kusami's exhibitions.

Kusami's joyful exuberant and colourful work is getting major recognition at the age of 80. Louise Bourgeois, who carried on working until her death in 2010, is best known for her large scale sculpture and installation art. She was given her first retrospective in 1982, aged 71, at the Museum of Modern Art. My work bears no comparison with theirs, but in my own small way I have been following the many small trails and tracks laid down by feminist artists before me in challenging and attempting to change the status quo.

Eastwood Lodge

In 2019 I was watching a political discussion on television about school exclusions. I was so angry as I heard the presenter describe how almost half of the children being permanently excluded in 2017 had special needs, yet children with special needs make up only 14 percent of the school population. One of the discussion panel described schools as "being lumbered with" these children. I thought back to happier days before the funding cuts brought about this debacle of social injustice.

By 2003 we were making real headway in the inclusion of students with disabilities and neuro-diversity at the University of Bath. As the numbers of students grew so did the number of staff in the Learning Support Department. We outgrew our old asbestos ridden accommodation and moved to newly re-furbished accessible accommodation on the edge of the campus. I put Mike Juggins' brightly coloured painting of a child wearing a dunce cap, with a window with prison bars in the background, in one of our rooms. It was at once vivid and disturbing and a representation of the feelings of a child with dyslexia being bullied in school.

Our windows looked out onto the campus grounds and our courtyard garden, and the light and airy self-contained space was welcoming and green, with plants inside and trees all around. Far from feeling 'lumbered' with the students, we were beginning to recognise the association between some conditions and exceptional ability. It was a privilege to work with the students and, as they taught us more about their life experience, we learnt from the obstacles they encountered, and the staff built up considerable expertise in a whole range of conditions.

Many of the academic staff were supportive and interested to know how they could improve things for their students. Amar came to arrange an appointment with his Director of Studies and our team to discuss his support needs. Amar was born in Iraq and contracted an infection that caused him to become blind when he was living in a refugee camp as a child. A beautiful young man with a kind and gentle nature, he gently described to his tutor how difficult it was to process the written information he was given on his course. Amar was studying computer science and he demonstrated the software he used for reading. This was of great interest to his tutor and their shared love of computer programming formed a bond between them. A couple of years later I was giving a talk at a conference and was challenged by a member of the audience, "How can you expect for example a blind student to study computer science?" he said. "It's just not possible." It gave me great pleasure to describe Amar's achievement and his award of a first class honours degree in computing science. We never know what is possible until we encounter the determination, hard work and commitment of students with disabilities and the staff who teach them.

Much of my work was in breaking down old barriers and boundaries to enable inclusion. I met with the estates department and, with the help of students, we conducted a campus wide access audit. There were previously unseen barriers everywhere. I went round the campus with Jan, a wheelchair user, and she showed me how impossible it was for her to get across campus from one lecture to another in the time provided. A reasonable adjustment was to take her needs into account and book a more accessible lecture theatre, but until now there was no system in place for this. The estates and room booking staff were keen to help, and although it would be some time before an accessible campus became the norm, plans were put in place to improve access. The campus in 2019 is vastly changed and the University is rightly proud of its record with inclusion, especially in the Sports Department where their status as a training ground for Paralympic athletes is highly regarded world wide, and has resulted in a bevy of medals of Paralympians from Bath.

To my great satisfaction the entry to the library was changed, as part of the initial access work, to an entirely new facia with accessible entrance. Libraries can be such inaccessible places for students with difficulties for many reasons. If you have difficulty with text, being confronted with walls of books can be overwhelming, and if you cannot master the alphabetic ordering of things, as is the case for many people with specific learning difficulties, you can never find the book you were looking for. When I was a child I enjoyed going to the mobile library with my mother, it was small and welcoming. When I was studying for my Master's degree the library in Cardiff was overwhelmingly huge. It was there that I ran up expensive library fines, hanging on to books until long after their due date to give me time to read them, and it was also there that I realised my ability with synchronicity often led me to the right book by a strange process of osmosis and recommendation. Sheila Page at Bath was a welcoming presence on entry to the library. Unfailingly helpful, her desk was bright with colourful information, and she engaged with students and helped them to overcome the psychological barriers. Sometimes staff from the Library and the Learning Support team shared a picnic lunch in the Japanese garden on the campus grounds. This manicured space with gravel paths and acer trees was an oasis, protected from wind and intrusion by its hedges. We sat on benches and shared stories in a healing respite from the non-stop hubbub of the University.

We have a tendency to box our education into separate paths from an early age. Many students with neuro-diversity find these separations difficult, their ability tends to overrun the notion of separation and to make unusual connections between things. At University the divide becomes physically obvious with different departments and subjects occupying entirely separate buildings, and with academic staff perceived as quite separate from administration and support staff. The divide enables focus and specialisation at depth but it often disables the ability for understanding between departments to grow.

Sometimes our breaking down of the barriers met with resistance. We traditionally separate physical health from mental health in our systems. When we first started to raise mental health issues as disability related at the University, it was the last great taboo. Liz, the Head of Student Counselling, came to see me to discuss Anna, a student in engineering who was suffering from depression and had been receiving counselling for months. "I'm rather concerned about how

Anna's lecturers are behaving," she told me. The lecturers had no idea Anna was ill and, due to the discrimination around mental health, Anna felt unable to tell them. The need to disclose in order to gain support, versus the need to maintain confidentiality and privacy to protect the student from the judgement that mental health attracts, is complex. We developed confidentiality policies and staff training, Liz brought a research paper to my attention, 'degrees of distress'. We were seeing students who had eating disorders, self-harm issues and conditions such as bi-polar and psychosis.

In our culture we are only just beginning to understand our error in separating physical health from mental health. Students with disabilities often develop mental health issues as a result of their life exclusion experiences. We are one body, and we all experience mental health fluctuation in the same way we experience physical health fluctuation. From mild depression or anxiety to the more severe and often debilitating issues, recent research is identifying direct physical causes for some mental health conditions. That will hopefully change forever the separation between the two in our health systems.

Staff also tended to hide their mental health difficulties. I had a phone call from Mac, a manager in Human Resources. "Mo, I know you don't usually deal with staff issues," he said, "but I'm hoping you can help me." A member of staff suffering from schizophrenia was having a psychotic episode. "I think you will help to calm her," he said. We found her in her flat, cowering in the kitchen, clearly terrified. We talked and calmed her down, and under advice from the psychiatrist we arranged for her to be sectioned under the Mental Health Act and taken to a secure facility. Had she been able to seek support for her condition sooner, such drastic action may not have been needed. And I was sad for her as the ambulance drove away, realising the students appeared sometimes to be in receipt of better support than the staff.

Occasionally I joined the interdisciplinary discussion group in the Claverton Rooms chaired by Jack Whitehead. Jack's work aims to bring emotional intelligence back into an academic system that has steadfastly excluded it. Jack's approach to action research as a living education theory inspired me, and the way he encouraged colleagues to live their values more fully in their practice influenced my work. I took these ideas to a team meeting where we were developing our annual plans. We sat around the round table in my office and I described how Jack uses the word 'love' as a positive value. "We're not sure about the word love" they replied, but we were able to develop and share our ideas and values and more clearly. If love is about positive regard, respect and attention, then this is what we all strove to give our students and each other. For most of the time we were successful in these aims and working with the team in Eastwood Lodge was a joyful experience, with laughter and tears as we managed the day-to-day challenges.

I was in my office with a mature student, Cathy, her lecturer David and her director of studies, John. John was a scientist and was struggling to understand the flexibility Cathy needed while she was undertaking chemotherapy. "What is the problem?" he asked Cathy peremptorily. Cathy, a little flustered and looking very pale, started to explain that her energy levels and ability to concentrate were fluctuating when she suddenly fainted and rolled off her chair onto the floor. I called our first aider in and ushered John and David out. They were shocked, and when we resumed our meeting a week or two later there was no difficulty arranging the flexibility Cathy needed. Until her collapse the academics had been unable to understand how ill Cathy was. Almost immediately after realising Cathy's needs were genuine, their attitude changed from judgement to support.

When you thrive in a system you often have no idea how excluding or forbidding that system is to those who find it difficult. The academic environment was about being rational, objectivity over subjectivity, and this very divide was perceived to create safety and security, separate from the random and uncertain qualities of spiritual and emotional sustenance. Even as the academe were beginning to identify the limitations of this approach and to recognise that nothing is fully rational - everything is influenced by our emotions and experience - computer systems were beginning to dominate the way our institutions run.

Nowhere was this more evident than in financial management. As computer systems developed across the University, practices began to change, especially those affecting accountancy procedures. Charmaine, the accountant, and I met regularly. "I can see every penny of your activity goes to the students," she told me as we waded our way through concertinaed piles of finance reports. The funding for Learning Support came from several sources, government funding to develop inclusion and University provision. Students had been described as 'units of activity' when I was working in Further Education, and now each student attracted funding both for their individual support needs and for the University provision. Charging University fees directly to students was not yet openly on the horizon, but what was happening as the systems changed is that accounts and budgets that had previously been fudged or managed more generally were becoming specific and detailed. Money was becoming an overriding value across the University. Words like 'transparent' and 'accountable' were used frequently and students became statistics, data.

Of course, in this environment I was keeping my feelings separate from my busy working life, my workaholism prevented me from dealing with difficult emotions and caused the erosion of my wellbeing. I had severe pain in my arm and went to see a cranial osteopath who found my neck was completely knotted with tension. I was coming through the menopause, any discussion around this and the effects was limited, even my GP had little to suggest. I was working hard to facilitate the inclusion of young adults at work while failing to support my son to thrive at home. Tom was ill with painful neuropathy, associated with Type One Diabetes. We went to see his consultant who told Tom he would be aggressive with pain – he gave Tom a high dose of Gabapentin that did knock out the pain but also knocked out Tom, so that for months he spent most of the day laid up in bed. Eventually Tom recovered but the experience had a damaging impact on him and I felt powerless to help. Watching the Learning Support tutors and academic support assistants help disabled students at work, I longed for the same support for Tom. It would be many years before he got to University and at last gained both the support and his degree.

When I went to a meeting with Government Advisors ostensibly to discuss funding for students with disabilities, I had an uneasy sense that times were changing, that profit overrode inclusion as a value in the system. Finance systems are in separate silos and it often appears to be more economic to cut support where there is the most need. To me this is a false economy, investment in inclusion leads to achievement and independence for disabled people. I was called to a meeting in the management offices and was introduced by the Vice Chancellor to the prospective Conservative parliamentary candidate. The narrow majority that would lead to the formation of a coalition Conservative and Liberal Government in 2010 was beginning to shimmer in the air.

Meanwhile, our expertise and the number of staff needed to manage the services continued to increase and we were once again faced with outgrowing our offices. My line manager Mike decided to move my office next to his in senior management, to give me a closer strategic working relationship with him and free up space to leave the operational aspects of the service under the day-to-day management of the team leaders. This would prove to be analytical methodology that had its flaws, but at the time it seemed eminently sensible and I sadly handed over my office in Eastwood Lodge and moved to Wessex House.

Scots Pine

The offices for Student Services were on the eighth floor of Wessex House. This tall block completed the University quadrangle of original buildings. A central corridor, reached by the small and unreliable lift at each end of the corridor, ran the length of the narrow building with offices on either side. One side looked down on the quadrangle below and east across to the North Wessex Downs, on a clear day you could see the White Horse of Westbury. The other side looked west to the Mendips and towards the aerial mast on the highest point that guided me home.

There was a sense of being displaced in an ivory tower unconnected from the ground below. On misty days we were cocooned in the unhealthy building with poor air circulation and old fluorescent lights that gave people headaches. I brought my design ethic, Anglepoise lamp and round table with me. "You know it's funny," Mike, the Head of Student Services, said - his office was opposite mine - "every time I come into one of your offices it has a calming effect." His office had a balcony that he used until all the balconies in the building were closed off after a student's death.

Adjustments to make this building accessible were not in place; the lift and the facilities were old and inaccessible.

Although I went to Eastwood Lodge for meetings, I gradually became separated from students and staff. This was the idea, the Team Leaders for Student Advice and the Assessment Centre would assume operational management day to day and I would be able to focus on the strategic aspects of my role. There was much work to be done, we were just starting a disability audit for the University and my time would be fully taken up in committee and department meetings, but I could not resist the feeling that my wings had been clipped and I missed the camaraderie of close working with my colleagues.

I had a meeting with Iain Biggs, the Director of Studies and Reader in Visual Art Practice at the University of the West of England. We were co-editing the papers from the Cascade conference and both of us were finding it hard to find time for the work. "I will have to hand the rest of this over to you," Iain told me. I felt strangely emotional, weak and weepy. In the evening I met with Andy at a furniture store, we were trying to choose beds for the children. Marie Claire and David came to stay every half term and for some of the school holidays and were rapidly outgrowing their bunk beds, we needed beds and a sofa bed. I tried to choose something but I couldn't think straight and made a choice that I knew was wrong as soon as I got home. The next morning I had a line of spots across my back and was promptly diagnosed with shingles, a serious, contagious and disempowering illness related to chicken pox. I cancelled the beds order and found myself unexpectedly home for several weeks. As I recovered my strength I was able to begin completing the Cascade book and to visualise the strategy for Learning Support more clearly.

Funding was available from the project to complete the book, including design and print costs. Our in-house graphic designer, Sue Fairhurst, and other staff at the University were enthusiastic and helpful. Mike viewed this activity as a separate issue to my job as Learning Support Manager and was uninterested when I told him the book was nearly complete. We held a book launch, reluctantly hosted by Mike and well attended by the excellent contributors and by staff across the University. It's still available in University Libraries in 2019 as well as online and attracts many positive comments. I think of it as a marker in the sand of developments in screening for and understanding the abilities of people with dyslexia.

I was asked to contribute to other publications, 'Dyslexia and Stress' and 'Dyslexia and Education'. One day Mike and I were having lunch on a bench overlooking the lake discussing writing. "I've always wanted to write, although you can't easily make a living from it," I told him. "I sometimes think I would like to just be a writer," he replied, "and then realise I can just leave and be that if I want to." I didn't understand the significance of his remark at the time, and I never saw him writing. I later realised he may have been encouraging me to leave.

A few years later when I was negotiating leaving the University, Bruce, a manager from Human resources came to see me. "You are a writer," he said. Despite the many positive comments about my writing, this was the first time anyone had said this to me, "Yes, I suppose I am," I replied. It was academic writing and, as such, for me it was separate from my creative writing, in the same way that my research dissertation had been separate from my poetry, and my designs for buildings separate from my paintings. Recognition as a writer was rare indeed.

At first all seemed to be going well in my new location – I thought we had a good senior management team. Introducing the new practices and procedures being brought in seemed to be sound practice. Mike seemed to have a healthy approach to life, eating raw salads, meditating and ensuring regular meetings with his team, and I was lulled into a false sense of security. New job descriptions were developed, and roles and responsibilities more clearly outlined, and away days held with the teams to ensure we were all familiar with new strategic developments. It was rational, clean and entirely failed to take into account the chiaroscuro of light and dark.

The staff teams were feeling insecure and we realised our new team leader had not gained the confidence of the team. I was responsible for supervising him through a series of probationary procedures in an attempt to support him to grow into the role. When this failed,

Mike stood over me as I talked to him and approved his dismissal.

It was a difficult decision, ultimately it was the right one for the team, but I had this sense of karma, an inner reminder to myself that what you dish out you will also receive.

The growing financial crisis plunged us all into recession and there was only one true agenda behind all the rational new management procedures, and that was cut costs, cut and cut again. Year on year the accountancy grindstone was milling out anything the system saw as unnecessary. The system, programmed to count only figures and data, did not take account human values and those values were invisible in the system. Learning Support provision, in fact all provision for people with disabilities, began to be eroded just at the time when expertise had grown and the Disability Bill and Human

Rights Act were coming in. By 2010 when the Conservative Party came to power and found the famous note telling them all the money had gone, all the social inclusion developments of the previous decade were becoming severely eroded and ultimately they were lost.

I came to see the continual new plans, structures and new role descriptions were something of a game of chess for Mike, where pawns could be easily disposed of and queens moved about the board. We appointed a new team leader and I felt positive, only in retrospect would I learn the political will behind the structural changes were underpinned by financial cuts that would ultimately reduce all services across the sector. There was just the hint of this beginning, something of the brave new world. Some of the new practice for students, meant to be efficient, seemed to show an apparent lack of empathy and made me feel uneasy and uncomfortable.

I was in my fifties but I had not encountered ageism before. Now the team leader was giving me advice on which creams to use to counter my wrinkles. "I don't mind wrinkles," I told her, "a smooth face is the face of someone who hasn't lived." I realised I was working in an institution full of young people, some of whom, the team leader included, viewed me as positively aged and out of date. This was a shock to me. I was beginning to feel vulnerable as my health was failing and was excessively tired and often shaky, but it was some months of visits to the GP before an overactive thyroid was diagnosed. I was then off work for some weeks and facing major treatment. By the time I came back Mike and the team leaders had made decisions and taken over most practical management issues, I had been deposed.

This was understandable, the symptoms for hyperactive

thyroid are unpleasant and my shakiness and absence had lost me the confidence of the team, like a prize stag I had been brought down. What I had not been prepared for was the malice with which attempts to get rid of me developed. Covert meetings and accusations of bullying were made. I was advised to make a counter claim against Mike and a whole series of toxic kangaroo court hearings ensued. "You couldn't have got it more wrong," I told Mike, "I will be proved right in the end." And I began psychotherapy sessions outside the institution.

Mike asked me to write a report on a number of disability related issues for our senior manager. I wrote a two-page document about the disability bill and student rights and University responsibilities. I got the feedback from Mike that they did not understand what I had written. I was nonplussed as I thought it was straightforward. In retrospect, I believe the cutting of those with expertise about disability law was necessary in order to implement the cuts of the services. The Human Rights Act and the changes it brought was not popular and the implications were viewed as expensive.

Yvonne, my union representative came to the hearings and was a tower of strength. "It's easy to see what they are doing, Mo" she said, "They just want to get rid of you. You're no bully," and she gave me a hug. The people accusing me of bullying began to bully me. I was trolled online with ageist abuse. This was massively upsetting, especially as the messages were timed to arrive before I went into hearings. I had to think about my practice, I was outspoken and a whistle blower, many women my age had to be strong to make progress, did this make me a bully? Education tended to be a bully culture, "robust" was the term used, often to discriminate against people with needs and I had counselled staff and students on their bullying experiences. It was devastating to think people might see me that way. The way to counteract bullying is not to suffer alone, but to tell someone and I told Angela, my friend, the University Chaplain. She advised me to speak with Human Resources and Bruce came to my support. Having read the messages he called in the University Computing Services.

Jackie my psychotherapist also helped me to restore my faith in myself and reminded me of the serenity prayer, to accept the things I cannot change. I was fighting a system that no longer wished to provide the services I was providing. My line managers knew they would have to get rid of me to get rid of the service. I had seen others deposed in my own and other institutions and I knew this was how the system worked, what I had not realised is how predicated this was. Some of the staff were required to give statements without being told this was to be used against me. Several told me later they were reluctant to do this and felt coerced into this practice, known as mobbing, in the way crows mob a buzzard. I was isolated and mocked, and in psychotherapy I revisited the resonance with my childhood experience. When Mike came into my office I told him I was being trolled and that Computing Services were looking into it. Within a day the trolling stopped.

My friend Jen reminded me to stay in touch with nature. I had a particular love of Scots Pine trees, a tree native to the UK that can live for up to 700 years. The bark develops fissures with age and the tree had some spiritual significance in Celtic times. There was a secluded part of the campus where I would go to lean against the trunk of a Scots Pine and process my thoughts. I found it healing and later learnt that Bach homeopathic remedies recommend Scots Pine for "those who blame themselves. Even when successful they think they could have done better, and are never content with their efforts or the results. They are hardworking and suffer much from the faults they attach to themselves. Sometimes if there is any mistake it is due to another, but they will claim responsibility even for that". [Bach: Twelve Healers and Other Remedies 1936]. I kept a photo of a Scots Pine tree by my desk. I also tried to renew my creative activity, bringing in a sketch book and trying to do a sketch at the start of every day. I was surprised how hard this was to maintain.

The stress took a severe toll on my health and thyroid condition. I was signed off on long term sick leave. The time off helped me to begin to recover my health and Occupational Health advised me that I was well enough to return to work, but the system had moved on and my post had been made redundant, enabling me to take early retirement and to duck under the retirement gate just before such options closed for all those a few years younger behind me.

From the highs of the achievements of our service, the inclusive development made by the University, and the wonderful working relationships I had enjoyed, I left with great sorrow knowing the change that was upon us and that much would be lost. Some colleagues thought I was exaggerating about the depth of the cuts that were coming, but I was indeed proved right in the end.

After leaving I was treated to a meal out and a presentation from the staff team that meant a great deal to me. I have many wonderful enduring friendships with former colleagues at the University, some of whom fully understood what I was going through and were the best of friends in enabling me to survive the experience. I know of others who have not survived this system, or who have been permanently wounded by it. One of the biggest issues is that confidentiality isolates and precludes you from talking to anyone. When settlements in such cases are made, the complicated and arduous procedure is often taken to the very door of the court hearing, only for a settlement offer to be made at the last minute with a gagging proviso, forbidding the recipient of the settlement from talking about their experiences. Thus the practice is maintained, with few understanding what has happened to the person who has left. It is a bitter legal legacy aimed at maintaining the status quo. The people who have signed the agreement often feel angry and disempowered, a lasting legacy.

A colleague told me that I was one of the few "real people" he knew in the University. I know many people were scared of entering the University domain because of its deliberately elevated status and I had wanted to bring a more emotionally intelligent element to education. Maybe my varied education experiences had given me this drive. One of the consequences of the high fees that students pay is that they feel more able to assert their rights. The only thing I left on the wall of my office was a quote regarding education being a right not a privilege, and education that has to be paid for does inevitably become a privilege.

I went home to my loving and supportive family, deeply grateful for all the help I received, all the good working relationships and all that together we had achieved.

The Parade

The Parade is the name for the courtyard that sits in the centre of the University of Bath. It comprises a long windswept rectangle raised above a lower level. The floor is supported like a bridge and surrounded on all sides by buildings that are post war sixties brutal architecture blocks.

One of my colleagues had a fantasy that one day we would see students wearing orange jumpsuits, like those worn in the notorious Guantanamo Bay Detention Camp, protesting and marching on the campus. They may not have been wearing orange jumpsuits, but when the students eventually came out in powerful protest, marching with banners on the Parade in 2017, I watched them on the national and local television news coverage with a mixture of relief that the truth had finally come out and sorrow that it had taken so long. What finally brought the students to protest was not directly the issues of social justice I was concerned with, rather the outrageous level of pay, £468,000 per annum plus expenses, house and car, received by the Vice Chancellor of the University, Professor Dame Glynis Breakwell.

Fifteen years previously, I'd been walking along the Parade and had shivers down my spine, a kind of premonition that nothing would be the same and that everything had changed.

I did not understand at the time the central position that the University I worked in played in these changes. The city of Bath has a strong Ministry of Defence presence, and students from the University were regularly recruited into military roles. I knew my shivers were somehow connected with the fact that, despite many protests, the UK had joined with the USA and we were now at war with Iraq.

I'd been to a meeting of the Equality Committee and was amazed, and deeply frustrated, to hear the statistics on the persistence of the huge disparity in pay between men and women. The meeting was in the Council Chamber where we were surrounded by classic portraits of previous Vice Chancellors, all white men. When I raised the poor message this gave out to a committee aimed at improving equality and diversity, the male Chair of the Committee expressed surprise while the female secretary smiled covertly at me.

Professor Breakwell, our first female Vice Chancellor, was appointed in 2001 - her appointment was meant to give us hope for change. When she took up her role she went round the University to meet the staff. I remember her coming into my office with the Dean of Students. They sat opposite me and, while we talked, Glynis looked directly at me and made a scything motion downwards with her hand, alongside the Dean. The Dean's appointment was terminated a year or so later. Professor Breakwell is a Social Psychologist, her publications include 'Coping with Aggressive Behaviour', 'The Psychology of Risk', and 'Changing European Identities: Social Psychological Analyses of Social Change'. She has worked closely with the military academy, and is adviser to Government on the use of psychological methods and theories. In January 2012 she was appointed a Dame Commander of the British Empire.

The UK financial crisis in 2007 led to a major recession and austerity measures were introduced in 2008. The Iraq war ended in December 2011. There is little reference to the connection between the cost of war and the country's financial crisis in the media. The so-called austerity measures rapidly proved to mean massive cuts to the most vulnerable in society and were used as a political football. The gap between the wealthy and the poor continued to increase at an extraordinary, exponential rate. This gap between the income of indebted students and the out of control pay at the most senior levels in the University had become unsustainable, and this led to the public outcry.

"A defining moment for Bath University" read the headline in the Guardian, reporting on the Vice Chancellor being urged to resign in November 2017. The article identified that Professor Breakwell chaired the committee that managed her own pay rises and how her pay had dramatically increased between 2011 and 2017. "There are porters at this University who earn less than she got in her last pay rise" said the Chair of the University's Unite branch. "For the first time in many years the community came together to embrace hope against the culture of fear that prevails here," said a member of the Senate.

The discussion raged at the highest levels, Lord Adonis actively campaigned for Professor Breakwell's resignation, four members of parliament resigned their posts associated with the University. Within the University, fifteen female senior academic staff supported the Vice Chancellor, their letter to the Guardian claimed "Being a successful woman seems to attract a disproportionate degree of negative criticism". Sixty-four female staff replied in their letter to the same newspaper, "Yes Professor Breakwell is a woman and a Vice Chancellor, something that is far too uncommon. However, it is her actions and not her gender that have led to a complete loss of confidence ... the few senior staff still willing to defend Professor Breakwell fail to consider how her use of power has affected women at the University. She could have taken action to eliminate our gender pay gap, which is significantly higher than the national average. She could have opposed the 16% real-terms pay cut that most of the staff have faced since 2011, which has left many female colleagues struggling to pay bills and some having to use food banks." The letter ends "Yes, we want to see women with power in universities, but not one woman who only seems to look after herself and a small clique of other senior managers. We want to see power spread across the organisation, with academics, support staff and students having a say in how our University is run."

I was naïve when, in 2008, an exercise to audit equal pay began at the University. I was full of hope that this would address the concerns raised in this letter ten years later. I believed the audit, that closely examined roles and responsibilities, would enable a significant move towards equality across the institution. Each member of staff had a long interview with the auditor, as well as their roles being compared across the University. How delighted and unsurprised I was when the results eventually proved that I had been underpaid and was at a lower pay grade than I should have been. In fact, I should have been on the same grade as my line manager for the past few years. Seeing that my line manager was less enamoured of the results than I was gave me pause for concern. Ultimately, shortly before I left the University I met with his line manager, one of top senior management in the hierarchy. Alone in his office, he advised me that under no circumstances would he have two managers on the same pay grade. I felt as though I had bumped into and broken the glass ceiling, briefly poked my head through, and promptly had my head cut off.

In October 2018 it has been identified that, at the current rate of progress, the gender pay gap will not close until 2073 in the UK. The persistence of resistance to change to secure the position of those at the top appears to be based on just this methodology. Cut everything right back and when the cuts are no longer sustainable make small changes and encourage hope. Allow growth to a certain level and then cut everything back again. In this way, people feel they are making progress while in fact they are being firmly held in check. Within two years of my leaving the University all the learning support services had been slashed back to a basic administration staff, agency outsourcing and/or non-provision of many services and limited online advice. I had hoped that when I left it would be because the service was no longer needed because there was a truly inclusive University. The news reports show this is not yet the case.

Initially I believed the University management did not understand what it was losing. I was wrong. I did not understand how severe the cuts would be, how long they would continue, and how much would be lost. When I realised, after one particularly difficult communication with my managers, that they did know and fully understood what they were doing I was devastated. I walked out into the grounds and sat on a bench facing the lake and wept. I called a friend from the Union and she came and sat with me. We had no idea then that the cuts we were witnessing for provision for people with disabilities, mental health issues and specific learning difficulties were just the tip of the iceberg for the cuts across the country for arts, education, social well-being and health. Lord Tugendhat was then the Chancellor of the University. His son Tom has recently been nominated as a potential future leader of the Conservative Party.

I remember a Professor telling me, "There's nowhere more political than a University, Mo". And I remember asking Dame Jocelyn Bell Burnell, shortly before she left the University, whether there was any hope for equality, and her rueful shrug as she replied "not at the moment in Bath, I'm afraid." Jocelyn became the Dean of Science at the University in the same year that Glynis was appointed. She is an astrophysicist and well known for her discovery of radio pulsars in 1967. Almost equally well known is the fact that Jocelyn was excluded from receiving the Nobel Prize in Physics for the discovery, which went to her male supervisor. In 2018 she was awarded the Special Breakthrough Prize in Fundamental Physics and gave the whole of the £2.3 million prize money to help women, ethnic minority, and refugee students become physics researchers. In the same year an ill-informed male Italian lecturer has been suspended from CERN, the European organisation for nuclear research, for claiming "women aren't as good at physics as men".

Jocelyn was very active in supporting equality and diversity across the University and her ethical, warm and honest approach was immensely helpful. She held no bitterness about the exclusion she'd experienced and played it down, recognising that is just how things were. She is a Quaker and her strong social values and lack of ego were a direct contrast to Glynis's approach. Her willingness to give time and consideration to facilitating change was invaluable and we were sad when she left in 2004 to become Professor in Astrophysics at the University of Oxford. In 2013 she was listed as one of the most powerful 100 women in the UK in the list compiled by BBC's Woman's Hour.

Every October I meet with former colleagues from the University for lunch. It is as though the start of the academic year is a rhythm in all of us, and we reconnect and share news. This year the very public news of both these strong women was published in the media was heartening. Both values have been recognised, the self-serving greed and bully culture versus the warmth of a social inclusion approach that shares wealth and power with others, have been very publicly acknowledged.

When I left the University I was almost inarticulate with rage, grief and frustration. I felt that all I'd worked for had been jettisoned. I learned there was a University of Bath survivors club and that many people had been through the demeaning procedures designed to belittle, contain, gag and exclude. In 2019 a BBC investigation into this practice by Universities in the UK revealed that £87 million was spent on non-disclosure agreements since 2017. Dozens of academics were beginning to break these agreements and disclose their experience of being "harassed out of their jobs". When I retired, all this was hidden on the surface but was an underpinning pulse that maintained the culture of fear where people are unwilling to speak out, an issue all too common in institutions.

Glynis tended to take a linear approach to management, with strict rules being followed and anything outside the guidelines being ignored or excluded. Everything that had a monetary profit was valued and anything that didn't was excluded. False economies were made, such as spending far more on excluding staff than on the salary cost that was saved. There appeared to be strong management and clean structures, only because of limited monetary values. In ecological theory this approach causes loss of habitat - open space or rain forests have no monetary value and are invisible in the system, whereas the financial value of a new road or crop can be calculated, and exists. The problem with this approach is that it is deliberate and consciously excludes anything non-monetarised, "non-valuable".

In contrast a lateral or holistic approach, such as Jocelyn's, includes values such as diversity, inclusion and human well-being, and includes the linear approach as one part of the whole. When I was first teaching the students about the left brain/right brain theories, I used to describe the linear approach as the segment of an orange, and the lateral approach as the slice across the whole orange. We now know there is more potential plasticity than this in the brain, but our education systems come from this bias, and many of the computer systems that run us are programmed as orange segments. It is like the old proverb 'fire is a good servant but a bad master'. We've allowed our procedural systems to become our masters rather than our servants and in so doing, we persistently exclude common sense, creativity and humanity.

Shortly after I retired I was in Bath, waiting to cross the road with my sister, when another parade came by. The parade of University Council personnel dressed in their robes, proceeding to a Graduation Ceremony. The Vice Chancellor was leading her group, she saw me and briefly caught my eye. It is fear that is at the root of so much exclusion, and love that is the heart of inclusion.

Road to the Isles 5

My tried and tested way of surviving the buffeting of life is to go to the Highlands, breathe deeply into the blustery wind, fill my lungs with pure air, cleanse spirit and soul and reconnect with my deeper self. There is nothing like the Highlands to put the small stuff of life into perspective. In the vast and ancient landscape, with its visible geology of deep time, many things become less important.

My sister and I scattered some of our mother's ashes in a roaring river in a Highland Glen. We are from the Munro clan, which goes back to the eleventh century. Both of our Great Grandfathers were called John Munro, a common name in Scotland - there are many thousands of John Munros - and people with Munro connections come from all over the world to visit Foulis Castle, the seat of the Munros.

On my maternal side there are three John Munros, the same name being passed on to the oldest son through the generations. My great grandfather John Munro was born in 1852, to his father John Munro who was a ploughman in Elgin on the Moray Firth. The conditions for workers in the Highlands and Islands were said, in Parliament, to be worse than the working conditions for slaves in the West Indies. Somehow John's parents survived the poverty and Highland

Clearances, which peaked in 1851, and supported their son in his education. He became a Schoolmaster and named his first son, my great uncle, John Munro.

The length of the Munro history pales into insignificance when compared with the geological history of Scotland. The Moray Firth, where Great Grandfather was born, is on the east coast of Scotland. A tributary, Dornoch Firth, points to Lairg where the centre of a meteor impact crater, 40 kilometres in diameter, was the first to be discovered in the UK, and identified in 2016. Dr Simms, the research scientist who discovered the site, said the impact released energy to the equivalent of 1,500 tonnes of TNT explosives. The evidence for the meteorite impact was first identified in 2008, through the deposits of green molten rock fragments mixed in with red sandstone found near Ullapool in Wester Ross. These sandstone deposits are almost 1.2 billion years old. As a beachcomber I intuitively sensed this history, rolling smooth red and green pebbles in my hand and wondering what story they might have to tell.

When I retired, Andy and I rented a cottage in Applecross, a village on the mainland of Scotland, opposite the Isle of Skye where the views of the volcanic structure of the island are dramatic. In 2017, the year following the discovery on the mainland, geologists found evidence of a second 60 million year old impact crater on the Isle of Skye. Dr Simon Drake believes the impact may have played a part in Skye's volcanological evolution. The spectacular sunsets dripped gold and rose over the mountains, and etched the shape of land on water and sky.

Gradually I was reconnecting the scattered parts of myself with my past, integrating my heritage with my sense of belonging, weaving together myth and fact. The road to Applecross took us to the spectacular Bealach-na-ba (Pass of the Cattle), famous for its hairpin bends and steep climb. It is considered to be one of the most dangerous and scenic routes in Scotland, and the world. When I innocently approached this challenge in blinding dense fog, I could not see where the road went and had to trust in fate on the steep hairpin bends, hands gripping the wheel, sweat on my brow, holding my breath and bearing tightly left hoping the wheels would find tarmac and not the steep drop over the side. At the summit the clouds cleared, far below we could see the archipelago of Applecross waiting to welcome us.

According to an article in the Guardian in 2018, there have been long queues of cars and camper vans, as thousands of tourists try to get onto and visit the Isle of Skye. The increasing popularity of Scotland has brought pressure and parts of the country are in danger of being overwhelmed by tourists. In Applecross there was no sign of such an invasion. The remoteness of the location, and the difficulty in accessing it, ensured all remained quiet – for the time being.

Walking the coast, listening to the sea shushing and drawing back over the stones, is like hearing the sound of the planet breathing. The Gaelic name for the peninsula, A'Chromaich (the Sanctuary), dates from 673 AD when St Maelrubha established a monastery and sanctuary in Clachan, second only to Iona in religious importance.

From the garden of our rented cottage came the pure high call of the skylark, and the views of the islands and the ever-changing light provided the healing I needed. The sea had startling clarity, in rock pools pink weed and coral waved invitingly, and I almost had to put my hand into the cold water to know it was there. On the strand the sand was ridged in small parallel hummocks and each silica grain reflected light, we were paddling in a sea of crystals. Here, where river and sea meet and merge in many tributaries and fluid connections, I am reminded of water logic and water memory. I know water logic will always outstrip the linear attempts to box us into canals or networks. We are constantly being channelled into ways of thinking that are binary and that frustrate some of us because we feel they are limited.

Andy and Sparky near Applecross

Sanctuary is a refuge and a place where wildlife is protected. The sighting book at the cottage held promise of seeing a pine marten, with reports from visitors to the cottage of seeing this elusive creature and encouraging its nocturnal attendance with bread and jam. Night after night we tried all sorts of treats - setting them on the outside table and watching from the window - we waited up into the early hours of the morning. We saw the stars of a dark sky and the Milky Way spreading her splendour above us until the sky slowly infused with soft colours of dawn, but we never saw the pine marten, although sometimes the treats had gone in the morning.

In 2019 there are estimated to be 3,800 pine martens in Britain. Mammals that were close to extinction in Britain in the 1970s are showing signs for recovery. Our willingness to act, to provide sanctuaries, stop using pesticides and pollutants and ban hunting, has helped their recovery. Their numbers, while much smaller than in the past, are showing increase in population. This is at a time when children are becoming activists for the Extinction Rebellion movement, by striking from school, attempting to reclaim their future and challenge adults to act now.

My sightings don't come to me when I look for them. They come to me unexpectedly when I'm not trying. In Australia, I tried and failed to see dolphins, but when Andy and I visited Gairloch and Red Sands a pod of bottle-nosed dolphins came to see us. It was after a storm and huge rollers were piling into shore from the Atlantic. The dolphins were surfing and leaping through the waves, their mouths curving in huge smiles. Their absolute joy communicated to us and we were somehow changed by the experience.

Another time we drove up with our elderly collie Sparky and wild camped on the stunning peninsula above Lochinver. There we shared our remote beach with a golden eagle. Disappointed tourists drove to a nearby Scottish estate hoping to see it but - like the dolphins - the eagle came to us. There are over 500 pairs of golden eagles in Scotland, and they are still a rare sight. This eagle soared and landed and hung out for an hour or two on a rocky outcrop, untroubled by our camp below. We had the soft white sands and burn entirely to ourselves, our dog and the eagle, in a timeless moment.

Sparky at Sheigra

In a river in Badachro we watched an otter fishing, with a large fish firmly clamped in his big paws he looked us straight in the eyes, as though he was showing his catch off to us, before swimming away to eat it in peace. Patrick Barkham says otter numbers are now estimated to be 11,000, when in the 1970s they were all but extinct due to hunting. I've seen otters several times, always unexpectedly and always bringing an energy and joy in life with them. Dolphins and otters play.

The wild cat I saw at Achilitibuie in my youth is my only sighting - Barkham says these are the mammals most likely to be imminently extinct in the UK. I guess what he is showing us is that there is hope. If we change our behaviour and protect and respect our wilderness and wildlife - it is not too late to change our relationship with the Earth. Free range and wilderness experience is becoming increasingly rare. 80% of our global population live in cities, and will never experience the call of a skylark or see the smooth wet coat of an otter's back.

I have stumbled many times in my attempts to make sense of, or improve, things. My Irish, Scottish, Jewish family history of loss and dislocation has taught me, the only things we can sometimes bring with us are our memories in stories and music, a Highland Fling or a Jewish lament. When we learn to play we find joy in life.

We humans are custodians and have been on this planet for such a short time in deep time. On a long long scale our existence is just seconds. Our survival depends on improving our relationship with each other, the earth and ourselves. Each of us walks in deep time - each walk is briefer than an outbreath, and each as important, valuable and eternal as the peat that holds the carbon or the sandstone in which the memory of the meteor is stored.

Geology in stone at Applecross

I am fortunate to have recovered my health and wellbeing, aided by the love of my friends and family. My creative process and belief in social justice sustain me, and I believe that those who have been supported to value and embrace their true selves will be the people who bring the changes we need for a sustainable future.

Bibliography

James Hutton (1726 -1797) Edinburgh geological society

Robert Burns *Where Braving Angry Winter's Storms*, BBC

Ian Hamilton Finlay, Scottish Poetry Library

Potter, Norman *What is a Designer: Education and Practice* 1969

Hollenberg, Donna *A Poets Revolution: The Life of Denise Levertov*
  University of California Press, 2013

Schumacher, E.F *Small is Beautiful: A Study of Economics as if People Mattered* Vintage Classics 1973.

Worthington, Andy *The Battle of the Beanfield*. Enabler publications 2005

Macintyre, Ben The Spy and the Traitor 2018

Bowlby, John *Attachment; Separation; Loss* trilogy first published 1969, 1972, 1980

Graves, J, Kiziewicz, M., in *Visual spatial ability and dyslexia: a research project* Central St Martins College of Art and Design 1999

Young, Michael *The Elmhirsts of Dartington*, Routledge 1982

Burkhauser, Jude Ed. *Glasgow Girls: women in art and design 1880-1920* Canongate 2001.

Kiziewicz, M and Biggs I (Eds.) Cascade: *Creativity across Science Art Dyslexia Education* University of Bath 2007

Kiziewicz, M *Supporting Dyslexic Adults in Higher Education and the Workplace* Wiley 2012

Guardian, The *A Defining Moment for Bath University* November 2017

Dame Jocelyn Bell Burnell awarded world's oldest scientific prize royalsociety.org 2021

Drake, Simon and Beard, Andy *Falling Skye* – The Geological Society www.geol.soc.org.uk April 2018

Images

Photos are by the author unless otherwise stated. Images in chapter order:

Cover Design by Westrow Cooper and Andrew Henon
 Front cover Five Sisters of Kintail, Northwest Highlands of Scotland
 Back Cover photo of Morag Smyth by James Howe, BPCAD

Part One, Belonging and Dislocation
 Path End painting by Helen Lees

Fault Line
 Path End woodcut by Helen Lees
 Morag as a baby in Path End garden by Howard Smyth

Tigh na Feile
 Joyce and Howard Smyth by Isaac Friend

Road to the Isles 1 : Sheila and Morag, Tiree by Howard Smyth; Arran by Isaac Friend

Hillfoots Way: Kate and Howard at Ladygrove by Peter Nesbit

Ladygrove: Ladygrove House, photographer unknown

Beau and Mini by Peter Nesbit
Alan and Morag, Ladygrove Garden by Howard Smyth
Morag Smyth with cousin Kay by Peter Nesbit

Part Two, Design and Romanticism: The Cottage painting by Martin Hursthouse

Snake Pass: Morag on her wedding day, Ladygrove garden, wedding photographer
Elizabeth Connal Friend by Joyce Smyth

Road to the Isles 2: Assynt, Highlands of Scotland

Somerset: The Cottage, 1975 with Joyce Smyth in doorway

The Folly: Ben, Mucky and Sunshine, The Cottage garden

Bath: Morag Smyth, Homestyle press photo, Jollys of Bath

Road to the Isles 3: Stac Pollaidh, North West Highlands of Scotland

Part Three Deconstruction and Transformation: The Mendips, water colour by Morag Smyth

St Michael's Hill: Baby Tom photo by Stuart

Chewton Mendip: Morag and Tom photo by Stuart

Szczecin: Hamlet in Poland

IMAGES

Road to the Isles 4: West coast Highland Scotland
 Stuart and Tom near Gairloch

West Moors: Spatial Design Studio, BPCAD photo by James Howe, BPCAD

Tarrant Launceston: Family at Tarrant Launceston by Andrew Henon

Bonnington Square: Tom in Trafalgar Square

Claverton Down: smoking room, University of Bath 1997

Blue Mountains: Joyce as a child with her father Isaac, photographer unknown

Poachers Pocket: Bodies by Andy and Morag at Café Bleu
 Morag's Den at Black Square Gallery

Road to the Isles 5: Andy and Sparky at Applecross
 Sparky at Sheigra
 Geology in stone at Applecross

About the Author

Morag Smyth was born in Scotland. Her free-range childhood gave her an intimate and lifelong connection with the natural world. She moved to England as a child and now lives in Somerset. Morag's poems have been published in journals and anthologies. She writes a column, *Electric Blue*, for the poetry journal *Tears in the Fence*.

Morag's first career was in interior design. Her research for her MA explored how we develop spatial ability. Morag worked in Higher Education for over 20 years, initially teaching Spatial Design, followed by Learning Support Manager for the University of Bath, working to develop inclusion for diversity in academia. Her writing on dyslexia and ability is published by Wiley.

MoragSmyth.co.uk

Testimonials

A Walk in Deep Time is a beautifully impassioned account of a woman's working and personal life as she embodies values of the heart and creative spirit in an educational and social system that all too often militates against them. Covering a period of intense change in roles for women – her nappy changing table doubles as a drawing board – and despite all the odds against her, Morag Smyth sustains a vision of humanity, inclusivity and love. This is made possible by an inspired link with the earth, especially the Western isles of Scotland, and a warm intelligence that never forgets the small, recent place we occupy. It leaves me full of hope and affirmation.
Rosie Jackson

A Walk in Deep Time is lively and evocative, thoughtful and well-researched. I find the story fascinating, moving and utterly engrossing.
Ama Bolton

www.ingramcontent.com/pod-product-compliance
Lightning Source LLC
Chambersburg PA
CBHW072045110526
44590CB00018B/3040